A CLASS OF THEIR OWN

By the same author:

Gadfly for God: A History of the Church Times, Hodder & Stoughton, 1991

High and Mitred: Prime Ministers as Bishop-Makers, SPCK, 1992

Reverend Rebels: Five Victorian Clerics and their Fight Against Authority, Darton, Longman & Todd, 1993

Men of Habit: The Franciscan Ideal in Action, Canterbury Press, 1994

A CLASS OF THEIR OWN

*Six Public School Headmasters who became
Archbishop of Canterbury*

Bernard Palmer

The Book Guild Ltd
Sussex, England

The Book Guild Ltd
25 High Street
Lewes, Sussex

First published 1997
© Bernard Palmer, 1997
Set in Times
Typesetting by Poole Typesetting (Wessex) Ltd, Bournemouth
Printed in Great Britain by
Antony Rowe Ltd,
Chippenham, Wiltshire

A catalogue record for this book is available
from the British Library

ISBN 1 85776 169 3

*To my children Nicholas and Rachel
who provided me with my last encounter
with education*

.

CONTENTS

FOREWORD
BY THE ARCHBISHOP
OF CANTERBURY

One of the things I have sought to do since becoming Archbishop is to encourage Bishops to develop their roles as teachers of the Faith. Coming as I and my three predecessors have done from a background of theological education, this has been a feature of the ministry of Archbishops of Canterbury over the last thirty-five years and the same has been true of a distinguished line of Archbishops of York.

In previous generations, as Bernard Palmer shows in this fascinating study, it was not the theological educators who became Archbishop of Canterbury, but a whole string of Public School Headmasters. Today we might think that such a role is largely an administrative one and far removed from the demands placed on a Bishop. Certainly curriculum development, discipline and financial management all feature in these pages, but a headmaster was also expected to carry out many of the duties we would now tend to link to the role of the Chaplain, both in terms of Pastoral Care, Confirmation Preparation and regularly preaching to the pupils Sunday by Sunday.

Such a pattern of pastoral oversight, administration and teaching the faith is not all that far removed from the New Testament's understanding of Episcopal ministry and it was that, perhaps, that provided the link into the series of appointments. Whatever the case, these six brief portraits provide us with some fascinating insights into the background of these men, and leave us with much to think about as we seek to work out how episcopacy should be expressed in our own generation.

13 May 1996

† George Cantuar

PREFACE

Casting around for a subject for a new book, I was urged by a friend to write about the great clerical headmasters of Victorian times. A quick search, however, revealed that the vast majority of Victorian public-school headmasters were in fact clerics, and that some restriction of the theme would therefore be necessary. Further thought suggested a fruitful demarcation line. It is a remarkable fact that, of the eight Archbishops of Canterbury who reigned from 1862 to 1961, no fewer than six had, earlier in their careers, been headmaster of a major public school. Three of the six – Frederick Temple, Benson and Fisher – could arguably be classed among the great headmasters, though not necessarily among the great archbishops. One, William Temple, was undoubtedly a great archbishop but not a great headmaster. The remaining two, Longley and Tait, come somewhere in the middle on both counts.

This book is therefore an attempt to analyse the six headmasterships. It investigates how the future archbishops coped with the miniature world of a public school before moving on to higher things; what persuaded them to embark on a schoolmaster's career in the first place and to abandon it when the time seemed ripe; how strongly they influenced their schools' religious and moral tone; and what factors they had in common with each other in interpreting the headmaster's role. The book also shows the many points at which their lives crossed each other. Tait urged the appointment of Frederick Temple as his successor at Rugby, though in the end Temple was his successor-but-one. Temple in his turn secured the appointment of Benson as the first Headmaster of Wellington, though his protégé got to Canterbury before him. Eight years after his death his son became Headmaster of Repton, and four years later the younger Temple secured the appointment of Fisher as his successor. In the fulness of time the two men were to succeed each other as archbishop. The educational world, like the ecclesiastical world, seems at times a small and close-knit one; but there is no denying that all the six subjects of this book were remarkable men who would have gone far in any profession. Its sub-title could well have been 'Six Archbishops in the Making'.

BERNARD PALMER
Charminster, Dorset

ACKNOWLEDGEMENTS

A book such as this must rely heavily on existing biographies and school histories. I accordingly acknowledge my deep debt to those in both camps of whose works I have made free. A full list of these and other relevant publications will be found in the bibliography at the end of this volume. I owe a particular debt to David Newsome's *A History of Wellington College 1859–1959* (published by John Murray), and to J.B. Hope Simpson's *Rugby since Arnold* (published by Macmillan), both of which volumes I have found especially helpful and of which I have made extensive use.

I am also indebted to Messrs Victor Gollancz for permission to quote extensively from the autobiographical work by the firm's founder, *More for Timothy*, in my chapter on Geoffrey Fisher; and to my namesake Dr Richard Palmer, the Lambeth Palace Librarian, for kindly allowing me to consult the transcript of the taped interview between Lord Fisher of Lambeth (as he by then was) and Canon William Purcell – an essential tool for anyone delving into the life of the archbishop.

I also express my gratitude to the Rugby School Librarian for his complimentary copies of the portraits of A.C. Tait and Frederick Temple; to Harrow School for permission to reproduce M. Gauci's lithograph of C.T. Longley; to Wellington College for the loan of the photo of E.W. Benson; and to the *Church Times* for the loan of the photo of G.F. Fisher.

Last but not least, I extend my warmest thanks to my wife for transforming my own messy transcript, for the fifth time of asking, into her usual fair copy for the publishers – and for much-needed encouragement along the way.

B.P.

1

PASTORS AND MASTERS

Public-school Heads in Holy Orders

Disciples of P.G. Wodehouse may recall the story in one of his earlier books about a headmaster who, under the stimulus of a tonic intended for animals rather than humans, paints a statue of one of the school's benefactors pink. As a result of his misdemeanour, he tells an accomplice, he risks incurring the wrath of the governors. The following piece of dialogue then takes place:

> 'They insist on my finding the culprit. Should I fail to do so, they hint at the gravest consequences.'
> 'You mean they will deprive you of your headmastership?'
> 'That is what they imply. I shall be asked to hand in my resignation. And, if that happens, bim goes my chance of ever being a bishop.'[1]

Those lines were published in 1927, by which time the dominance of the clergy among public-school headmasters was almost at an end (though Geoffrey Fisher still ruled at Repton). But the image of the clerical head still persisted in the popular mind, so the words of Wodehouse would have seemed perfectly natural to his first readers.

It was in the nineteenth century that the clerical headmaster had come into his own. That was the age of the really great heads – men of the stamp of Warre of Eton, Vaughan of Harrow, Temple

1

of Rugby, Thring of Uppingham and, supremely, Thomas Arnold. All had been ordained. It was Archibald Tait, Arnold's successor at Rugby, who described the schoolmaster's calling as a 'proper profession' for a clergyman. 'My opinion', he once wrote, 'is that there is no situation of so directly pastoral a nature as mine.'[2] And Christopher Wordsworth, who succeeded the future Archbishop Longley as Headmaster of Harrow before rising to be Bishop of Lincoln, took up his headship 'with very high and noble aims, with a longing to unite religion and scholarship in education'.[3] He was convinced that to separate the two was like setting a man to climb a mountain and then depriving him of a guide. Arnold himself maintained that education and religion were really two aspects of the same thing – a system of instruction in striving towards moral perfection. To idealists such as these the taking of holy orders seemed a natural aid to putting their principles into practice.

Arnold symbolized his own acceptance of the link between the roles of schoolmaster and clergyman by proceeding to priest's orders on his appointment to Rugby after many years as a deacon. For much of the nineteenth century that link was regarded as essential for any ambitious schoolmaster aiming at a headship. Even as late as 1898, when the headmastership of Cheltenham fell vacant, it was an 'open secret' that one candidate on the short-list was not elected solely because he did not happen to be in holy orders. About the same time the more prescient H.M. Burge, an Oxford college fellow, delayed taking orders till he was thirty-five – by when his name was being mentioned as a promising candidate for a public-school headship. He was appointed first to Repton in 1900 and then, after only two terms there, to Winchester; 18 years later he returned to Oxford as its bishop.[4] A cynic might have observed that Burge's forethought had paid good dividends. It was all very well for a late-nineteenth-century Headmaster of Harrow, J.E.C. Welldon, to remark that 'as a general rule it is not especially valuable for a headmaster to be in holy orders' – but then, Welldon was already a clergyman at the time of his appointment and might not have secured the job if he had been a layman.[5]

Why was it considered so advantageous, if not essential, to have a cleric for a headmaster? In his analysis of the issue in *Tom Brown's Universe* J.R. Honey suggests that it was because the special problems of boarding-school communities were thought to call for 'the exercise of functions which could only be looked for in a clergyman'. These functions were preaching in chapel, preparation for confirmation and religious teaching generally. In fact, says Honey, the headmaster's role as a preacher was considered to be one of his most important duties and the 'key weapon in the armoury with which the school equipped the boys to cope with moral evil'.[6] As this book will show, the sermons preached by the two Temples had a profound effect upon their pupils, as did, to a lesser extent, those of Tait, Benson and Fisher. But the paradox of the situation was that lay headmasters could, and sometimes did, preach almost as powerfully as their clerical counterparts. And some critics argued the unfairness of a system which insisted on an ordained headmaster as an essential safeguard for the religious and moral content of education in a boarding school, while allowing housemasters who might well be laymen to act as his delegates in teaching their pupils divinity and preparing them for confirmation.

It was not even as if clerics necessarily preached better than laymen. Welldon, for instance (he who had cast doubt on the need for a headmaster to be ordained), was no great preacher. That astute critic, Hensley Henson, described his pulpit manner as slow and monotonous, and his matter as scarcely ever original – 'platitudes put forth with extraordinary appearance of sincerity'.[7] And the Headmaster of Eton, Thomas Balston, was reduced to special pleading when taxed by the Public School Commissioners in 1862 with his failure to preach regularly to his pupils:

Boys are so easily influenced and so easily impressed with anything which is said from the pulpit, that it requires great consideration whether the man who is placed over them as Head Master should be the man who should influence them so extensively as I consider the Head Master would have the power of doing if he had the right of preaching to them. I think it would rather tend to destroy the purity and freedom, and therefore the thorough simplicity, of their religion.[8]

3

The proportion of clergy to laity among assistant masters at public schools dropped substantially during the final quarter of the nineteenth century. The result was an increasing number of able laymen aspiring to headmasterships. But, though many felt themselves called, few in fact were chosen until after the end of Victoria's reign – at least as far as the major public boarding schools were concerned. The turning-point came in 1903 when a talented layman, Frank Fletcher, was appointed Headmaster of Marlborough, to the astonishment of the educational world and only a few months after his headmaster at Rugby had prophesied that none of the great boarding schools would accept a lay headmaster during Fletcher's lifetime.[9] Fletcher may have fancied himself the exception rather than the rule. At any rate it was he who urged the appointment of one of his bright young colleagues at Marlborough, the Rev. Geoffrey Fisher, to succeed William Temple as Headmaster of Repton.

Progress thereafter was slow but sure. Although Tonbridge appointed its first lay headmaster in 1907, Sherborne in 1909, Wellington in 1910 and Charterhouse in 1911, Repton had to wait till 1932, Eton till 1933, Winchester till 1935 and Westminster till 1937.[10] But, even in the dying years of the breed, the surviving clerical heads often had a profound influence on their charges. Although Fisher at Repton had his critics among the boys, others (as will be seen in due course) thought highly of him. And at Rugby Albert David, the future Bishop of Liverpool, left an indelible impression on the young William Plomer, whose housemaster David had been as well as his head. Plomer points a memorable contrast in describing a photograph of a concourse of Anglican bishops:

> There they sat, row upon row, like a school of sleek sea-monsters washed up on the rocks, their faces mostly wearing an expression of blank complacency and self-importance as if the world depended on them. It seemed extraordinary that these pink magnates should have anything to do with people's souls.... But among all those faces one face stood out. It seemed to me the face of an exceptional man and an exceptional Christian, as long before it had seemed the face of an exceptional schoolmaster.[11]

The educational historian A.F. Leach observed in 1913: 'There is probably no position in English civic life where a single individual exercises such uncontrolled power as does the headmaster of a successful Public School.'[12] And, in the English ecclesiastical life of the nineteenth century, the same could be said of a diocesan bishop. So the progression from the headmaster's study to the episcopal bench seemed a natural one. In fact, however, such promotions were not as common as might have been expected. Of the hundred or so English diocesans appointed during the reign of Queen Victoria, fewer than a dozen had first presided over a public school. By the middle years of this century the narrow stream had slowed to a trickle.[13] Now it has almost dried up completely. It is significant, however, that, of the half-dozen headmaster-archbishops discussed in this book, no fewer than four had connections with Rugby – Tait and Frederick Temple as headmaster, Benson as assistant master, and William Temple as pupil and subsequent governor. Rugby, one might say, was a nursery for future archbishops (which would no doubt have rejoiced the spirit of Thomas Arnold). It was William Temple who (in a letter to his wife) remarked of his old school:

> The great glory of Rugby is not the brilliancy of its results – it has few Cabinet Ministers and so on – but the incomparably high level of usefulness reached by its average products. Eton will produce, say, two or three Viceroys; Rugby will produce twenty or thirty first-class provincial administrators. But before all comes its influence on other schools. Here it far surpasses any.... Rugby has done a wonderful lot in training the men who have guided the other schools.[14]

The concept of the headmaster-bishop did not win universal approval in Victorian times. In a comment on the appointment of the Rev. W. Inge (father of the future Dean Inge) to be Provost of Worcester College, Oxford, the *Journal of Education* observed that it was 'as absurd to promote a country vicar to the Mastership

of a College as to make a headmaster a Bishop'.[15] And a few
(like H.A. James of Rugby) actually turned down the offer of a
bishopric.*

* * * * *

What actually *is* a public school? Some would claim today that
representation on the Headmasters' Conference establishes a
school's right to the title. But the HMC includes 200 or so schools
in its membership, not all of which would strike observers as
being obviously 'public schools'. The title was bestowed with
equal freedom in the nineteenth century until the Clarendon
Commission, appointed in 1861 to enquire into the state of the
public schools, narrowed the number down to a mere nine:
Charterhouse, Eton, Harrow, Merchant Taylors', Rugby, St
Paul's, Shrewsbury, Westminster and Winchester. A question-
mark even hung over one or two of the mystic Nine. The captain
of the Shrewsbury cricket eleven, for instance, proposing to his
opposite number at Westminster a match between the two
schools, received a crisp rebuff:

> The Captain of the Westminster Eleven is sorry to disappoint
> Shrewsbury, but Westminster plays no schools except Public
> Schools, and the general feeling in the school quite coincides with
> that of the Committee of the Public Schools Club, who issue this
> list of public schools – Charterhouse, Eton, Harrow, Rugby,
> Westminster and Winchester.

The Public Schools Club of those days was an embryo attempt at
exclusivity which never in fact got off the ground; but the disappointed Shrewsbury cricket captain gave as good as he got, arguing his school's right to the title of 'public' and ending: 'I regret
to find from your letter that the Captain of the Westminster Eleven

---

* C.J. Vaughan, the great Headmaster of Harrow, was technically in this class. But it has now
been revealed that his decision to decline the offer of at least two sees from Palmerston was
due to the threat of exposure of a homosexual affair he had had with one of his pupils if he
accepted. Vaughan was forced by the same threat to resign his headmastership. He ended up as
Dean of Llandaff.

has yet to learn the first lesson of a true public school education, the behaviour due from one gentleman to another.'[16] Even the Clarendon Commission recognized that its choice of schools might be considered arbitrary, and that newer foundations such as Marlborough, Cheltenham and Wellington might have a justifiable claim to the title of 'public'. Today there are between 30 and 40 leading educational establishments which most people would regard as public schools. Of these Repton, the school over which William Temple and Geoffrey Fisher successively presided, is certainly one. The other three schools discussed in this book are Longley's Harrow, Benson's Wellington, and the Rugby of Tait and Frederick Temple.

The period covered by the book spans the change of ideals which accompanied the transition from the mid-Victorian to the late Victorian age – a change which, as David Newsome remarks, was 'reflected in the difference commonly discerned between what Thomas Arnold taught and what Thomas Hughes, the creator of *Tom Brown,* practised'.[17] Newsome defines the contrasting worlds of Arnold and Hughes as 'godliness and good learning' and 'godliness and manliness'. Longley and Tait belonged to the first era, Frederick Temple and Benson to the beginning of the second. Nearly 40 years separated the end of Benson's reign at Wellington from the start of William Temple's at Repton. The twentieth century was by then well into its stride, and the school over which first the younger Temple and then Fisher presided would have had a great deal more in common with the public schools of today than with the Harrow which caused such miseries to Anthony Trollope.

The stage has now been set. It is time for the major actors to appear.

C.T. Longley: drawn on stone by M. Gauci from a drawing in chalk by Mlle. Romilly.

2

TEACHER OF TROLLOPES

Charles Thomas Longley: Headmaster of Harrow, 1829–1836

'Dr Longley never in his life was able to say an ill-natured word.'[1] The tribute to the man who reigned as Archbishop of Canterbury from 1862 to 1868 came not from a fellow ecclesiastic but from the novelist Anthony Trollope. Young Anthony's schooldays were not the happiest days of his life – far from it. And the least happy among them were the years he spent at Harrow first under Longley's predecessor, George Butler (Byron's 'Pomposus'), and then under Longley himself.

Our knowledge of Trollope's ordeal at Harrow is based mainly on the account of it he gives in his autobiography. It is not an entirely trustworthy account: some of the alleged facts in it were contradicted by former schoolfellows who claimed that the novelist did protest too much. But he undoubtedly had a raw deal at Harrow, even though it may not perhaps have been quite as raw as he himself alleged; and the picture he paints is graphically descriptive of the school over which Longley had once ruled. The basic cause of Trollope's unhappiness was the fact that he was one of the handful of boys at the school known as 'home boarders'. Under the school's statutes instruction was available free to the sons of Harrow residents. Trollope's father, a man much given to economies, decided to avail himself of this privilege. Although intending to send his four sons in due course to his own school,

Winchester, he built himself a house at Harrow. This qualified him to send his sons as day boys to the school until they were old enough to go on to Winchester.

For his sons their free education was a doubtful blessing, the home boarders being despised by their more affluent fellows. To Anthony it was a purgatory. He was only eight when he entered the school for the first time in 1823, but his extreme youth was no defence against the taunts of his fellows. He was bullied without mercy, his appearance being held against him not only by the boys but by the masters too.

> I remember well, when I was still the junior boy in the school, Dr Butler, the headmaster, stopping me in the street and asking me, with all the clouds of Jove upon his brow and all the thunder in his voice, whether it was possible that Harrow School was disgraced by so disreputably dirty a little boy as I![2]

After three years at the school (according to his own account, though the school records imply that it was only one year) Trollope was removed on the advice of his tutor, who suggested to his father that 'my juvenile career was not proceeding in a satisfactory manner at Harrow'[3] and that the future novelist would do better at a private school at Sunbury, Middlesex, which happened to be run by the tutor's brother. Trollope had a happier time of it there, but after two years went on to Winchester, where (partly because of unpaid bills deriving from his father's poverty) he endured miseries similar to those he had experienced at Harrow. Trollope senior's financial affairs were now in such a mess that he was forced to return to Harrow and Anthony to avail himself once again of the benefits of a free education.

His second spell at the school was no happier than his first. Indeed, it was even more miserable in that his father had moved to a 'wretched, tumbledown farmhouse' at Harrow Weald, three miles from the town, which involved young Anthony in a long and arduous journey each day to and from school. Looking back in his autobiography 40 years on, he complains of those later Harrow days:

Perhaps the eighteen months which I passed in this condition, walking to and fro on those miserable dirty lanes, was the worst period of my life.... I had not only no friends, but was despised by all my companions.... What right had a wretched farmer's boy, reeking from a dunghill,. to sit next to the sons of peers – or, much worse still, next to the sons of big tradesmen who had made their ten thousand a year?[4]

There was one consolation, however. At least he now had a head-master whom he could respect – even if the headmaster may not have thought all that highly of *him*.

Charles Thomas Longley had succeeded George Butler as head in 1829, two years before Trollope was readmitted to the school. The fifth of the 17 children of John Longley, a Rochester magistrate, he had been born in 1794 and educated first at a private school at Cheam, Surrey, and then at Westminster and Christ Church, Oxford.[5] His mother is said to have discouraged his desire to become a clergyman as she had a large family to bring up, a husband who lived beyond his income, and no church influence. But young Charles was determined to enter the ministry, and so disregarded the maternal advice.[6] He took a first in Greats (one of his examiners being John Keble) and was ordained to a title at Cowley, a village outside Oxford, under Thomas Vowler Short, who was later to be Bishop of Sodor and Man and of St Asaph and whom Longley succeeded as incumbent in 1823. He combined his cure with tutorial work at Christ Church and soon became a popular don; but in 1827, tiring of the Oxford ambience, he accepted from one of his pupils in whose gift it lay the living of West Tytherley, near Stockbridge. His stay in Hampshire was brief, however. Early in 1829 Vowler Short proposed his name for the headmastership of Harrow, vacant by the resignation of Butler.[7] He was elected by the governors on 21 March and took up residence at the school at the beginning of the summer term.[8]

According to Archdeacon W.W. Phelps, at that time an assistant master at the school, Longley was chosen primarily because he was an outsider. At least two other members of the staff were among the possible candidates for the headship. There was a strong 'Harrow party' who favoured the appointment of Harry Drury,

Trollope's old tutor; and an 'Evangelical party', headed by the Vicar of Harrow, J.W. Cunningham, who backed Samuel Batten, a housemaster who had fitted up his house for the reception of a 'rather aristocratic class of boarders'. In the end the governors resisted the blandishments of both parties and opted instead for Longley as one who was totally unconnected with the present staff. According to Phelps's biographer, Longley 'was believed by competent critics to be the man of all others for the post'.[9]

His inheritance was a tricky one, the school in recent years having been plagued by a series of so-called 'rebellions'. It had been founded in 1571 by a local worthy, John Lyon, who had laid it down that the master in charge was to 'take pains with all indifferently, as well of the Parish as Foreigners, as well of poor as of rich'.[10] Unfortunately, over the years, the founder's ideals had been whittled away, so that, by the time that Anthony Trollope attended the school as a home boarder, the 'Foreigners' (the non-local boys) vastly outnumbered the locals. And the 'poor' boys, even the moderately poor ones like Trollope, were by now so thin on the ground that they were looked down upon by their more affluent contemporaries and had a pretty thin time. As Trollope put it in his autobiography: 'I might have been known among all the boys at a hundred yards' distance by my boots and trousers.'[11] In another passage he complains:

> The indignities I endured are not to be described. As I look back it seems to me that all hands were turned against me – those of masters as well as boys. I was allowed to join in no plays. Nor did I learn anything – for I was taught nothing'.[12]

The wealthy boarders tended to persecute the day boys on principle, taking the line that such a tenuous link with the founder's intentions was one which deserved to be forgotten.

The first of the 'rebellions' took place in 1771, when the governors appointed as head an Eton master, Benjamin Heath, in preference to a member of the Harrow staff, Samuel Parr. The boys protested against what they regarded as an insult to the school, but their petition was ignored. Disorder broke out, and the coach belonging to one of the governors was rolled down the hill to the common and smashed to pieces. The governors were not amused. They dismissed all the pupils to their homes for a week and expelled the ringleaders of the revolt – including eleven-year-old Richard Wellesley, who was later to achieve fame in India as the Marquis Wellesley and whose younger brother Arthur achieved even greater fame on the Continent as the first Duke of Wellington. (Both the Wellesley boys were then sent, ironically, to Eton.) The unfortunate Parr withdrew from Harrow in a huff and set up a rival establishment at Stanmore; he took with him 40 ex-Harrovians, but his school survived for only five years.[13] His successful rival, Heath, soldiered on without further disaster until 1785, when he was succeeded by Joseph Drury*, founding father of a dynasty of Harrovian masters, his son, grandson, brother and nephew all serving on the staff. Indeed, it was the failure of the governors to appoint his brother Mark to succeed him that sparked off a second 'rebellion' when he retired in 1805. The governors were evenly divided between Mark Drury and George Butler, a Fellow of Sidney Sussex College, Cambridge, and an outstanding classical and mathematical scholar. In accordance with the statutes, they were reduced to calling on the Archbishop of Canterbury to give a casting vote; he cast it for Butler, and the result was mayhem. The ringleader of the revolt was the poet Byron, then nearing the end of his time at Harrow. He wrote some satirical verses on the new appointment, in which Drury was lauded as Probus and Butler as Pomposus. He also helped to lay a train of gunpowder with a view to blowing up the headmaster's house, but the powder misfired and no harm was done – nor Byron's part in the plot discovered.[15]

The most serious of the three rebellions occurred three years later, and was provoked by Butler himself, who curtailed some of the privileges of the monitors, including their right to cane other boys without reference to the head. Butler confiscated the canes. The school (surprisingly, perhaps) sided with the monitors and a

---

* The school at that time was a nursery for statesmen. Four future Prime Ministers – Goderich, Peel, Aberdeen and Palmerston – were pupils there under Joseph Drury, as was the poet Byron. 'There goes Byron like a ship in a storm,' Mrs Drury remarked on one occasion, 'without rudder or compass.'[14]

four-day 'strike' took place. The keys of the birch-cupboard were seized, communications with London cut and a main road blockaded. But the revolt soon fizzled out. Seven of the ten monitors were expelled, and King George III 'was pleased to express approval of the way the disturbance was repressed'.[16] Those were indeed stirring times in which to be a public-school headmaster, but by the time Longley took over from Butler* things had quietened down, though the numbers at the school had sunk by now from a peak of 295 to a mere 128.

He was by now a man of thirty-five, and rather below the average height. But he had a fine head which, though prematurely bald, was flanked at the sides with strands of black hair. His eyes were of the deepest black and his mouth well formed – 'with, on occasion, a pleasant smile'. This last detail is supplied by Bishop Henry Lascelles Jenner in an essay appearing in Howson and Warner's *Harrow School*. Jenner (whose abortive episcopal career may have embittered his personality†) adds sourly:

> *On occasion*, for the boys had but little experience of *this* side of Longley's manner, which, indeed, was seldom exhibited in the relations between a master and his boys at this period. There was no apparent sympathy between them; no approach to kindly familiarity or confidence. And thus, one of the strongest agencies that a master possesses for developing the character of his boys was lost.[19]

Jenner's contemporary, Anthony Trollope, would have disagreed with this assessment. Recalling in his autobiography the gibe of Longley's predecessor, Butler, about his extreme scruffiness, Trollope remarks: 'Dr Longley might with equal justice have said

---

* Butler himself was a charismatic character. Besides being a classical and mathematical scholar, he was also a musician and linguist and skilled at riding, skating, fencing and swimming. In his seventieth year he plunged into a half-frozen river and rescued a woman from drowning.[17] His Harrow pupils included (besides Trollope) Sidney Herbert, the future Cardinal Manning and Anthony Ashley Cooper, the philanthropist Earl of Shaftesbury.[18]
† He was elected Bishop of Dunedin, New Zealand, in 1869, but, on arrival in his see, was accused of favouring Tractarian practices and, unwilling to become a focus of controversy, returned home after a few months. He formally resigned the see in 1873, but was never offered another.[20]

14

the same thing any day – only that Dr Longley never in his life was able to say an ill-natured word.'[21] That tribute rings true. Queen Victoria referred to the Archbishop on his deathbed as the 'worthy and amiable Longley',[22] and his general benevolence was certainly apparent at Harrow, one of his nicknames being 'Good-natured Longley'.[23] Another nickname was 'Jacob' (after a favourite parrot), though, according to J.G. Cotton Minchin in *Old Harrow Days*, 'it was the boys who beguiled him, and not he the boys'.[24] He certainly tried to govern by kindness and personal influence. Even Jenner admits that he was popular with the boys.

> It is true that he failed to inspire them with enthusiasm, but he certainly gained their respect. He possessed qualities which boys are always quick in discerning and appreciating; those, for instance, of a perfectly well-bred and courteous gentleman who knew how to treat his boys as gentlemen.[25]

But of course there was an obverse side to the coin of Longley's good nature: the less scrupulous boys took advantage of it. He was a poor disciplinarian. Minchin admits that during his reign 'skylarking' was the order of the day. 'The greater part of this skylarking was pure fun, but alongside of, and under cover of it, many practices were indulged in that were neither manly nor innocent.'[26] Or, as John Fischer Williams puts it in *Harrow*, 'in truth the School got rather out of hand in those days, and the government forgot the cardinal duty of keeping order'.[27] Yet another historian, Percy M. Thornton in *Harrow School and its Surroundings*, agrees that the moral fibre of the school became loosened during Longley's reign, 'and it is agreed on all sides that too mild an exercise of authority had led to a mischievous laxity in discipline'. Thornton admits that the headmaster possessed a 'peculiar power of attracting mankind towards himself', but points out that such a quality is appreciated more by adults than by schoolchildren: 'boys are apt to take advantage of the charity which hopeth, believeth and endureth all things'. Thornton goes on:

A tendency to benignant judgment when independent decision was possible naturally prompted the school monitors to adopt similar easy-going methods of rule, and, as some would say, led them to doubt whether they would be supported in exercise of their authority. But Dr Longley was so courteous and bending to the staff of masters that, though not a strict disciplinarian himself, he nevertheless gave way to the most experienced of them as regards making rules and enforcing obedience, so that delinquents by no means always got off scot-free.[28]

The various histories of Harrow abound in Longley anecdotes. On one occasion a boy stole into the headmaster's larder and abstracted the inside of a pie, leaving the outer crust intact: the feelings of Longley's guests when he cut through the crust only to encounter a vacuum may be imagined. But, when the culprit owned up, the head's comment was merely a mild 'I am so glad you told me'.[29] On another occasion he caught a boy out of bounds at night-time. The boy wriggled out of his grasp, but left one of his coat-tails behind him. Longley's triumph, however, was short-lived. The next morning fifty boys appeared in coats short of a tail.[30] A favourite trick was to let a number of cockchafers out of a box when the headmaster was reading house prayers beside the only candle in the hall. The insects in-variably made a beeline for his bald pate – and Longley invariably believed that they had entered by the open window.[31]

Thornton reports a 'ludicrous scene' wherein the future arch-bishop was hauled up towards the upper story of his own house by young miscreants who believed a basket of forbidden provender to be attached to the rope. 'Rumour has it that a recalcitrant youth dropped the rope in horror, exclaiming in his surprise, "By Jingo, it's Jacob!".'[32] But at least the indulgent Longley nerved himself to stamp out one forbidden pastime – the notorious 'Jack o'Lanthorn'. This was a kind of nocturnal hare-and-hounds and involved 30 or 40 'hounds' creeping out of the house at night and running across country after a lantern carried by a swift-footed 'hare' who, by means of his lantern, would lure the 'hounds' into every pond and ditch along the route.[33] The egregious Jenner records: 'Eventually the thing came to the ears of Dr Longley; and the indignant oration, in which he somewhat pompously

16

announced his determination to "put a stop to this system of Jack o'Lanthorn", was long remembered.'[34]

*   *   *   *   *

Apart from being kind to his pupils, how did Longley shape as Headmaster of Harrow? He was certainly successful in increasing the numbers at the school and introducing more frequent examinations. His chief service to Harrow, however, was the reform of the school's curriculum. As with the other public schools of the period, classics took precedence over other subjects, the study of Latin and Greek being considered the be-all and end-all of educational existence. Looking back on his own schooldays under Longley, Bishop Jenner agreed that such a policy left much to be desired. While not contesting the supremacy accorded to the classics, Jenner considered it overdone.

> There is no question that the absence ... of all instruction in modern languages, and in mathematics, as parts of the school system, was a fatal mistake, and entailed serious after-disadvantages. The same may be said of history, which formed a very minute part of the teaching.[35]

But it was not only the emphasis on Latin and Greek at the expense of other subjects that seemed wrong in retrospect: the actual teaching methods were gravely at fault. Anthony Trollope claims that, when he finally left Harrow, he had received no education in the formal sense. He records in his autobiography:

> No attempt had been made to teach me anything but Latin and Greek, and very little attempt to teach me those languages... When I think how little I knew of Latin or Greek on leaving Harrow at nineteen, I am astonished at the possibility of such waste of time.[36]

Further light on the teaching (or lack of it) at Harrow in Trollope's day is contained in an article he contributed in 1865 to the *Fortnightly Review*. While nominally a critique of the report of a commission set up to investigate the state of nine major English public schools, the article is in effect an indictment of the teach-

17

ing system then in vogue at those schools. Trollope is particularly scathing on the 'intellectual training' considered suitable for sixth-formers at Harrow. Lessons in class, he recalls, consisted simply of selected boys being summoned by the headmaster to translate whatever passage by a classical author such as Thucydides or Sophocles they had been told to prepare. Longley's good nature impelled him, apparently, to call only on those boys who were likely to show skill in construing the chosen passage.

> That he very rarely – almost never – called upon me, who was certain to fail, I impute to him as no blame. When I failed, what could he do? What he did do was to undergo a look of irrepressible, unutterable misery at the disgrace which I brought upon his sixth form, and bid me to sit down with a voice of woe! How well I remember his face when he was thus woful [*sic*]! How I reverenced him and loved him – though he could never have loved me! And I love him and reverence him now.[37]

Trollope's hero-worship of his old headmaster was reflected in his portrait of Bishop Yeld in *The Way We Live Now*, based on Longley and published in 1875.[38] And, in his *Fortnightly* article, he goes on to wonder whether 'the calling up of bishops who won't believe the Old Testament is pleasanter work than was the calling up of boys who wouldn't get up their Thucydides'.*[39] Then, maybe thinking that he might be accused of having gone too far, he continues:

> Dr Longley, if he should take this as an accusation – which I trust he will not do – and should condescend to answer it – which of course he will not do – would doubtless say that his business, when the sixth form was before him, consisted simply in hearing, and not in teaching, and that he endeavoured to communicate to the work in hand as much of the nature of a lecture as the time would permit. He would also say that the boys were supposed already to have studied the subject of that hour's lesson with the assistance of their tutors in the pupil-rooms.[40]

---

* A reference to J.W. Colenso, whose deposition as Bishop of Natal in 1863 because of his allegedly heretical views provoked a furious controversy. By then Longley was Archbishop of Canterbury. By a strange irony he had himself engaged Colenso to teach mathematics at Harrow shortly before he left. See below.

Trollope then comes to the nub of his complaint about the teaching methods current at Harrow in his day. He claims that the studying with the tutors in the pupil-room was a process exactly similar (except that it was done still more quickly) to that which took place afterwards in the school-room.

> There was no teaching – nor was there any possibility that the masters should teach. These men, who were tutors in their pupil-rooms, were also the masters in the school... This pupil-room work, therefore, was the quickest possible gabble of construing – and of course those boys were made to do it who could do it, and not those who could not.

The effect, according to Trollope, was that the precocious boys were pushed ever onwards at the expense of their less able fellows, who received no teaching at all. 'How should there have been teaching when a master was sorely tasked to hear all the lessons he was called upon to hear, and to read all the exercises he was called upon to read?'[41]

There is no reason to doubt the general accuracy of Trollope's analysis, though he may have exaggerated his own intellectual deficiencies. According to the sixth Earl of Bessborough, who, as Frederick Ponsonby, was at Harrow from 1830 to 1833,

> Mr Trollope [as he recalled many years later] must have forgotten the weekly themes wh ... Lord Bessborough had reason to remember, because, having taken extraordinary pains with one for which a small prize was to be given, he went anxiously to Dr Longley for his decision, having, as he believed, done fairly well. 'You did well,' replied the headmaster, 'but, you see, Trollope writes better English than you do, at present.'[42]

Even then, it seems, the future novelist was showing signs of a literary promise which his headmaster was shrewd enough to perceive.

Both Trollope and Ponsonby were at Harrow during the early part of Longley's headmastership, and so missed the extension of the curriculum which he introduced towards the end of his reign. The pioneers in the French and mathematical trail-blazing were a pair of brothers, Jacob and Jacques Marillier. Jacob had been appointed by George Butler as early as 1819 to teach writing. Seven years later he was given permission to coach pupils in mathematics – though only on Fridays. According to P.H.M. Bryant in *Harrow*, quoting an anonymous Old Harrovian, 'he lived the life of a dog and was received with hallooing and hooting whenever he appeared'.[43] And Sir William Gregory recalls in his autobiography: 'Of Euclid and Algebra I was entirely ignorant; there was, it is true, a French and Mathematical master, the same man performing the double function, but good-natured, laughing M. Marillier was a perfect Gallio as regards tuition. He "cared for none of these things"'.[44] Jacob, being a Frenchman, insisted on referring to maths as 'les mathéma*tiques*' – so both he and his subject were inevitably dubbed 'Teek'.[45] In 1834 Longley made both French and 'Teek' compulsory parts of the school curriculum and brought in Jacques Marillier to take over the teaching of the former subject from his brother. Bishop Jenner claims that both brothers were pleasant and genial, and general favourites with the boys.[46]

When it came to Divinity, however, Jenner was more critical. He says in his memoir that it consisted merely of an hour's study of the Greek Testament on Sundays, sometimes with the aid of a commentary. 'The writer can recollect no other religious teaching.'[47] There was no school chapel in those days, so the boys resorted on Sunday morning and afternoon to the parish church, where they occupied two enormous galleries. The preacher was usually the Vicar of Harrow, John William Cunningham,[48] a bigoted Evangelical whose views were anathema to many of the masters and who served as a model for the unctuous and dishonest hero of *The Vicar of Wrexhill*, a novel by Anthony Trollope's mother Fanny.[49] Longley would certainly have liked to have brought more religious teaching into the school, but his efforts were hampered by the absence of a chapel. According to Percy Thornton, 'custom did not allow of the Harrow head-master occupying the pulpit [of the parish church] except on special occasions'.[50] No doubt Longley envied Thomas Arnold, his contemporary at Rugby, who relied on his sermons in the school chapel each Sunday for propagating his high moral ideals among his pupils. In the absence of a chapel Longley had to rely more on personal contacts with individual boys. It may well have been the lack of such an aid to making religion a prominent force in school life that helped him in his decision to exchange his headmastership for a bishopric after only seven years in the post.

*　　*　　*　　*　　*

It is one of the delicious ironies of history that a man who was to cause Longley immense problems in the years ahead should actually have been appointed to the Harrow staff by the future Archbishop of Canterbury as a master of great promise. The man was John William Colenso, at that time an obscure mathematical don at Cambridge. He it was whom Longley, on the lookout at Cambridge for a young mathematician to serve under Jacob Marillier, was advised to engage as the most promising recruit available. Colenso came from an impoverished home in Cornwall, and had only been able to pay for his four years at St John's College by taking in private pupils, translating classical texts and writing a small textbook on mathematics. But he had a brilliant mind and was placed as Second Wrangler in the mathematical tripos of 1836. At the time of his appointment he had not yet been ordained, nor had his theological views broadened out from their Evangelical base; and the ever-trustful Longley could have had no possible inkling of the theological storms that lay ahead. In fact, he spent only a term at Harrow with Colenso before moving on to higher things. Colenso soldiered on at the school for a further six years, resigning in 1842 to take up a tutorship at his old college.[51]

In 1853 he was appointed Bishop of Natal in South Africa, but became a hero or a bogeyman (according to your point of view) in the ecclesiastical circles of the 1860s. This was because, in published works, he had not only rejected the doctrine of eternal punishment but had also questioned the Mosaic authorship and literal accuracy of the early books of the Old Testament,* thereby scandalizing the faithful on two counts. His papers on the Pentateuch and the Book of Joshua were condemned as heretical

---

* He demonstrated, among other things, the mathematical impossibility of the account in Leviticus of the 600,000 men who constituted the whole assembly of Israel being gathered at the door of a 1,692-square-yard tabernacle.[52]

21

by both houses of the Convocation of Canterbury. In 1863 he was deposed from his see by his metropolitan, Bishop Gray of Cape Town. The Judicial Committee of the Privy Council declared the deposition null and void, whereupon Gray pronounced a solemn sentence of excommunication on the erring prelate.[53] It fell to the lot of Longley, by then Archbishop of Canterbury, to attempt to sort out the mess during the first Lambeth Conference, which met for four days in September 1867. Fifty-six out of seventy-six bishops present signed a declaration accepting the spiritual validity of the sentence pronounced on Colenso by Gray. But Longley, moving quietly behind the scenes, was instrumental in preventing the Conference from officially condemning Colenso as a heretic. And the outside world knew little or nothing of the arguments expressed, as the proceedings of the Conference were never published.[54] Its president must have wished at times, however, that Colenso had remained an obscure teacher of mathematics at Harrow.

During their respective spells at the school the two men fared very differently in material terms. Harrow was at the top of the public-school league when it came to the emoluments of its headmaster. By the early 1860s his gross salary was £10,000 a year, as opposed to the Eton head's £6,000 and the £3,000 awarded at Rugby and Winchester. The Harrow head's enormous pay-packet arose from a complex relationship between the number of boys at the school and the profits made from running a house for boarders. Longley was said to have saved as much as £30,000 out of his salary during his seven years as headmaster. Poor Colenso, on the other hand, after six years at the school found himself £5,000 in debt. Although he received a reasonable salary as an assistant master, he was saddled with the cost of fitting out two boarding houses in succession, the first having been destroyed by fire very soon after it had been built. It was his crippling financial position which forced him to leave Harrow and return to St John's, Cambridge, as a tutor. In his efforts to redeem his debt he produced a best-selling book, *Arithmetic for Schools*, which, for a generation of schoolchildren, was a household word.*[55]

---

* After the author had become notorious for his allegedly heretical views the novelist Charlotte Yonge made one of her characters decline to do the sums in her textbook because it was written by that 'dreadful Dr Colenso'.

*　　*　　*　　*　　*

When Longley took over the headmastership of Harrow in 1829, its fortunes were at a low ebb. Under his predecessor, George Butler, who reigned from 1805 to 1829, its numbers had sunk from a peak of 295 to as low as 128 – a fall of over 50 per cent. A Harrow historian, John Fischer Williams, ascribes the steep decline not so much to the faults of the headmaster as to a number of external circumstances: the financial crisis in the nation at large; growing opposition to a purely classical curriculum; and an increasing hostility to the rigours, amounting at times to barbarism, of a public-school education.[56] Longley at first succeeded in halting the decline. By 1833, half-way through his benevolent reign, the numbers at the school had doubled from 128 to 259, though he was unable to maintain his initial impetus. By the time he left in 1836 the numbers had fallen to 165. But at least he ended the day, as it were, with a credit balance of 37 over his original inheritance.*[57]

In 1836 he was forty-two and well settled into his head-magisterial routine. He might well have ended his days at Harrow had it not been for the fact that he had married into an influential family. His wife Catherine was the daughter of Sir Henry Brooks Parnell, later the first Lord Congleton, who had the ear of the then Prime Minster, Lord Melbourne; and it was his father-in-law who suggested Longley's name for a bishopric. He was appointed to the new see of Ripon, the first to be founded in England since the Reformation, and there he was to spend the next 20 years of his life. He expected to end his days at Ripon,[†] but in 1856 was prevailed upon to accept the offer of the bishopric of Durham. By now he had made a name for himself as an elder statesman, and it

---

* The fluctuation in numbers continued to an even greater extent under Longley's successor, Christopher Wordsworth, who went on to be Bishop of Lincoln. Rising initially to 190, they then fell so steeply that, when Wordsworth left in 1844, he had only 69 boys to hand over to his successor, Charles John Vaughan – an outstandingly successful headmaster under whom the numbers rose to almost 500.[58]
† Longley's oath of allegiance at the act of homage following his consecration was made to William IV. No sooner had he risen from his knees than the King suddenly adjured him in a loud voice: 'Bishop of Ripon, I charge you, as you shall answer before Almighty God, that you never by word or deed give encouragement to these d — d Whigs who would upset the Church of England'.[59]

23

was no surprise when Palmerston nominated him in 1860 for the archbishopric of York.

In September 1862 the Archbishop of Canterbury, J.B. Sumner, died. Gladstone suggested to Palmerston that the succession should fall on 'someone who from moderation as well as piety and learning should carry real weight not with any party in particular, but with the Church at large'. There was only one possible candidate in Gladstone's view, and that was Longley – 'whose praise for wisdom and goodness is in all parts and all borders of the Church'.[60] Palmerston took the hint, and Longley was chosen. *The Oxford Dictionary of the Christian Church* dismisses his primacy as 'rather undistinguished', but at least he managed to hold the diverse strands of Anglicanism together without disaster – in contrast to his successor and fellow-ex-headmaster, Tait, who provoked intense conflict in the Church through the ill-advised Public Worship Regulation Act. Longley was indeed the calm before the storm at Lambeth.

His death took place at the end of October 1868. Had it occurred a few weeks later, when Gladstone rather than Disraeli was Prime Minister, Wilberforce and not Tait would almost certainly have succeeded to the primacy – and the future progress of the Church of England would have taken a very different turn.*

---

* The real-life situation had been curiously foreshadowed 11 years earlier by Anthony Trollope in *Barchester Towers*, when Archdeacon Grantly is hoping for the succession to his dying father as Bishop of Barchester but is robbed of the prize by the fall of the government; the incoming premier appoints Dr Proudie instead.

A.C. Tait: from the portrait by J.R. Swinton, 1857.

3

IN THE SHADOW OF ARNOLD

Archibald Campbell Tait: Headmaster of Rugby, 1842–1850

The future Archbishop Tait was appointed to Rugby against all the odds. If we are to believe his earliest biographer, A.C. Bickley, it was only on the last day on which applications for the head-mastership – vacant by the sudden death of Thomas Arnold – could be sent in that he was finally persuaded by his friends to become a candidate. But even then he was a highly reluctant candidate. He complained that, even if he did apply, his application would arrive too late to be considered. His friends were quick to reassure him. If he would but pen his application, they said, he could safely leave it to them to see that it was delivered by the midnight deadline. So Tait was persuaded, almost against his own inclination, to apply for the vacant post. The immediate sequel can be told in the words of Bickley:

> A man was waiting on horseback for it [the letter of application], and, before the ink was well dry, it was speeding over the country as fast as the horse's legs would carry it. Though the man lost no time on the way, it only wanted a few minutes to twelve when he got into Rugby, and the clock was actually commencing to strike as he knocked at the door of the place of delivery. It was just in time, however, and in a few days Dr Tait was both astonished and delighted to find that, out of all the eminent men who were candidates, he was the one chosen to fill the important position of headmaster of Rugby.[1]

His astonishment was justified, as he was by no means the strongest of the applicants for Arnold's mantle. But, before considering how such a comparative outsider came to win the race, it is time to say something about the man himself.

Archibald Campbell Tait was a Scot, born in Edinburgh on 21 December 1811. His father, Craufurd Tait, was a gentleman of straitened means, having squandered his capital on unremunerative agricultural experiments. Archie was the youngest in a family of six sons and three daughters. His mother died when he was only three, and his childhood was spent in the care of a devoted nurse. He had been born club-footed, but overcame the disability with the aid of special tin boots prescribed by a Lancashire farrier. At the age of seven he all but died of scarlet fever. At the age of nine he was enrolled as a pupil at Edinburgh High School, and three years later became a foundation member of the newly opened Edinburgh Academy. In 1827 he entered Glasgow University, rising at 4 a.m. and seldom working less than ten hours a day; he was an ambitious youngster, and in 1829, at the age of eighteen, won an exhibition to Balliol College, Oxford. From now on England rather than Scotland was to be the scene of his endeavours; moreover, soon after his arrival in Oxford, he abandoned the Presbyterianism in which he had been brought up and was confirmed as an Anglican. He had been called 'the little bishop' as a boy; so perhaps it was hardly surprising that, when passing through London to take up his exhibition, he should have visited Lambeth and, on being asked the reason, replied: 'Well, I wanted to see how I shall like the place when I get there.'[2]

Lambeth Palace, however, was nearly 40 years ahead, and meanwhile there was Oxford to conquer. Tait shone as a scholar of Balliol, then, with Oriel, one of the two foremost colleges in the university. In 1834, a year after graduating with a first in classics, he was made a fellow of Balliol and a year later (aged twenty-four) tutor. He was ordained deacon in 1835 and priested the following year. His journals, which give signs of a constantly deepening reflection and fervency, show that he regarded his college work as a truly sacred ministry.

His early pupils included a number of Old Rugbeians who came to recognise his quality. Among them were A.P. Stanley, later Dean of Westminster and the biographer of Arnold; W.C. Lake, later Dean of Durham; Benjamin Jowett, later Master of Balliol; and E.M. Goulburn, later Tait's successor at Rugby and afterwards Dean of Norwich. Two other of his pupils were Matthew Arnold, son of the late Headmaster of Rugby, and Frederick Temple, a second future headmaster. It was indeed a close-knit Rugby circle among whom Tait ministered at Balliol; and it is hardly surprising that some of his former pupils should have pressed him to apply for the headmastership when it fell suddenly vacant in 1842.

By this time he was well known to the public at large – and particularly to the Church public – through his opposition to the *Tracts for the Times*, now coming rapidly to the boil at Oxford. What caused him finally to explode into print was the publication on 25 January 1841 of Newman's notorious *Tract* 90, 'Remarks on Certain Passages in the Thirty-Nine Articles', which interpreted the Articles in a Catholic sense. The tract caused a storm of controversy in which Tait soon found himself involved. He was persuaded to draft the famous 'Protest of the Four Tutors' against it. The 'protest' played a large part in persuading Newman to discontinue the *Tracts for the Times*; and, as the weightiest of its four signatories, Tait shot into prominence as a cleric with a future. His Broad Church sympathies had brought him to the notice of the Rugby School trustees and undoubtedly helped his candidature when the headmastership fell vacant.[3]

It was by no means plain sailing, however, as there were other candidates in the field with higher claims than those of the anti-Tractarian Tutor of Balliol. Conspicuous among these were a number considered his superiors in scholarship. They included Bonamy Price, a former pupil of Arnold's who was now an assistant master at Rugby; J.W. Blakesley, later Dean of Norwich; Herbert Kynaston, later High Master of St Paul's; and Tait's chief rival, C.J. Vaughan, another Old Rugbeian who was later to be an outstanding Headmaster of Harrow.[4] In the face of such powerful opposition Tait was fearful of submitting his own application. But he had some persuasive would-be sponsors, chief among whom were Lake and Stanley. Lake admired Tait as a man both of powerful intellect and of high moral tone. He discussed with Stanley who ought to succeed Arnold and later wrote:

We had very little doubt from the first that the right man would be Tait, who had been our own tutor at Balliol, and I believe the result confirmed our judgment. Though Tait had no experience whatever of an English public school, he had already given indications of that tact in dealing with men which distinguished him through life… It was evident that the trustees would give great weight to the opinion of Arnold's warmest friends and pupils, and a short visit which Stanley and I paid to the leading trustee, Lord Denbigh, in which we dissected all the testimonials, practically settled the matter.[5]

The only snag was that Stanley, a man known for his vacillation, changed his mind at the last minute about Tait's being the right man for the job. He found himself, however, in a difficult position over this particular nomination. He was regarded as the most distinguished, academically, of living Rugbeians,* had been a confidant of the late headmaster and was now the trusted advisor of the Arnold family. He had been pressed to stand for the vacant headship himself; and, though he resisted that temptation, he could hardly resist giving his opinion on the merits of the rival candidates. Vaughan and Price as well as Tait were his personal friends – which may help to account for his sudden change of heart. On the whole, says his biographer,

his voice was for Tait. But he could not disguise that, in some points, which at times he was disposed to regard as of paramount importance, he thought him unquestionably inferior to either Vaughan or Price. The eve of the election found him in one of his fits of despondency as to Tait's qualifications in the matter of scholarship. In a fever of excitement he wrote hither and thither, endeavouring to procure Tait's withdrawal.[7]

And what meanwhile of Tait himself? On 23 June 1842, 11 days after the death of Arnold and a few hours after his last-minute

---

* According to Lake 'Stanley was, if ever a boy was, a book (though a very bright one) in breeches; and though I myself had been an idle boy, and devoted to every sort of game before I came under Arnold's influence in the sixth form, I gave them up almost as a matter of course when I became an intimate friend of Stanley.'[6]

28

decision to stand, he wrote in his diary: 'O Lord, I have this day taken a step which may lead to much good or much evil. Do Thou suffer me to succeed, only if it be to the good of my own soul, and to Thy glory.'[8] (Those eminent Victorian churchmen so often tempered their ambition with pious reflections of this sort.) But Tait cannot have been much comforted by a letter he received from Lake a few days before the election: 'O my dear Tait, I do not envy you if you do get it. I quite quake for the awful responsibility, putting on that giant's [i.e., Arnold's] armour.' While emphasizing that he really did believe Tait to be 'far the best' candidate, Lake went on: 'My main fears are for your sermons being dull, and your Latin prose, and composition generally, weak, in which latter points you will have, I think, hard work.'[9] Tait himself wrote to a friend on the day before the election:

> The near approach of the day has brought so vividly before me the deeply responsible nature of the office for which I am a candidate that I shall be able to make up my mind to failure. The responsibility of such a situation seems to me every day more awful; but all situations are responsible just in proportion to their usefulness, and, if it were in my power to keep up that system which Dr Arnold has begun, I should certainly think my life well spent.[10]

In the event everything went well. According to Tait's sister, Lady Wake, the trustees had all placed Tait's name either first or second on their lists. The issue was finally narrowed to a consideration of the relative merits of two of the youngest among the 18 candidates, Tait and Vaughan. The latter was undoubtedly superior to his rival in technical scholarship and his equal both as a vigorous personality and as a capable administrator. In the end it may well have been Tait's recent emergence as a Broad Church Michael battling against the Tractarian dragon that swayed the vote in his favour. It was not until after long and anxious debate, says Lady Wake, that the decision was arrived at and Tait was elected in Arnold's room.[11] The election took place on 28 July, and the news reached the successful candidate the following day. He hastened to confide the tidings to his diary, and to reassure the Almighty:

Let me view this event, not as success, but as the opening up of a fresh field of labour in Thy vineyard. Now I may look forward to dedicate my whole life to one object – the grand work of Christian education. Let me never forget that the first requisite for this is to be a true Christian myself. Give me a holy heart. Give me boldness and firmness in Thy service. Give me unfailing perseverance. Banish all indolence. Give me freedom from worldly ambition. O Lord, I have much labour before me – much to do of a secular character. Grant that this may never draw me from regular habits of devotion, without which the Christian life cannot be preserved within me.[12]

But he cannot have been best pleased to receive a letter from the fickle Stanley, spurred on by the news that Tait's appointment had aroused ill feeling among some of the assistant masters at Rugby (fortunately it did not last). Stanley began by referring to the 'awful intelligence of your election' which had just reached him. He continued with a short lecture:

Lay aside every thought for the present except that of repairing your deficiencies... Read Arnold's sermons. At whatever expense of orthodoxy (so called) for the time, throw yourself thoroughly into his spirit. Alter nothing at first. See all that is good and nothing that is bad in the masters and the Rugby character.[13]

A few days later Stanley was having qualms about his initial reactions and wrote again:

Forgive me if, in the first agony of distress, when your election brought before me what I had lost – not only in him at Rugby, but in you at Oxford – I may have spoken too sadly. You must not expect that I could go scatheless through so terrible a convulsion as this has been.[14]

Luckily for Stanley's peace of mind he was able to immerse himself for the next two years in the compilation of his *Life and Correspondence of Thomas Arnold*, a massive two-volume work which played no small part in perpetuating the Arnold legend.

*   *   *   *   *

It is time to pause for a moment to consider the nature of Tait's inheritance, and in particular the character of the educational titan in whose steps he was to follow.

Rugby School had been founded in 1567 by Laurence Sheriff, a freeman of the Grocers' Company who supplied provisions to, among others, Queen Elizabeth I. He endowed the school in his will, his massive bequest forming the basis of its later affluence. It underwent a temporary eclipse towards the middle of the seventeenth century and closed for a period. It picked up again under Henry Holyoake the younger, appointed in 1688, and began to attract the sons of the nobility as well as local lads. Numbers increased considerably during the eighteenth century, and trebled during the headmastership of Thomas James (1778–94), who was ahead of his times in declaring that he governed by 'the principles of justice … rather than by the terror of the rod'. The pendulum swung right back under James's successor, Henry Ingles, known for his extreme severity as 'The Black Tiger'. His harsh rule resulted in a rebellion by the boys which had to be quelled by the local militia. Some of the ringleaders were expelled and others flogged. Ingles's successor, Thomas Wooll, was equally rigorous in his attempts to maintain order and discipline.[15] But the Rugby regime of those unenlightened times was no worse than that experienced in other public schools. Eton under John Keate, a contemporary of Ingles and Wooll, was stigmatized by Lytton Strachey as harbouring 'a system of anarchy tempered by despotism … in which licensed barbarism was mingled with the daily and hourly study of the niceties of Ovidian verse'.[16] And Harrow, as we have seen, was no better. In public schools as a whole there was little supervision outside the classroom and practically no organized games; the boys' leisure time was devoted mostly to fighting, drinking, racing and poaching.

It was this unhappy and anarchic state of affairs that Rugby's most famous headmaster, Thomas Arnold, was determined to rectify. He was appointed in 1827 on the recommendation of Provost Hawkins of Oriel, who predicted (correctly) that Arnold would 'change the face of education all through the public schools of England'. He achieved his aim not by attempting to alter the basic educational curriculum, which continued to rest firmly on the study of Latin and Greek, but in more subtle ways. For the free-and-easy system of the past he substituted a more disciplined regime. He forbade entry to any place where dogs, guns or horses could be obtained. He encouraged organized games. He greatly increased the powers of prefects, whom he taught to co-operate with himself in maintaining discipline. Above all, he endeavoured to improve the pattern of public-school life by basing education on a background of religion and morality. He believed that the formation of character mattered more than the mere acquisition of knowledge, and that the Christian standpoint was all-important. 'It is *not* necessary', he once remarked, 'that this should be a school of 300, or 100, or of 50 boys; but it *is* necessary that it should be a school of Christian gentlemen.' His feet were planted firmly enough on the ground for him to add: 'My object will be, if possible, to form Christian men, for Christian boys I can scarcely hope to make.'[17]

One hundred and fifty years after his death Arnold remains a controversial and enigmatic figure. Opinions vary as to how much he actually did achieve. Stanley's hagiographic biography was followed in the fullness of time by the famous denigratory essay of Lytton Strachey. The truth, as always in such cases, lies somewhere between the two extremes.

Certainly Arnold was loved and admired by his pupils to a far greater degree than was customary at the time. Tait's sister, Lady Wake, paints a touching picture of a party of boys she observed piling into the carriages of a train at her local railway station in June 1842:

'Who where they?' 'The young gentlemen from Rugby!' was the reply. Evidently it was no holiday. 'What brought them there?' 'Arnold is dead,' passed from mouth to mouth. Their hushed voices and subdued looks told evidently how suddenly the blow had fallen, and how it had affected each one of them.[18]

Part of Arnold's attraction to the young lay in his energy. He threw himself with ardour into all the pursuits of his pupils. Isabel Quigly maintains that most of his achievement stemmed from his personality rather than from his ideas.

It was his presence that made Rugby boys change, masters admire, parents believe in him; and, later, it was the memory of that presence in those who had known it that made other schools follow. His fervour, his company, his preaching, his whole cast of mind – these were what made his ideas seem memorable and alive.[19]

Arnold was an idealist. His priorities at Rugby were, first, religious and moral principle, and, secondly, gentlemanly conduct. Intellectual ability came last – though he once declared that 'the first, second and third duty of a schoolmaster is to get rid of unpromising pupils'[20] As John Chandos comments:

> He thought that the exaltation of the intellect alone, without regard to moral and religious values, was a dangerous course; at the same time he felt that the retention at school of big older boys who were dull-minded, probably bullies, but, perhaps, good at games, was a bad and morally subversive example to younger ones.[21]

Chandos remarks elsewhere: 'Arnold was ambitious in a natural, worldly sense for himself and the school, and was, in practice, primarily interested in clever boys and in the fruits of success. It was a normal choice for a diligent headmaster to make.'[22] At the same time 'he was determined to make his chosen few, at least his sixth form, shine and radiate his kind of moral effulgence'.[23] This of course sometimes made for priggishness in those at the receiving end of the educational process. In the words of James Fitzjames Stephen, 'A Rugbeian never tied his shoes without asserting a principle.'*[24]

Arnold was once described as 'the first headmaster who made the school chapel the centre of the school'[26] – and the religious atmosphere at Rugby was, at least in its headmaster's eyes, its most significant challenge to other schools. Though his own religion was hard to classify, and although he felt uneasy about a number of traditional dogmas, there was no doubt about his genuine piety. As David L. Edwards comments:

---

* Another eminent Rugbeian used to remark that it took a Rugby boy who had been in the sixth form under Arnold ten years to recover his health both physically and intellectually.[25]

Any boy's approach to irreligious levity or impertinence was checked with a glance, or a white face, or if necessary a terrible word or a judical blow ... Sunday by Sunday he preached to the boys, sometimes weeping in the pulpit, sometimes denouncing their faults, sometimes warning them of death and hell, sometimes proclaiming Christ as the only Saviour for them, sometimes holding up the vision of a nobler life for man and nation.[27]

To sum up: Arnold's achievement at Rugby was more moral than material. Tait's great friend, W.C. Lake, admired his idealism but claimed that conditions at Rugby were much the same at the end of Arnold's reign as at its beginning and that 'it would be a mistake to suppose that his influence materially changed the character of school life for the ordinary boy'.[28] A modern commentator, John Chandos, says that it is difficult to resist the conclusion, on the evidence, that 'Arnold's much-publicised pronouncements made more impression on the outside world than they did on the school as a whole. His reputation worked, in the end, mainly to the advantage of Rugby.'[29] The last word on the subject can come from Bernard Darwin:

When he died ... he had done what Dr Hawkins of Oriel had prophesied of him ... if not in education, technically so called, at any rate in morals and decency, or, if we prefer a less generous word, in respectability. Even if we cannot quite see how he did it, nothing can take away the solid honour of that achievement.[30]

*   *   *   *   *

This long digression must be forgiven if for no other reason than that Tait's initial handicap as Headmaster of Rugby lay simply in his not being Thomas Arnold. As Lake had remarked to him before the election, the new headmaster would face 'the awful responsibility of putting on that giant's armour'. The first hurdle he had to face was his official inauguration in the school chapel on 14 August. The pulpit and desks were still hung with black in memory of Arnold. Tait felt that he could not face the ordeal of preaching himself, so delegated the task to Stanley. The latter, still in two minds about whether he had backed the right horse, wrote in a letter to his sister:

> The first moment of seeing Tait in the study was overpowering; but then all seemed to me natural. It was true that the rightful master of the house was gone; but I rejoiced to think that his labours were over... When I turned to look at his successor, I really felt that there was a moral dignity about him, and a consciousness of the shadow of the past, which in itself fitted him for his great position, and held out the happiest prospect for the future.[31]

Shortly after preaching his valedictory sermon Stanley wrote again to report the effect it had had on the congregation:

> You will be glad to hear how deeply impressed the boys were by the service yesterday. I am told that, when the sermon began, there was a burst of sobs from some, and that the Sixth were in tears almost all the whole time, and that many more, who had always kept their eyes fixed upon him, held their heads down, unable to look up.[32]

Tait recorded his own feelings in his diary immediately after the service:

> Gracious Lord, accept my heartfelt thanks for the mercies of this day. May the words which Stanley spoke be fixed deeply in my heart, and in the hearts of all who heard them. Oh may the solemn responsibility which has this day come so fully upon me make me a man of prayer. Without incessant prayer I am lost, and, if I perish, how many souls perish with me.[33]

It was not long before he found someone with whom to share his 'solemn responsibility'. Or, as his earliest biographer remarked with a touch of the male chauvinism characteristic of the period: 'He had not been many weeks at Rugby before he found out, practically, that it was absolutely necessary that a headmaster should have a wife to relieve him of the trouble of attending to domestic matters.'[34] The lady on whom his choice fell was a certain Catharine Spooner, the youngest of the five daughters of William

35

Spooner, Vicar of Elmdon, Warwickshire, and Archdeacon of Coventry.* She had first met him a few years previously at the house of her uncle, Gerard Noel, who had jokingly remarked to her on seeing her busied on a piece of embroidery: 'I suppose you are making those slippers for Mr Tait!'[35] She was now twenty-two and 'exceedingly beautiful in face and form'. On being reintroduced to her when she visited Rugby in November 1842, three months after his arrival there, the new headmaster was at once captivated by her charms. She for her part was at first inclined to resist his advances. As a cousin of Samuel Wilberforce she was High Church in her sympathies. Indeed, she had been so incensed at Tait's organizing the 'protest of the four tutors' against *Tract* 90 that she hoped that the Rugby headmastership would fall to Charles Wordsworth, a Tractarian sympathizer (and later Bishop of St Andrews), rather than to Tait, the Broad Church Tutor of Balliol. However, as Tait himself reflects in the memoir of Catharine which he wrote after her death: 'It was a strange turn of fate which made her open her heart next year to the very candidate whose success she had deprecated, and become the happy partner of his life.'[36]

They were married at Elmdon on 22 June 1843 by Gerard Noel, who remarked to his niece: 'So, Kitty, you were, after all, making those slippers for Mr Tait!'[37] They spent the school vacation on a prolonged honeymoon (or 'marriage tour', as Tait described it) which took them first to Derbyshire and then to the Lowlands and Highlands of Scotland. Back at Rugby, Catharine took to her new duties as to the manner born. She soon won all hearts; and for once the cliché, 'as good as she was beautiful', was justified. Her mind was intelligent and sympathetic and her enthusiasm for religion deep and genuine. Every day she attended Morning Prayer at the parish church before breakfast, returning in time for family prayers with her husband and other members of the household. She insisted on teaching the basics of the faith to her younger maids and on preparing them for confirmation. But she found herself unable to

---

* William was the grandfather of his more famous namesake, William Archibald Spooner (1844–1930), Warden of New College, Oxford, and inadvertent originator of the 'spoonerism'. The younger Spooner may well have been named after his uncle by marriage, Tait.

share the Broad Church sympathies of some of the masters or to appreciate their disrespectful references to those of differing views. On one occasion an Oxford don on a visit to Rugby gave voice to an unorthodox theological opinion which gravely offended her. She at once left the company, shut herself in a spare room and recited aloud the Apostles' Creed.[38]

If her husband in later years came to be regarded as a bogeyman in Tractarian circles, he might perhaps have been even less restrained without the irenic influence of his wife. In his own memoir of Catharine, based mainly on correspondence, William Benham claims that

> a whole multitude of evidences tell how she was worshipped by the boys, the chivalrous, romantic admiration of her youth and beauty being joined to their grateful sense of her kindliness, and her manifold acts of sympathy and affection rendered to them when they were in sickness, or in any way needed her watchful care.[39]

She often gave tea parties for the younger pupils and entertained the sixth-formers to dinner. She also encouraged the boys to help her in her charitable work for the sick and needy in the neighbourhood. She allowed neither her mind nor her body to go to seed. According to her husband, 'she was never more happy than when helping me to get up my history lessons or when galloping by my side in the green lanes and over the meadows'.[40] Although she was to produce eight daughters and a son, the family was slow in making its first appearance – which enabled the Taits to enjoy a two-month tour of Italy during the summer vacation of 1845. Their eldest daughter Catharine ('Catty') was born in 1846; and Mary ('May') and Craufurd followed during the years at Rugby.

A touching picture of Catharine soon after her arrival at the school is given by A.P. Stanley in a letter to his sisters dated September 1843:

> I ... visited the school house and, finding Tait in school, sent up a message to Taitia to announce my arrival. Immediately there appeared a little creature, pretty, gentle, with a fund of merriment, and taking a great and brimming interest in the place. We gradually advanced in intimacy, which was marked by the gradual reiteration

on both sides of 'Archie' for 'Dr Tait'. This was at last completed by the arrival of Archie... The little creature playfully rebuked her husband for his attacks on Oxford, and perhaps she inclined too much to the notions of her cousin Samuel Wilberforce altogether to suit my notions of one who should occupy the house of Rugby.[41]

On another occasion a curmudgeonly old man of whom the neighbours went in terror was so captivated by Catharine that he presented her with a bunch of the choicest flowers from his greenhouse and declared: 'Monstrous fine woman, Mrs Dr Tait!'[42]

Meanwhile, what of Tait himself, and how was he shaping as Arnold's successor in the headmastership? According to Catharine his face 'assumed a businesslike look the moment we came to our home at Rugby',[43] and certainly he devoted himself heart and soul to his scholastic duties. He was always in school, winter and summer, 'before the first stroke of the clock at seven'* and was seldom in bed before midnight. He regarded himself primarily as the conservator of his predecessor's work and as building on the foundations which Arnold had laid. He was both conscientious and hard-working, and during his reign the school numbers rose gradually to a peak of 493. One of Rugby's earlier historians, W.H.D. Rouse, suggests that he may have pushed Arnold's methods too far, 'and it is to be feared that there was too much introspection and too little naturalness in the type of character which he fostered'.[45] He was not totally wedded to Arnold's principles and methods, however, and was prepared to deviate from them if necessary. 'We have other things to do at Rugby,' he once observed, 'besides exalting the Arnold tradition.'[46] His pupils appear for the most part to have liked and respected him; and, when he left in 1850 to take up the deanery of Carlisle, the trustees expressed their satisfaction that he had 'fully maintained the character and reputation which the School obtained under the distinguished man who preceded him'.[47]

---

* Unlike his predecessor Thomas Arnold, whose dislike of early rising, according to Lytton Strachey, amounted 'almost to a constitutional infirmity'. Arnold overcame the weakness eventually, though early rising continued to be a daily effort to him.[44]

Official approbation, however, must usually be taken with a pinch of salt; and of course, as a schoolmaster, Tait could in no way measure up to the stature of Arnold. As one of his former colleagues, J.C. Shairp, who went on to be Principal of St Andrews, remarked, he 'was certainly by no means a born schoolmaster'. He was handicapped to some extent by not having himself been to an English public school, his sympathies and powers of influence lying more with young men than with boys. Shairp observes that many of the assistant masters had been devoted pupils and friends of Arnold, 'and they were apt to fancy themselves exalted beyond other men by their contact with him'.[48] Such hero-worship of his predecessor cannot have eased the task of the new headmaster. All along, Tait's work at Rugby tends to be damned by faint praise. George Bradley (later Dean of Westminster), while conceding that his teaching was 'thoroughly good in the main' and that he 'always left on the mind of the Sixth the idea of conscientious and thorough work', cannot refrain from adding somewhat cattily: 'He was not, of course, remarkable as a scholar.'[49] And Arthur Butler, later the first Headmaster of Haileybury, claimed that Tait's 'teachings, sermons, govt. [were] all good and sensible, but somewhat cold and repressive; of a kind rather to create respect and confidence than affection and admiration'. Butler had in fairness to add, however: 'Behind his reserve and dignity there was, we all felt, a deep fund of power and feeling, which it only needed the occasion to bring forth.'[50] A modern historian of Rugby, J.B. Hope Simpson, feels that the reserve in the attitude of the assistant masters to their new chief was due primarily to the fact that he was not Arnold.[51]

Tait attempted to emulate his predecessor in the importance he attached to the school's religious observances. Bradley maintains that he 'exercised a great deal of religious influence on the school' and that his sermons were 'very earnest and devout. No one could sneer at them; no one did, I think. They were sometimes really impressive.'[52] Butler recalls that there was usually little in Tait's sermons either to arouse or to stimulate. 'But on touching occasions, such as the death of a boy or master, he gave rein to his feelings, and moved us as deeply as he was himself moved.'[53] A significant sidelight on Tait's own attitude to his religious opportunities is contained in a letter to his future wife, written on Good Friday 1843, in the course of which he remarked:

> Many people think that a schoolmaster's is not a proper profession for a clergyman. My opinion, on the contrary, is that there is no situation of so directly pastoral a nature as mine. How very few clergy have parishioners who are so willing to be led as my boys![54]

As for what 'my boys' thought of their headmaster, such evidence as there is implies (at least to begin with) that, though his wife inspired affection, Tait himself was a more remote figure who was regarded merely with respect. He left the 70 inmates of the School House, for whom he was responsible as their housemaster, very much to themselves. He rarely interfered, and took little interest in the boys' leisure activities. Although he was reluctant to punish transgressors, he never hesitated to do so if the offence was sufficiently heinous. When a boy who had been gated broke out and was found riding on a circus elephant he received no more than a severe reprimand ending with the immortal words: 'Remember, I won't be disobeyed, even for an elephant!' But, when a group of senior boys had been caught drinking, two of them were expelled and four others demoted to the form below.[55] Arthur Butler, who was a pupil at Rugby under Tait, recalls that his admonitions might begin seriously but would end with a twinkle of the eye and a 'Don't let it occur again!' Butler recalls Tait as a

> most dignified and courteous gentleman with a grave manner, an impressive voice and an occasional sparkle of deep feeling or quiet humour, which we felt lying in the background, ready either to flash out upon our faults or make allowance for our shortcomings. Everything about him was dignified, kind and trustful.[56]

Another former pupil, giving his recollections years later in a magazine article, wrote that Tait

> was certainly regarded with respect and esteem by those who did not know him well enough or possess insight enough to wax enthusiastic in his praises. He was never gushing himself, and he had scarcely yet developed that freedom of manly speech which he

attained in a new position, and after trial in the fire by his crushing sorrows at Carlisle.[57]

One of the planks of the Arnold system of school government which Tait successfully reformed was the overlordship exercised by the sixth form over the rest of the school. The praepostors of the sixth had been raised by Arnold to a pinnacle of power and influence which caused resentment and hostility among their less-favoured fellows. Tait defused the situation by fixing limits on the power of the sixth to punish; by giving a right of appeal to any junior boy who felt himself aggrieved; by abolishing some of the sixth's more arcane privileges; and by frequently impressing upon them the desirability of tempering justice with mercy.[58]

The event which was to bring about a significant improvement in the relationship between Tait and his pupils was a sudden illness which all but killed him in February 1848. For some time before then he had been complaining of frequent bouts of fatigue and drowsiness which he refused to see as a warning that he might be working too hard. A succession of comments in his diary drew attention to these attacks as symptoms of a weakness to be overcome. 'O Lord, save me from indolence,' he exclaimed. 'My body becomes so wearied that I cannot pray to Thee as I ought. Forgive me, O Lord, and give me strength for Christ's sake.' On another occasion he confessed in his diary to have been 'sadly drowsy. This is the very sin which I most called to mind this morning at the Holy Table. Yet so weak am I that this very afternoon it has been overpowering me. Last night I felt it and deplored it deeply. O Lord, deliver me from it.'[59] Soon nature had her way, and the over-diligent headmaster succumbed to a severe attack of rheumatic fever. His heart and lungs were affected, and the doctors were in despair. On Ash Wednesday, 8 March, he was expected to die at any moment. He made a new will, dictated a letter of farewell to the sixth form and dispatched special messages to his friends.[60] Luckily it proved a false alarm. He turned the corner and slowly recovered his health, though it was to be many weeks before he was able to leave his bed; nor was he ever again as physically strong as before.

Throughout the period of his illness Catharine proved a tower of strength. She kept constant watch beside his bed, was ready to pray with him and repeat helpful texts and hymns (she could recite almost every psalm by heart), and guarded him from over-excitement at the political news which was convulsing the continent of Europe during that revolutionary year of 1848. Nor was her help confined to holding his hand and ministering to his spiritual needs. She was of a practical turn of mind and, from the early days of her marriage, had relieved her husband entirely of the care of the school accounts (this was before the age of bursars). She now really came into her own. Tait, believing that he was about to die, was concerned lest certain intricacies in the accounts should baffle his executors. His two brothers, both experienced businessmen, undertook to examine the books – but soon found that they were beyond their power to unravel. Catharine then appeared and, in the words of her husband's official biographers, 'quietly and composedly sat down to the task, and, with a calmness which amazed them all, made everything clear and simple.'[61] The brothers were profoundly impressed.*

It was from his sickbed that the ailing headmaster was able to exercise a profounder influence on his pupils. Two episodes in particular struck observers as symptomatic of the growth of a more affectionate relationship. The first was when, at a critical point in his illness, he dictated a letter to the head of his house in which, as a dying man, he begged the boys to think seriously of the great issues of school life and never to go to bed at night without reading a passage from the Bible. Arthur Butler well remembered the impression made by this 'simple, earnest appeal to our higher nature':

The response to it was general. Not only then, but for a long time after, there was an unwonted silence after evening prayers in the long schoolhouse passages, as singly, or by two or threes, we read

---

* As were others. In his memoir of his wife Tait reveals that his brother-in-law, Sir Charles Wake, 'scrutinising her accounts with the preconceived feeling that a lady's habits of business were not much to be trusted, was obliged to confess that nothing could be better managed'. And the manager of Coutts's Bank in London complimented one of Catharine's brothers on the way in which she conducted her husband's financial affairs.[62]

our Bibles. Nothing could better show his influence. There was no talking about it, no parade; but every one at once did what 'dear old Tait' asked us to do from his seeming deathbed.[63]

The second episode was when a 'revolution' was about to break out in the school against the 'Thirty Tyrants' of the sixth. Lists had been drawn up assigning various assailants to each 'tyrant'. In the event the sixth received advance warning of the proposed revolt and appeared in strength in the quadrangle just as the rebels were assembling. In the words of a modern Rugby historian:

There might still have been a considerable riot had not the sudden realisation spread, apparently spontaneously, through the throng that the noise involved might have a serious effect on the sick headmaster; and by the time a master, Bradley, appeared on the scene, tempers had cooled and he was able to disperse the assembly peaceably.[64]

Relations between headmaster and boys improved still further in June when, for the first time since his illness, Tait appeared in the Close during a game of cricket, still very weak but on the road to recovery. 'Instantly,' Arthur Butler recalls, 'every bat and ball was laid aside, and such a cheer arose, again and again repeated, as may well be imagined.' Butler continues:

It was the beginning of a wholly new relation between boys and master. It was the first expression of a popularity which went on increasing till he left us, and which, I believe, has been rarely equalled at any public school. It was not that he had changed outwardly to any great extent. He was always rather the statesman than the schoolmaster, the ruler than the friend. But everything between us took a warmer tone. We had been drawn to him in his illness; we understood him better.[65]

Tait's popularity reached its apogee two years later when, having been appointed Dean of Carlisle, he left Rugby for the last time and the boys took the horses out of the carriage and dragged it to the station themselves. 'Wasn't it a queer way of showing regret?' one of them exclaimed. 'It was as if you were glad to be rid of him.'

But another wondered: 'How shall we ever get on without him?'[66]

The move to Carlisle was dictated by Tait's health. Although he had seemingly made a good recovery from his illness, his physical powers were clearly no longer equal to the strains of a schoolmaster's immensely busy life: a deanery, by contrast, was considered a post of comparative ease. He struggled on for two anxious years; but then came the offer from the Prime Minister, Lord John Russell, and it was at once accepted. In fact Tait was the Premier's second choice, as the deanery had been offered first to Arthur Stanley – partly, as Russell's letter stated, as a 'tribute of respect' to the memory of Stanley's father, the late Bishop of Norwich. Stanley turned down the offer, however, preferring to remain as a fellow of University College, Oxford, so the deanery went to Tait instead. On hearing the news Stanley wrote to Benjamin Jowett:

> I feel myself more than repaid for the many other anxieties I may have had about the refusal by its having issued in this delightful appointment of Tait. I am sorry that Rugby is to be again at sea; but, for his sake and with the great risk of his continuance there, I cannot imagine a place which would suit him better. I reflect upon it with curious joy every hour of the day.[67]

It is one of the more intriguing 'ifs' of ecclesiastical history to imagine how the Church of England would have fared if Stanley rather than Tait had become Dean of Carlisle. Tait would almost certainly have been spared the tragedy which marred his last months in the deanery; but he would not then have attracted the sympathy of Queen Victoria, which helped him to obtain the prestigious bishopric of London, and he might well have ended up in some inferior position to that of Archbishop of Canterbury.

As the headmaster of a public school he was dubbed by one observer 'hardly a success'. That is the verdict of his friend Dean Lake, given many years after Tait's departure from Rugby. He suffered, in Lake's view, from the double handicap of succeeding a man of 'real genius and extraordinary force of character' and of being 'anything but a finished scholar'; and he therefore had to run the gauntlet of a good deal of severe criticism. Nevertheless, says Lake, though Tait's life at Rugby was the least marked period of his career, it greatly developed some of his best qualities and proved the happiest time of his life. It offered him a more congenial and more independent sphere than Oxford, and 'gave a great scope to his tact and his natural power of dealing with men'.[68] If Tait's achievement at Rugby can be summed up in a word, it was evolution, not revolution. Such changes as he introduced were progressive and gradual rather than spectacular. Like Arnold he made the chapel the focus of the school and used its pulpit for the most important part of his instruction. In his dealings with both boys and masters he showed tact and humour, while maintaining a firm discipline.[69]

Arthur Butler, recalling the day before Tait's final departure from Rugby, praises the 'perfect speech' he made in reply to one from the head of the school, G.J. Goschen – afterwards a Cabinet minister and, with C.L. Dodgson (Lewis Carroll), the most distinguished of the 1158 Rugbeians to enter the school under Tait. Nearly 40 years on, says Butler, 'I can recall many of the tones and gestures with which he stirred and thrilled and carried us along as he dwelt on the great work begun by Arnold which he had striven, however imperfectly, to carry on.' No subsequent oration by Tait, in Butler's view, ever came up to the 'grace and fire and dignity of that last speech at Rugby.'[70]

*   *   *   *   *

Tait, unlike his predecessor, usually refrained while Headmaster of Rugby from plunging into public affairs unconnected with the school. But, as a cleric, he could not resist having a say in two or three of the ecclesiastical controversies of the day. He intervened with marked effect in 1845 in the dispute caused by the publication of W.G. Ward's *Ideal for a Christian Church*. This had aroused a storm of protest at Oxford because of its author's denigration of the Reformation and praise of the Roman Catholic

Church. The public outcry was such that a Convocation of the University was summoned to consider three resolutions. The first of these declared the book to be utterly inconsistent with the Thirty-Nine Articles and with Ward's good faith in having subscribed to them; the second annulled the degrees of BA and MA conferred on Ward on the strength of his subscription; the third imposed for all future graduates a new form of subscription to the Articles with a view to avoiding any possibility of such pro-Roman interpretations as Ward and his Tractarian supporters had put upon them.

As one of those who had signed the 'protest of the four tutors' against *Tract* 90 three years before, Tait was confidently expected to champion the three resolutions. He disappointed the anti-Ward faction, however. He reluctantly agreed to his being deprived of his degrees, since he was 'a Roman Catholic in everything but the name'. But he took exception to the third resolution and published a pamphlet, in the form of a letter to the Vice-Chancellor, to explain why. Such a test as was proposed, he declared, could do nothing but harm. 'There is no need of our narrowing the limits of the Church of England because some amongst us wish to make it too wide.' The university authorities were furious at Tait's action ('You have indeed, most prudent of men, put your foot into it', wrote Lake); but Ward, an old friend of Tait's, appreciated the tone of the pamphlet and thought it would do great good. In the event it was largely responsible for the withdrawal of the 'test' resolution by its proposers and the substitution for it of a motion conveying the formal censure of the university upon the principles of interpretation adopted in *Tract* 90. But even this watered-down version failed to get through Convocation. The two proctors (one of whom was Richard Church, afterwards Dean of St Paul's) exercised their constitutional right of veto, and the proposal automatically fell to the ground. And even the resolution depriving Ward of his degrees only scraped through by a handful of votes. To Tait, however, his victory was clouded by regret over the virulence of party spirit exhibited on both sides throughout the contest. Writing to Arthur Stanley a few days after the vote he referred to 'black Thursday – a dreadful day, full of the most painful thoughts of any day I have known for long, and making me

46

melancholy ever since'.[71] He was to have his full share of this type of melancholy in the years ahead.

Three years later Tait played a small part in the 'Hampden controversy', the dispute surrounding Lord John Russell's nomination of Dr Renn Dickson Hampden as Bishop of Hereford. Hampden had already come under fire 11 years earlier, when Melbourne had appointed him Regius Professor of Divinity at Oxford, for his allegedly heretical views; and the controversy was reopened on his nomination to a diocese. Over half the bishops on the English bench signed a letter of protest to the Prime Minister. Tait was among 250 members of the university who signed a counter-petition in Hampden's favour. Although he had no liking for Hampden's 'frigid and somewhat shallow and uninspiring theology', he saw nothing very unorthodox in his opinions and thought that he had been unjustly abused, In a letter to his brother James, Tait conceded that Lord John would have done much better not to have appointed Hampden in the first place; but 'I am fully of the opinion that no case of heresy can be made out after the explanations in Hampden's subsequently published writings.'[72] The dispute dragged on for months, but in the end Hampden was duly consecrated – and laboured blamelessly in his rural see for the next 20 years.

The final ecclesiastical controversy in which Tait found himself involved shortly before his departure from Rugby was one much nearer home: it concerned a book written by one of his own assistant masters, Henry Highton. The book was the subject of a hostile review in *The Guardian*, an influential Church of England weekly, whose anonymous reviewer criticized the character of the religious teaching given at Rugby. He accused the school of being a 'refuge of heresy and latitudinarianism' and claimed that 'the spirit now paramount in the place is that of a sectarian and a freethinker'. Tait at once leaped to the school's defence. 'I ought not lightly to allow this great place of religious educa-tion to be vilified,' he declared in a letter to the paper's editor. He continued:

As to the words 'sectarian' and 'latitudinarian', and even 'heretic'
... I believe that coming from you they will be rightly understood

by the public to mean simply that the person to whom these epithets are applied differs from your particular views in interpreting the formularies of the Church of England, though he may be supported in his interpretation by the authority of many of the wisest and most pious of those whom the Church delights to honour.

The Guardian's reviewer, however, hit back in a further article which accused some of Tait's subordinates of professing opinions of the 'laxest kind', and suggested that there was no political or religious theory on the so-called liberal side which might not find its supporters at Rugby. 'Not that Dr Tait is a freethinker any more than Dr Arnold was a freethinker ... but the tendency of a system of education conducted by either of them is to a false and irreligious liberality.'[73]

*   *   *   *   *

During his six years as Dean of Carlisle Tait cleaned up the cathedral's worst abuses, reorganized its grammar school and handed over its estates to the Ecclesiastical Commissioners. But he also found time to serve on the royal commission appointed by Lord John Russell to reform the University of Oxford and sweep away many of its abuses. Four more daughters – Charlotte ('Chatty'), Frances, Susan and Lucy – were born to Catharine during their years at Carlisle. But, only three weeks after Lucy's birth in February 1856, disaster struck and Chatty went down with an acute attack of scarlet fever – the same malady which had almost carried off her father as a child. One after another Chatty's sisters caught the infection (all except baby Lucy); and one after another, within the space of five short weeks, they died. Tait wrote in his journal after the last of the five pathetic little coffins had been laid in a common grave: 'When last I wrote I had six daughters on earth; now I have one, an infant. O God, Thou hast dealt very mysteriously with us.'[74] But, though he and his wife continued to mourn the loss of their daughters for the rest of their lives, the cloud had, if one may so put it, a silver lining. The tragedy had aroused nationwide sympathy – including, most importantly, that of Queen Victoria. She pressed for the appointment of Tait to the vacant bishopric of London,* far away from the tainted air of Carlisle.

By now Palmerston was Prime Minister. In his episcopal nominations he looked for advice to his *éminence grise*, Shaftesbury, who strongly favoured the appointment of Evangelicals. But Shaftesbury was prepared to concede that the Broad Church school of thought should at least have a token representation on the bench. He selected Tait as (in the words of his diary) 'the mildest among them' and (as he told Lady Wake) 'by very much the best' of the dangerous followers of Thomas Arnold. The Queen was strongly in favour of promotion for Dean Tait in his bereavement; and this was no doubt the crucial factor in persuading Palmerston to appoint a man not yet in episcopal orders to a diocese second in importance only to Canterbury. 'This is certainly *not* the post which I should ever have dreamed of for myself,' Tait recorded modestly in his diary.[75]

As Bishop of London he soon acquired a reputation as an able and conscientious administrator, and he was offered the succession to Longley as Archbishop of York in 1862 when the latter was translated to Canterbury. However, he declined Palmerston's offer of a post 'at once of greater dignity and of less work' than London, on the ground that he might find the distant and untried duties at York less congenial.[76] He had no such inhibitions six years later when Disraeli offered him the succession to Canterbury on the death of Longley. His promotion to the primacy in fact came on the insistence of the Queen and against the wishes of the Prime Minister. For days they argued the toss, the Queen praising Tait as an 'excellent, pious, liberal-minded, courageous man' and Disraeli castigating him as 'obscure in purpose, fitful and inconsistent in action and ... a prey to constantly conflicting convictions'.[77] But the Queen got her way; and Tait repaid her championship in 1874 by drafting, at her instigation, a Public Worship Regulation Bill

---

* Two more daughters were born to the Taits after their move to London: Edith (who was to marry the future Archbishop Randall Davidson) and Agnes. Their son Craufurd survived the scarlet-fever epidemic, but died prematurely, aged twenty-nine, in 1878. Catharine's touching if highly emotional account of the last days of the five doomed sisters forms the centrepiece of *Catharine and Craufurd Tait*, published soon after her own death.

and assisting the Premier to steer it through Parliament. The Bill was an attempt to suppress the growth of ritualism in the Church of England, but it failed in its purpose and was eventually discredited – though not until after years of bitter conflict which resulted in a number of ritualist priests being gaoled for refusing to toe the establishment line.

Tait's final years were saddened by the deaths in 1878 first of his son Craufurd and then, six months later, of his wife. But he enjoyed a final triumph when, on his own deathbed, he persuaded the well-known ritualist priest, A.H. Mackonochie, to resign his living of St Alban's, Holborn, which had been the subject of a protracted series of lawsuits, for the sake of the peace of the Church. Though Tait's proposal could be criticized as a form of moral blackmail, it displayed the same combination of tact and firmness as had characterized his eight-year reign as Headmaster of Rugby.

Frederick Temple in 1858, at the time of his appointment as Headmaster of Rugby.

4

BENEVOLENT AUTOCRAT

Frederick Temple: Headmaster of Rugby, 1858–1869

Tait had secured the headmastership of Rugby in the face of strong opposition. There was no such problem for Frederick Temple. He was incomparably the favourite candidate to succeed Tait's successor, E.M. Goulburn, when the latter resigned in 1858. Temple could indeed have succeeded Tait direct in 1850, had he so chosen. Tait had pressed his name on the trustees as the ideal candidate. But Temple, who was then in his late twenties, had only recently been appointed Principal of Kneller Hall, an experimental training college for teachers in elementary schools, and felt that he could hardly abandon his new duties so soon. He confessed to Tait, however, that the headmastership of Rugby was 'the post on earth which he would most like to fill'.[1]

In 1858, with the resignation of Goulburn, his chance came again. By now his circumstances had changed. Kneller Hall had been closed down in 1855, so his ties of loyalty no longer existed. He had become an inspector of schools, but felt no particular dedication to his new job. Tait, by now Bishop of London, again pressed Temple's name on the Rugby School trustees. 'I have no hesitation', he wrote, 'in saying that I am acquainted with no man in England so fit for it [the headmastership] as he.'[2] His praise was echoed in other quarters. R.R.W. Lingen, Secretary to the Committee of the Privy Council on Education, forecast that the

51

appointment of Temple to Rugby 'would mark an epoch in the public education of this country not less notable than that which followed the appointment of Dr Arnold.'[3] Arthur Stanley, then a canon of Canterbury, assured a young Rugbeian of his acquaintance that , in Frederick Temple, 'you will have the best headmaster in England.'[4] Even Matthew Arnold, who might have been expected to doubt the ability of any man to measure up to his father, had no doubts on this occasion. 'In the most important qualities of a schoolmaster,' he wrote, 'in the union of piety, energy and cheerfulness, in the faculty of governing the young, in the power of commanding at once the respect and the affection of those under his charge, Mr Temple, more than any other man whom I have ever known, resembles, to the best of my observation and judgment, my late father.'[5] Such testimonials from his intellectual equals would no doubt have gratified Temple had he ever read them (which, according to his sister, he did not). He would have been still more pleased, however, at a tribute from one of his older pupils at Kneller Hall who happened to meet a Rugby boy on his way home for the holidays just after the appointment had been announced. 'What do you know about him?' the boy asked the ex-pupil, now a fledgling teacher in a local elementary school.

'Oh, he's all right,' said the pupil teacher. 'I remember one day he came down to visit us when we were set to clean out the pigsties, and one of us went up to him and said, "Am I forced to do this dirty work?" "I suppose not," he replied; "you are not exactly *forced*." "May I go, then?" said the other. "Yes," was the answer. "Give me the rake." The man was just handing him the rake when he saw Mr Temple beginning to take off his coat; so he stopped and said, "I don't want you to do it, sir." "Someone must do it," said Mr Temple, so my friend did it and never grumbled any more.'[6]

*   *   *   *   *

Who was this paragon who was to step so effortlessly into the shoes of Thomas Arnold? He had been born on 20 November 1821 in the unlikely setting of Santa Maura (now Leucas), one of the Ionian Islands. The islands had been occupied by Great Britain since 1815, and remained virtually British colonies until they were handed over to Greece in 1864. Frederick's father, Major Octavius Temple, was the official 'Resident' on Santa Maura at the time of his son's birth and then, for a brief period, held a post on Corfu. By 1825, however, he had saved enough money to buy a farm in Devon and return home with his family to take up a new career as a minor landowner. Unfortunately, he soon found that farming did not pay enough to enable him to educate the eight of his fifteen children who had survived infancy; so, in desperation, he accepted the lieutenant-governorship of the colony of Sierra Leone in West Africa. He left his family behind him, but within ten months of his arrival in the colony was dead. That notoriously unhealthy part of Africa had indeed assured him a white man's grave.

The care of the family now devolved on his widow Dorcas. Until he was twelve Frederick had no education apart from two hours a day supervised by his mother. By then she had scraped together enough money to send him to Blundell's, Tiverton, at that time a small grammar school which was able to give him a thorough grounding in classics and mathematics. He proved an eager pupil – though such an independent-minded one that his headmaster observed to him on one occasion: 'Temple, I do believe that you are the most impudent boy that ever lived.'[7] But he was obviously making his mark, as, on another occasion, one of the school's trustees told him: 'Temple, I cannot say what you are going to be, but this I am sure of: that, if you live long enough, you will be one of the greatest men in England.'[8] (In the fullness of time the prophecy was to be fulfilled.) It was at Blundell's that he acquired that capacity for hard and independent work that was to remain with him for the rest of his life. Many years later he paid tribute to the Blundell's system when he remarked: 'We were not made merely to listen to a teacher but to learn ... there is a real and special value in throwing a boy on his own resources and allowing him to learn.'[9] It was a principle which he was to apply in due course at Rugby.

A knowledge of the classics and the ability to study independently were not the young Frederick's only acquirements at Blundell's. It was while he was at school that he was able to develop his prodigious powers as a walker. He used to boast that

53

he had for many years been able to cover six miles an hour with comparative ease – and that on one occasion, while on holiday in Wales, he had walked 18 miles in three hours before breakfast. On another occasion, when, as an undergraduate, he had been invited to meet Thomas Arnold, he tramped the 48 miles from Oxford to Rugby in a single day.[10] Another of his athletic pursuits was climbing trees. He achieved instant popularity among Rugbeians when, on his arrival at the school, he claimed to the boys of his house that he could run a hundred yards, climb a tree or jump a brook with any of them.[11] It was no idle boast. He had been struck by the obvious temptation offered by the elms in the Close to anyone fond of climbing; but, before issuing an edict forbidding such escapades, he confirmed the truth of the temptation by going out one evening in the dusk and scrambling up every elm in succession. Nor did he confine his climbs to his own school. On a visit to his friend and former colleague Edward Benson, Headmaster of the newly-founded Wellington College, he was taken by his host to view a magnificent beech tree in the school grounds.

> Temple admired it very much, and, after looking at it for some time close at hand and at a distance, cried out to Benson, 'I can't resist the temptation – look out!' And, before Benson could turn round, Temple had made a rush and a leap, and was scrambling up the bole of the tree. In a few seconds Temple had succeeded in reaching the first stage whence the magnificent limbs diverge in all directions, and was grinning with delight at his success.[12]

To the day of his death Temple delighted in his farming background and retained the rough accent of his childhood. His hands were horny enough to pass as working-class. He made up for his lack of small talk by a directness of mind and speech which left little to the imagination. Above all, he was an immensely robust man who was able to work long hours and beaver away at wearying chores without any effect on his health.[13]

His phenomenal energy was put to good use when he moved from Blundell's to Balliol College, Oxford. He would rise as early as 3 or 4 a.m. and work (with a single break for chapel) until 3 in the afternoon – and then again from 6.30 or 7 p.m. until 10.30 at night. His immense industry paid off with a double first in classics and mathematics. But he had a hard time of it in making ends meet. Although he had won a scholarship to Balliol, the amount was not enough to keep him, and had to be supplemented by an annual £50 gift from a local benefactor.[14] Throughout his time at Oxford he knew real poverty. He once told a Church Congress:

> I have experienced many privations in my time. I have known what it was to be unable to afford a fire. I have known what it was every now and then to live upon rather poor fare; and I have known – what perhaps I felt most – what it was to wear patched clothes and shoes.[15]

He could not afford to drink wine or to use his oil-lamp in the evenings. He was reduced to sitting on the staircase night after night in order to read his books with the aid of the public light. But, in spite of his poverty, he enjoyed his time at college and was popular with his fellow undergraduates, who respected his integrity even if they could not share his wine. He was able to bask in the heady religious atmosphere of the Oxford of the early 1840s. Tait and Ward were among his tutors at Balliol, and Newman was still an Anglican and holding congregations spell-bound at St Mary's.[16] Bliss was it in that intellectual dawn to be alive, even if one happened, like Freddie Temple, to be short of material possessions. Almost immediately after taking his degree he was elected to a fellowship of his college and to a lecturership in mathematics and logic. In 1845 he was appointed Junior Dean, and the following year was ordained by Bishop Samuel Wilberforce, who is said to have marked him down as a man of special promise.

Temple was too ambitious and too vigorous to be content to stay at Oxford for long. Teaching clever undergraduates was all very well, but he hankered after wider educational pastures. He determined to devote his career to training the minds of boys from the humblest class of society. With this aim in view he entered the service in 1848 of the newly-formed Educational Committee of the Privy Council, and for a year worked as an examiner in the

Education Office. Then came the opportunity for which he was looking. In 1849 he was appointed the first principal of Kneller Hall Training College, which had been built by the Government on an estate near Twickenham formerly owned by Sir Godfrey Kneller, the painter. The purpose of the college was to train schoolmasters to teach boys from the workhouse in elementary schools.[17] Sadly, however, the scheme proved a failure. It was unable to attract sufficient pupils to make it viable. The Government soon lost confidence in its latest brainchild and declined to give it the funds necessary for its survival. Temple lost his initial enthusiasm and resigned in 1855 to take up a new appointment as an inspector of training colleges. Three years later came the offer of the headmastership of Rugby, an educational post very different from the one on which his youthful idealism had originally been set. But it was at Rugby that he was to find his feet, and to make for himself a reputation as one of the greatest headmasters in the country and one fully worthy to have followed in the footsteps of Thomas Arnold.

His predecessor, Edward Goulburn, had been a man of very different stamp, who had been chosen to succeed Tait primarily because of his known hostility to liberalism in either Church or State. His most formidable rival among the 20 candidates for the headmastership had been W.C. Lake, the future Dean of Durham. Lake was a recognised disciple of Arnold, and (as we have seen) a friend of both Tait and Stanley. He was also reputed to be a Puseyite, so was anathema on that score to some of the trustees. But he had wide support in the country at large – and Goulburn himself would have withdrawn from the contest had his father not pressed him to continue to stand. The news of his election was received with dismay by the friends of Lake. Stanley in particular was devastated. He wrote to Lake: 'Our poor servant who brought it [the news] in concluded, I suppose, from my expression of grief and dismay, that it was tidings of another death.' He then reassured the disappointed candidate: 'You have been defeated not from any fault of your own ... but from the hostility of personal enemies combined with other causes in so extraordinary and unexpected a manner as almost to give to this fatal decision the character of a providential dispensation.'[18] Lake took the news more philosophically. Writing to Tait shortly afterwards, he declared: 'Depend upon it, this is not the sort of thing I should ever allow to annoy me for long… As to Goulburn, my hearty wish would be to act with him, or at least support him, heart and head.'[19]

Goulburn's reign marked a low point in the fortunes of Rugby School. The school's most recent historian ascribes the decline in numbers during the 1850s to the headmaster's conservative convictions and to the moderate ritualism which he introduced into the chapel services. His religious views were contrasted unfavourably by many parents with the liberal opinions of both Arnold and Tait – which meant that the school's trustees, by preferring Goulburn to Lake, had backed the wrong horse. In the words of Goulburn's biographer, 'it was apparently impossible that the School could flourish on distinctive Church principles'. Later Goulburn observed that he had expected too much advance in holiness from schoolboys – and had been disappointed.[20] By 1856 numbers had fallen from almost 500 to barely 300, though an upswing to 365 in his last year implied that the tide was turning. But by then it was too late. Goulburn was no disciplinarian, and showed no desire to carry out necessary reforms in the school's curriculum or in its financial organization. Much work, therefore, awaited his successor; nor was Temple slow to take advantage of his opportunities, and to bring the school once more to the crest of the wave.

The contrast between the outgoing headmaster and his successor was at once apparent to the boys. Henry Lee Warner observed the two men together in the Schoolhouse shortly before Goulburn's departure: 'the one dignified, sweet-voiced, cassocked, almost pompous; the other with a wide shirt-front, a rasping voice and an elastic spring as he bounded up the stairs'.[21] When he arrived to conduct evening prayers Goulburn had been preceded by his butler carrying a silver candlestick and bowing as he left him at the door. Temple, wearing neither gown nor cassock, would walk in by himself, blowing out his candle as he entered. The old headmaster dined in a grand silk gown, the new headmaster in a gown green with age.[22] Already, on his first arrival in Rugby, Temple had caused a triple shock to the locals by walking up from the station in a swallowtail coat and carrying his own bag.[23] This was not the kind of behaviour to be expected of the headmaster of a prestigious school like Rugby. But it was in keeping with the image which Temple, consciously or unconsciously, wished to create. Quite apart from his urge to climb trees, he thought nothing of taking his own boots to the cobbler to be mended or, when fire had broken out in one of the boys' houses, of directing the fire-engines from a post of vantage on the roof. But there was strength behind the outward homeliness of dress and demeanour – and woe betide the boy who attempted to take advantage of a seemingly easygoing headmaster. When a sixth-former, for instance, failed to treat him with proper respect, Temple crushed the offender with a withering 'Conduct like that will alter the relations between us.'[24] The pupils of Rugby soon discovered that no one could presume on the new head's good nature with impunity. But, once that was recognized, all was well. As Lee Warner put it:

> We soon found that we had to do with a strong and humorous man, absolutely fair and simple in method, as penetrating as truth itself in his judgments; and, though it was remarked playfully that his alpaca gown would be the better if it caught less often in the coal-barrow as he hurried into school, we felt his natural dignity, and the era of hero-worship soon set in.[25]

*　　*　　*　　*　　*

In spite of his curt speech and brusque manners, Temple was basically kind-hearted. He might, occasionally, wound the feelings of an over-sensitive boy with an abrasive comment, but the testimony of one of his former colleagues that he 'was immensely and hugely genial' is echoed by other witnesses. One Old Rugbeian commented: 'The one thing that I should like to say about him is that the general impression that he was very severe and stern as a master is quite wrong.'[26]

Of his many qualities one of the most conspicuous was his capacity for hard work. On one occasion, when the masters were grumbling about the extra chores imposed on them by the introduction of grammar papers into the school curriculum,

58

Temple immediately declared: 'Very well, then *I* will look them over.' He was as good as his word, and settled down to correct the papers over a single uninterrupted stretch of 17 hours. At the end of his long stint he looked a little grey and wrinkled, but was still sufficiently relaxed to be able to exchange jokes with a passing visitor.[27] A similar experience was recalled by Arthur Butler:

> I have seen him during an examination, after sitting up through a whole night and working for eighteen consecutive hours, as bright and cheerful at the end as if he had done nothing. He just passed his hand over his face with a rapid movement, as if rubbing away something, and then turned to you with the usual smile of kindly greeting. This constant and unfailing cheeriness in the midst of work, and under great pressure, was his special characteristic. It was partly natural, partly a matter of duty with him. I have heard him preach about it. 'A true Christian should be a happy man, and he should show his happiness in his face.' This was his teaching, and his example illustrated it.[28]

This capacity for hard work remained with him all his life. Henry Scott Holland recalled his energy while Bishop of London: 'He worked like six horses; he let everybody else work; he believed in his men – believed in them, indeed, to an extent which astonished and bewildered them.'[29] By that time in his career he had learned to treat his subordinates with a proper consideration. At Rugby he was more sparing of his praise – and sometimes disappointed those who looked in vain for the occasional kindly word of encouragement. Sometimes, however, his colleagues failed to take account of his keen sense of humour. As F.D. How observed in *Six Great Schoolmasters*: 'It must often have happened that a word spoken with a twinkle in the eye gave offence to one on whom that twinkle was thrown away.'[30] By all accounts he was a great laugher, and a former colleague recalls an occasion when he used his laugh as a means of making a youthful delinquent ashamed of himself.

> A very small boy was once 'sent up' to him for smoking. Dr Temple looked at him and said, 'What! you smoking!' and lay back in his chair roaring with laughter, which doubtless made the small boy feel rather smaller still, and was no little part of his punishment.[31]

One of Temple's most prominent characteristics was his sense of fair play. He felt passionately about this, and once remarked that, if he could be shown a monkey with the most elementary idea of justice, he would believe that that monkey might in time become a man.[32] And he treasured, as the highest compliment ever paid to him, a boy's postscript in a letter to his father: 'Of course Temple's a beast, but he's a just beast.'[33] He was quick to repudiate a suggestion made to him that he should compile a 'black list' recording the misdeeds of every boy as they occurred. 'Certainly not,' he exclaimed. 'I shall try to forget all about them as soon as they are dealt with.' His philosophy of justice was summed up by an Old Rugbeian in a magazine article written years after he had left the school:

> We saw that he was a right good fellow who was absolutely just, who cared for us, and who always put the best construction on all we did, and who, if ever he made mistakes, always made them on the side of too favourable a judgment.

But in this Temple acted on principle. 'Nine times out of ten the kindest judgment is the right one,' he used to say.[34] Like Thomas Arnold before him, he always insisted that a boy's word should be taken on trust. But, even when there seemed overwhelming proof of an act of wrongdoing, he would give the alleged miscreant the benefit of the doubt if he persisted in his denial. Nor would he allow a boy to be punished if he had simply misunderstood a master's directive. He always felt that it was better for a misdeed to go unpunished than for a single act of injustice to be perpetrated. Truly a 'just beast'!

With his love of justice went an urge to perform acts of personal kindness. No trouble was too much for him if he felt that he could be of use. An example of his practical compassion was when, over a considerable period of time, he went daily to the house of a poor widow in the town in order to lift her son, who was ill with rheumatic fever, off his bed. The woman was too weak to lift the boy herself and too poor to employ a nurse, so Temple was content to perform this daily service for her.[35] On another occasion, when the widowed mother of four boys at the school fell sick and had to go abroad to convalesce, Temple at once wrote to her with an offer of hospitality:

> I presume I may take it for granted that your four sons will look upon School House as their home for next Christmas and will come here for any time that is not taken up with invitations elsewhere. It will give me real pleasure to see them.

One of the four boys, Arthur Haslam, spent a holiday in the Lake District with Temple in 1866, which excited the envy of his sister: 'Dr Temple's company would make a coal-cellar a pleasant sojourn, but Temple and the Lakes together!'[36]

*   *   *   *   *

What was Temple like as a teacher? According to the Rugby historian, J.B. Hope Simpson, he was both a great teacher and a supremely great headmaster. 'He induced an atmosphere of cheerfulness and serenity in work and engendered a lively interest.' He never expected too high a standard from less-able boys. 'All your questions are too hard,' he once told a young colleague. 'Why do you frighten your boys so?'[37] He had an equal dislike for the 'forcing' system which concentrated most of the masters' attention on likely scholarship candidates at the expense of their less-intellectual fellows. Temple's aim was to raise the average standard of his pupils. Although he looked on the classics as the essential foundation of a proper education, he never regarded the ability to turn out a neat set of Latin verses as the be-all and end-all of scholastic endeavour. As one who had himself studied science at the university in addition to classics and mathematics, he was anxious to extend the Rugby curriculum. He was continually introducing fresh subjects in order to broaden the minds of his pupils and interest them to a greater extent in the world at large.[38]

F.E. Kitchener's 'Rugby Memoir' in Archdeacon Sandford's collection of biographical essays contains a number of assessments of Temple's teaching powers by those who had either sat under him as schoolboys at Rugby or been his colleagues on the staff. H.G. Hart, later Headmaster of Sedbergh, spent two and a half years in

61

the sixth and considered that it was because Temple was so great a man that he exercised such power as a teacher. And, in an analysis of his teaching methods, he remarked that Temple hurried his pupils forward

> at a speed that enabled us to gain that which is so often lost in classical work at school, namely, a general comprehension of a treatise or a play, though he might thereby be taxing the powers of the slower thinkers to the utmost... But, if a boy had even average ability and a real desire to learn, he had great opportunities... He [Temple] simply poured forth his thoughts in a mighty stream which, while it might leave a few stranded on the shore, carried the main body of the Form with it.[39]

Henry Lee Warner, another of Temple's sixth-formers, thought that the best effect of his teaching was the impression he created of the general character of an author's meaning and style, and of the possibility of mastering it.

> But the analyses of chapters and books which he made in our presence were the most masterly and illuminating weapons he used for our instruction... His method of teaching was to create an impression of ease in the task, whilst carefully disentangling all the difficulties.[40]

To B.E. Hammond, a boy at the school from 1856 to 1861 and afterwards a lecturer in history at Trinity College, Cambridge, Temple was, quite simply, 'the greatest teacher I ever knew among living men'. Hammond had been particularly impressed by his masterly ability to analyse a difficult classical author. 'He taught us methods of teaching ourselves... He used to analyse every didactic or historical work that we read in form .. In commenting on my essays weekly, he was admirable in exposing any inconsequence in thought or wobbling in the meaning of words.'[41]

The schoolboy eulogies of Temple's teaching methods are balanced by the more critical comments of some of his colleagues. They considered that he had not the qualities of an ideal classical teacher – and they appreciated the gibes current in the universities at the time concerning his 'rough-and-ready scholars'. T.W. Jex

Blake, a later Headmaster of Rugby who went on to be Dean of Wells, compared him with his illustrious Rugby predecessor: 'If Arnold had not Temple's positive shrewdness, Temple had not Arnold's consummate literary taste and skill.'[42] Arthur Butler, a house tutor in the early days of Temple's headmastership and afterwards Headmaster of Haileybury, thought that he had never become a 'really great teacher in the highest sense... He was more of the statesman and ruler dealing with things present than the man of imagination transporting his hearers into times long since passed away' – though Butler was prepared to concede 'how the Sixth felt the power and stirring influence of his lectures on St John'.[43] Archdeacon Sandford, while admitting that Temple lacked the future Archbishop Benson's 'delicacy of intellectual touch', declared that his 'broad, human treatment of intellectual subjects was a deathblow to pedantry and it held out a hope of mental salvation even to the dull'. It broadened the intellectual interest and outlook of the pupils, so that they were able to understand social problems and experience a 'sympathy with the conditions of the lives of poor people ... we learnt to be in bondage to no party allegiance; and to reverence conscience as the voice of God'.[44]

*   *   *   *   *

Temple might be genial and just and (to his pupils at any rate) a superb teacher. But he had also to maintain discipline. He never shirked this side of his duties. When he had to be stern, he *was* stern. As Henry Lee Warner observed: 'When he made up his mind to be angry, there was no mistaking it. But he never punished without leaving on your mind the sense of shame at having forced him to show his anger.' Sometimes, Lee Warner adds, if he found a lesson unprepared, 'he would put his victim through a miserable ordeal of self-exposure and leave him to the mercy of his fellows, who were kept in school till they were a quarter of an hour late for breakfast.'[45] He would stand no nonsense from his pupils. 'I have seen him quell disorder with a look,' says Lee Warner. ' "You are getting rude", was all he said.'[46] And he was firm in insisting that every boy, however exalted, must conform to school discipline. There was one noted episode when an athletic 'swell' was reported to the headmaster for skimping his work. Temple sent for the miscreant at a time 'accidentally' fixed to coincide with the start of an important match in which the boy was due to take part. He found the head busy with his correspondence, and was forced to stand in the study for a full hour until Temple was ready to deal with him. His eyes wandered in agony between the headmaster's pen and the game proceeding on the field outside the study. The match at last ended and Temple looked up from his desk. 'Now you may go,' he said (but was there perhaps a twinkle in his eye?). He had made his point without the need for a specific punishment.[47]

Sometimes, however, words (or even the lack of them) were not enough. Although Temple personally disliked flogging, occasionally he felt that he had to beat a boy. But he would not resolve to inflict the extreme penalty without repeatedly asking himself the question, 'Is it just?' One witness of a flogging remembers the occasion vividly:

> I had to mount the fatal steps up the turret staircase to the room in which boys were birched. I was one of the Sixth Form boys on duty to see fair play. The Headmaster seemed to feel his position more acutely than the culprit. But, in spite of the tears coursing down his cheeks, Temple inflicted on the boy a good sound licking.[48]

Temple showed an extraordinary reluctance to resort to punishment. Arthur Butler recalls that he would always prefer to rely on force of character and moral influence. 'If we had properly impressed boys there would be no need to punish,' he once remarked. Masters, says Butler, would be required to sit in with 'lazy and dull boys who had failed in their lessons, to hear them over again, shaming (it was to be hoped) the one and helping the other'. Butler remembers Temple himself, when hard pressed, finding time to hear a lazy boy his lesson day after day before going into school. 'He wished to try everything before punishing... He succeeded to a remarkable extent in giving moral weight to punishment: and also in making his own feelings of right and wrong generally pervade the school.'[49] What really broke his heart, however, was when a boy betrayed his trust. J.H.

Crowfoot was a sixth-former under Temple and recalls such an occasion:

> He always treated us as if we were in all respects what we ought to be. One day one of us, soon after he had come, proved untrue to that trust. He [Temple] began to talk to us about it; but after a few words he put his head into his hands and broke down utterly in tears. No one who was present will ever forget what he then felt.[50]

*   *   *   *   *

If Temple was a hero to many of the boys at Rugby, he was equally revered by the masters. One Old Rugbeian who was not personally warm towards his old head conceded that he had been 'intensely venerated' by his subordinates and that the sister of one of the housemasters had always referred to him as 'our glorious chieftain'.[51] Arthur Butler claimed that he could never remember a time when the confidence and enthusiasm of the masters for their chief had slackened for a moment. To Butler Temple had appealed, first and foremost, as a great administrator.

> All the various parts of a complicated system were made by him to work easily and comfortably, without hitch or hindrance, so as to give the idea of an intelligent and self-working machine... He combined the mastery of detail ... with a cheery vigour and sympathetic treatment of difficulties which delighted and inspired every one who came about him.[52]

Another Temple devotee among the staff, E.A. Scott, went even further in adulation: 'I loved him too much to criticize, even. It never occurred to me he could be wrong; he was so fertile and so conciliating to everybody and on every point.'[53]

Temple never attempted to introduce changes into any aspect of the school's organization without first discussing them with his colleagues. Masters' meetings were held in the library every month for this purpose. As Temple put it to the Public Schools Commission: 'We repeatedly discuss the working of the school among ourselves, make changes as they seem needed, and are ready to make more to the best of our ability.' Of course, it was not always plain sailing. Some of the headmaster's proposals met with strong opposition on the part of his colleagues. But, as Kitchener remarked in his memoir, 'it was always understood that the decision lay with the Commander-in-Chief'.[54] A typical example of the way in which Temple would go through the motions of consulting his subordinates and then ignore their opinions was when he was considering the launch of a school rifle corps. Almost all those present at the meeting at which he mooted the idea were opposed to it. 'Is that so?' Temple blithely remarked. 'Then we must certainly try it!'[55] Such curt disregard of staff opposition was so blatant that it was apparently greeted with a round of (surely ironic!) applause. Temple must indeed have exercised a profound influence on his colleagues to have induced them to submit to his benevolent dictatorship without exciting any more than token opposition. Occasionally a 'rebel' master was goaded into print, as when J.M. Wilson set forth his views in a letter to the headmaster highly critical of the Rugby system. The nub of his attack came in his comment on the masters' meetings:

> We are, in fact, a 'council of suggestions', and nothing else. Your despotism is beneficent, but it is unlimited; and I cannot but think it would be for the good of the school if we more frequently took the initiative as members of the school council, and considered ourselves less as mere operatives in particular departments.

Temple was unmoved – though he had the letter printed and circulated to the other members of the staff.[56] In spite of his autocratic rule, however, he allowed his colleagues a free hand in running their forms in their own way and trying their own experiments. Nor did he allow his sense of humour to desert him in moments of controversy. When, for instance, he was contemplating a reorganization of the timetable to allow more room for the teaching of non-classical subjects and the mathematics masters were urging their claims, he broke into verse:

Mathematics will flourish, and x, y and z
Will dethrone Greek and Latin and rule here instead.
Ye Mathematicians, so this is your plot:
Catch a weazel asleep, but asleep I am not.

Temple himself was not a truly great scholar,* though his scholarship was sound enough. Nor was he averse to improving it: as soon as he had been appointed to the headmastership he immediately set himself the task of reading through all the classical authors likely to be encountered in the school curriculum.[59] In spite of his sympathy with those anxious to introduce new subjects into the curriculum, he still looked upon the classics as the essential foundation of a true education. Mathematics in his opinion was an admirable discipline in precision of thought and science in cultivating a love of order and beauty, but the classics were on an altogether higher level. He told the Public School Commissioners in 1861 that the classics in his view were 'decidedly the best instrument' for giving the highest kind of education. The plea advanced on behalf of maths and science was their utility. Nevertheless,

those who use this plea seem to forget that the world in which we live consists quite as much of the men and women on its surface as of the earth and its constituent materials... If, therefore, we are to choose a study which shall pre-eminently fit a man for life, it will be that which shall best enable him to enter into the thoughts, the feelings, the motives of his fellows.[60]

Having said that, however, Temple was quite prepared to supplement the classical core of his curriculum. In a further answer to the Public School Commissioners he declared:

A boy ought not to be ignorant of this earth on which God has placed him, and ought, therefore, to be well acquainted with geography. He ought not to walk in the fields of total ignorance of

---

* He was once caught out mistranslating a Greek verb in a lesson with the sixth form. As Henry Lee Warner recalls the incident: 'It was decided that it was the duty of the Sixth to call his attention to this grave dereliction of duty. I shall never forget the candour with which he acknowledged his mistake, said his Greek was somewhat rusty, and begged us to catch him out in any further mistake. But we did not.'[58]

what is growing under his very eyes, and he ought, therefore, to learn botany. There is hardly an occupation in which he can be employed where he will not find chemistry of use to him.[61]

He gradually enlarged the Rugby curriculum. In 1864 natural science was made a compulsory subject for all boys below the Upper School, its main constituents being chemistry, geology, botany and physics. In the following year English language and literature were introduced as form subjects throughout the school. Temple also encouraged the teaching of music and drawing, doubling the number of teachers for both arts and providing special accommodation.[62] In extending its outreach in this way Rugby was very much in the forefront of the English public schools of the period.

*   *   *   *   *

It was in a sense religion rather than the classics which Temple regarded as the keystone of the educational arch. This particular 'subject', however, was dealt with in the chapel as much as in the classroom – and by one who practised what he preached. To T.W. Jex Blake, for many years a colleague of Temple's, 'his religious fervour and preaching power were felt instantly in the school chapel; and very soon he held the school, masters and boys alike, in his hand'. Jex Blake recalls a significant remark made by Edward Benson, then a young colleague but shortly to become the first Headmaster of Wellington: 'Temple's ideal of the Church of Christ appeals to me strongly; it is truer than Arnold's: I accept it almost entirely.'[63] Thus one future Archbishop of Canterbury in a salute to his successor.

Temple followed the Arnoldian tradition of preaching to the school every Sunday.* His sermons were lapped up by his youthful congregations. In a remarkable testimony to their power, H.G. Hart recalls that the headmaster would 'utter the deepest thoughts that

---

* In a letter written in 1831 to the chairman of the Rugby trustees Arnold had written: 'Whoever is Chaplain, I must ever feel myself, as Headmaster, the real and proper religious instructor of the boys. No one else can feel the same interest in them, and no one else ... can speak to them with so much influence.'[64]

were in his heart; and he uttered them – often with the tears streaming down his face – in a manner that went straight to the hearts of his hearers'.[65] Hart's tribute is echoed by others. 'I could never take my eyes from his face from the first word of the sermon to the end,' declared W.O. Moberly, while Henry Lee Warner commented: 'No man who ever heard him preach in Rugby Chapel on Good Friday or Easter Day can ever forget the depth of conviction which vibrated in his voice.'[66] Perhaps the most considered testimony to the power of Temple's pulpit oratory came from Arthur Butler:

> No one indeed could listen to his sermons … without being deeply moved by them…. It was the warm soul of a strong man speaking in the name of his Master (often with tears flowing down his cheeks), with the naturally somewhat harsh voice softened and vibrating with emotion, which stirred his young hearers like a trumpet-call. I have heard some old Rugbeians speak of them in a way that would sound to many an exaggeration. I have never heard anyone question their universal influence.[67]

Temple took immense trouble over his sermons: the preparation of each one never occupied him for less than three hours, though it might take a bare quarter of an hour to deliver. The sermons were rarely polished productions in the conventional sense: they lacked 'purple patches', but they came straight from the heart and, as has been shown, exerted an enormous influence on their hearers. As Kitchener remarked: 'It was the conviction of boys and men alike that, compressed into that short address … was the force by which they were to live till the next Sunday came round.'[68] But Temple had no illusions about the nature of his task. He was always afraid of 'out-running the religious feelings of the boys'. He once declared: 'I do not think the diminution of religious zeal an evil; I think much of it unhealthy. What I want is a quiet sense of duty.'[69] But at least he recognized his own powers as a preacher. When he published his first volume of sermons and Butler forecast that they would stir people strongly, he disagreed: 'No,' he said, 'written sermons rarely do that; it is the man behind the sermon that stirs.'[70]

He was a firm believer in the value of confirmation not only for the individual schoolboy but as a factor in raising the moral tone of the school. The Bishop of Worcester conducted a confirmation service each spring, and Temple used to comment that the effect did not wear off until the following Christmas. But he came down with a firm hand on any candidate who adopted a flippant approach to the ceremony. He once overheard a boy remarking to a friend, 'Oh yes, I'm entered for the Confirmation Stakes!' 'Well,' said Temple, 'you're scratched now!'[71] He also made a practice of helping boys prepare for the services of Holy Communion that took place on three Sundays each term. He would hold a service in the chapel late on the preceding afternoon and address the boys in an entirely informal manner. An eyewitness recalls:

> Dr Temple always came in alone from his study, his well-known Bible in his hand... Nearly every communicant came, in any dress – football or cricket, how they pleased – and sat where they liked. Nobody noticed who was present. Often the chapel was nearly dark: no lights were lighted. And what a rough-and-tumble assemblage it was! Dirty often from the football scrimmage, they crept silently under the pulpit – and listened.[72]

Butler too recalls these Saturday afternoon services.

> It was a striking sight to see them [the boys] lend themselves to the magic influence of the earnest, soul-stirring preacher. Never was he more eloquent than on these occasions; every eye was fixed on him. No one who did not hear him can judge of what he was in his power over boys.

The power that he wielded on these occasions, according to Henry Lee Warner, 'was the power of a man who, having his eyes on God, was not looking about for followers or converts, but was rapt as it were into a trance as he talked with his Creator'.[73]

It was in his chapel addresses that Temple really let himself go. But they were supplemented by divinity lessons in classes which were themselves memorable experiences. His lectures on the Old and New Testaments brought the Bible to life; they were simple, graphic and suggestive, though never eloquent in the sense of his pulpit sermons.[74]

*　　*　　*　　*　　*

Temple always remained a boy at heart – as witness that sudden decision of his to clamber up his fellow headmaster's beech tree at Wellington. So he did all he could to encourage the playing of team games, in which he took a keen interest throughout his time at Rugby. But he valued games not only as a form of recreation but for their potential role in character-building. In Kitchener's words, 'the slackness that led a boy to drop a catch at a critical point of a match, or to shirk the game on the last day of a big foot-ball match, was as much to be expelled as that which led to false concords or incorrect reasoning'.[75] Temple frequently watched football matches in the Close, where his harsh voice might be heard shouting excitedly, 'Take your drop! Take your drop!'[76]

He never shrank from stamping out what he considered abuses on the playing-fields. His two most celebrated reforms were the abolition of the traditional customs of keeping goal and intentional hacking. The first of these was steeped in Rugby history. As readers of *Tom Brown's Schooldays* will recall, those who were not allowed to take part in a game of football were obliged to stand behind the goal posts on the off chance that a rare turn in the game's fortunes might call them into play. Any attempt to escape from this tedious duty was regarded by the sixth form as a deadly offence, and punished accordingly. Temple saw at once that such a custom was bad for health, discipline and character (the more mischievous goalkeepers would even attach lighted crackers to the coat-tails of unpopular praepostors). Within a year of his arrival he abolished the practice, except for three formal occasions in the year retained out of respect for the feelings of Old Rugbeians.[77] Intentional hacking suffered a similar fate. The practice had arisen from the large number of players involved in a 'Big Side' match. Any boy of a certain standing in the game had a right to take part in such matches – with the result that the ball might have to be driven through a scrum of as many as fifty players. This was easier to do with the aid of 'hacking', in other words, kicking shins, but it was

71

a vicious if legalized abuse. On one occasion, when the father of a boy had been watching with amazement a vast crowd of footballers inextricably mixed up in a gigantic scrimmage, he had turned to the headmaster and asked, 'Do you ever stop this sort of thing?' 'Never.' was Temple's reply – 'short of manslaughter.' But his flippant answer did little to disguise his growing dislike of a barbarous practice which often got completely out of hand. On one occasion he threatened to make a particularly notorious 'hacker' take off his boots and play in slippers for the rest of the afternoon; and before long he had declared the practice illegal.[78] He showed a similar determination when he ruled out the use of fireworks on Guy Fawkes' Day. In announcing the ban to the school he began with the remark, 'I never could see why we should remember, remember the fifth of November,' continued with a historical address on the Gunpowder Plot and a reference to a serious fire the previous November, and ended with the stark injunction, 'And you are not to do it.' Surprisingly, the announcement of the ban was greeted with loud cheers by the assembled boys – which caused an American visitor to the school to remark: 'That man is the biggest demagogue I have met in England!'[79] Temple's attitude to tradition was summed up thus in *The Meteor*, the Rugby School magazine: 'If he is the first to touch anything that is utterly bad, he is the last to cut down the tree which may still bear fruit.'[80]

*   *   *   *   *

The abolition of hacking and fireworks might cause Old Rugbeians to turn in their graves or write impassioned letters to *The Times*; but of course there were more important things for Temple to put right at Rugby. The impetus of Arnold's reforms had to some extent worn itself out under the more relaxed regimes of Tait and Goulburn; and the task faced by Temple was to build on those reforms and carry them several stages further. His most immediate problem was to cope with the increase in the number of boys at the school – which, as his reign proceeded, was threatening to become an unmanageable flood. He told the Royal Commission on Public Schools in 1862: 'I refuse twice as many as I take because I have not room. I have three times as many applications as I can take into the school.'[81] There was an urgent need for more masters and for more classrooms – both of which cost money which Temple often had to wheedle out of reluctant trustees.

Arnold had introduced both mathematics and modern languages into the school curriculum. But (incredibly by modern standards) he had required both the new subjects to be taught by the same masters who were responsible for teaching classics. This certainly saved money, but it was hardly a recipe for sound learning – truly a case, as Kitchener remarked, of putting new wine into old bottles and requiring an impossibly encyclopedic knowledge on the part of Arnold's hard-pressed subordinates.[82] Not surprisingly, the Arnoldian system was condemned as a failure by the Public School Commissioners:

> To exact from the accomplished classical masters of the year 1836, selected without reference to knowledge of French, the duty of giving grammatical instruction in a language for the correct teaching of which the 'Grammaire des Grammaires' is not a superfluous instrument, was perhaps the requirement of a man ready to do wonders himself, and sanguine in his expectations from the zeal and versatility of others.[83]

Temple at once saw the absurdity of expecting his colleagues to be polymaths capable of teaching a number of unrelated subjects. He began to recruit a staff of specialist teachers for the new subjects in the curriculum. Thus, whereas Arnold at the time of his death had required only nine colleagues, Temple, when he left in 1869, was assisted by no fewer than twenty-two masters, of whom eight were teaching modern subjects.[84]

There was also the allied problem of staff salaries. Early in Temple's reign he had persuaded the masters, by a self-denying ordinance, to agree to a rearrangement and limitation of their salaries so as to admit of the enlargement of their numbers. But masters' financial expectations had risen over the years, and Temple found it increasingly hard to recruit men of the right calibre. As he remarked in 1862 to the Public School Commissioners:

I noticed that three years ago I had only to ask a man to come, and he came. This year I asked four men to come, and they declined, on the ground that the money was not enough; and this was in consequence of the reductions made in 1858.[85]

Temple might have been able to charm his existing staff into accepting lower pay, but those not yet subject to his spell were a tougher proposition. The answer, as it must inevitably have been, was a substantial increase in pupils' fees. Temple also found himself engaged in constant battles with the school's trustees over the need to provide new classrooms and laboratories to cater for the new subjects creeping into the curriculum. But he usually got his way in the end.

*   *   *   *   *

The middle years of Temple's headmastership coincided with the sittings of the Royal Commission on Public Schools. This had been appointed in 1861, under the chairmanship of the Earl of Clarendon, to 'inquire into the revenues and management of certain colleges and schools, and the studies pursued and instruction given therein'. Rugby was one of the nine schools investigated, so Temple found himself much involved in the work of the commission. His subordinates were each required to describe what he taught, how he taught it, what books he used, how he used them and what time was spent on each. Not surprisingly, some of the masters were slow in compiling their returns; and Temple found himself having to defend his colleagues to the secretary of the commission, Professor Montague Bernard. Luckily he had established good relations with Bernard, so was able to write to him in suitably informal terms:

Now I will deliver my soul of a long, loud, savage growl at you. Have you no consideration for busy men that you only give us seven days to send you back the proofs? But we could easily do it if you had only the bowels to send us down a copy each. If you only knew the gnashing of teeth which you cause us… If you decline for no reason [to send us twenty copies] we shall turn crusty and decline to give you any more evidence, oral or written. Bow-wow-wow.[86]

74

In 1864 the commission issued its report, which bore eventual fruit in the Public Schools Act of 1868. Rugby fared well in the report, which described the classical teaching there as unsurpassed and the teaching of history as second to Harrow alone.[87] The report also praised the system of government by praepostors:

> It has largely assisted, we believe, to create and keep alive a high and sound tone of feeling and opinion, has promoted independence and manliness of character, and has rendered possible that combination of ample liberty with order and discipline which is among the best characteristics of our great English schools.[88]

Among the many recommendations made by the commissioners in their report was one concerning the composition of Rugby's governing body; and here Temple forcibly disagreed with their proposal. The governing body was intended to replace the trustees; and the commissioners recommended that four of its members 'should be elected for eminence in literature or science'; that the governors as a whole 'should take a much more active part than heretofore in the management of the school'; and that the powers of the headmaster should be increased in some respects, limited in others, but in every way more precisely defined. In a memorandum of dissent Temple fiercely attacked the proposal to hamper a headmaster by subjecting him to constant interference from his governing body. In particular he took strong exception to the election of four members eminent in literature or science:

> The four gentlemen elected for their eminence in literature or science would be perpetually tempted to justify their election by doing what the Headmaster ought to do, and, if he is fit for the post, can do better than anyone else. They would often be tempted to push the interests of their own particular study to the detriment of general education. They would be almost certain to encourage an amount of interference which, if it hastened or even introduced improvements at the time, would purchase them at the dear price of diminishing the Headmaster's sense of responsibility and freedom of action. I am confident that in the end the school would lose much more than it gained.[89]

Any executive smarting under the restraints of an over-zealous board of directors will sympathize with Temple's sentiments. But he was conveniently to disregard his own advice when, by then himself a member of the Rugby governing body, he played a leading part in ousting his successor, Henry Hayman, from a disastrous headmastership. The episode forms a fascinating chapter in Hope Simpson's history of Rugby and gave rise to much comic literature at the time.* It was said of Hayman: 'If a headmaster can't teach and can't preach and can't organize, he ought to be either a scholar or a gentleman.'[91]

Another recommendation of the Public School Commissioners which caused controversy related to Rugby's local responsibilities. Free education had always in the past been given at the school to the children of parents resident within a certain distance of Rugby. The commissioners now proposed the abandonment of the school's local responsibilities and the establishment of open scholarships out of the funds released. The townsfolk bitterly resented the prospect of losing their privilege. Temple's solution was a middle course whereby a 'Lower School' would be set up in Rugby at which a semi-classical and commercial education would be made available free to the children of local residents and from which the cleverer boys would pass on by means of closed scholarships to Rugby School. The compromise proposal pleased neither the commissioners nor the residents; but the 'Lawrence Sheriff School' was set up under the terms of the Public Schools Act of 1868 and to a large extent satisfied local needs.[92]

*   *   *   *   *

In his private life Temple was both frugal and hospitable. The fare at his table might be of an almost spartan simplicity, but the conversation more than made up for it. Two evenings a week at least

---

* Including a verse parody of which a typical stanza read:

> Who killed poor Hayman?
> I, said *Froddy* [i.e., Frederick Temple];
> With my Governing Body
> I killed poor Hayman.[90]

76

were given up to dinner parties at which the headmaster entertained his friends and colleagues. One observer commented of these parties: 'The astonishing versatility of the host was what has since surprised me. Often somebody was down staying with him, always somebody worth having met. But it was always he who drew the stranger out.'[93] Equally memorable were the Sunday afternoon tea parties at which Temple was able to relax after preaching in chapel to the boys. For most of his time at Rugby his widowed mother was a member of his household, as was his sister Jennetta ('Netta'), who kept house for him. Mrs Temple was by now an invalid who spent most of the day in her bedroom. Her son and daughter would take tea with her there, and later in the evening, if there were guests for dinner, she would often come down to welcome them in the drawing-room. Just before she retired to rest Temple would go to her room again to recite the 51st Psalm and the Lord's Prayer by her bedside.[94] Mrs Temple died on 8 May 1866. Netta continued to manage his household both at Rugby and afterwards in the early years at Exeter.

A highlight of Temple's headmastership was the school's three hundredth birthday. This was celebrated on 26 June 1867 with a service in chapel, ceremonial lunches, speeches in Big School and a celebratory dinner in the Town Hall presided over by Dean Stanley. Here the men at their tables below and the women accommodated in a special gallery above sat through no fewer than nineteen speeches over their meal. The final toast was to 'The Ladies' – which, as the ladies were meant to be seen but not heard, was responded to by a gentleman.[95] Rugby, like nearly all such institutions, gloried (if unconsciously) in its male chauvinism. How surprised those guests at the tercentenary banquet would have been could they have foreseen that, within little more than a century, girls would be gracing the sixth forms of many of the major English public schools for boys.

*   *   *   *   *

During his headmastership Temple found himself involved in one major ecclesiastical controversy not entirely of his own making. The dispute, which was to affect him far more seriously when he was appointed Bishop of Exeter, followed the publication in 1860 of a book that was to become notorious, *Essays and Reviews*. He was the author of an introductory article in the volume which he had agreed to contribute before his appointment to Rugby. The book as a whole came under fire on account of its liberal ideas on theology, and in 1864 was condemned by the Convocation of Canterbury as 'containing teaching contrary to the doctrine received by the United Church of England and Ireland in common with the whole Catholic Church of Christ'. The irony was that Temple's own essay was relatively blameless. It was in fact a Rugby School address which had been reworked into a sermon delivered before the University of Oxford. Its subject was 'The Education of the World', comparing the growth of an individual with the growth of mankind. Though some of the author's interpretations of biblical texts were questionable, the essay was basically inoffensive from the standpoint of orthodoxy. But of course, in the climate of the times, it was inevitable that Temple's contribution should be dubbed every bit as bad as those of his less orthodox fellow essayists and that he should be tarred with the same heretical brush. The result was that he was driven to defend himself on three fronts: before the boys, before the masters and before the school's trustees.

He told the sixth form that he had been asked to contribute to the book long before he had come to Rugby (in fact, it owed its origins to some conversations he had had with Benjamin Jowett on the great amount of reticence in every class of society in regard to religious views). 'It was perhaps a blunder in me not to reconsider my decision of letting the essay be published when I came to Rugby, but, inasmuch as it was a past act, it never occurred to me to reconsider it.' After seeking to justify the book's publication on the ground that its opinions had long been lurking in corners but should now be dragged into the open, he concluded with a warning to the boys 'against entering on the speculations contained in that book in a light or cursory way, and against supposing that I agree with all that is said in that book'. He must have convinced at least one of his audience who, in response to an anxious enquiry from home, added his own reassurance: 'Dear Mother, Temple's all right, but if he turns Mahometan all the school

78

will turn too.' Temple had certainly alarmed a good many of the parents. He admitted as much to a friend, adding frankly:

> I think I made a blunder in one respect, and in one alone. I ought not to have done anything which would encourage those boys to plunge into critical speculations before their time. I did not realise the attractions that would be conferred upon a book for the boys by my having written about it.

Temple made a similar point when he defended himself before his staff at a masters' meeting in February 1861, by when the controversy was really getting into its stride. There was only one thing, he told his colleagues, which made him regret having contributed to the volume:

> This is that as Headmaster here I made a mistake in doing so, a great mistake, on account of the boys, many of whom may be led to read the book because I wrote in it, before they ought to enter on such questions as are discussed in it; but, so far as the Sixth is concerned, I hope to prevent its being thus read. I also made a mistake on account of the parents, to many of whom the outcry and panic must undoubtedly cause great anxiety and alarm.

Temple's key task was to reassure the school's trustees, many of whom had become alarmed by the adverse publicity and who might conceivably have sought the dismissal of their allegedly heretical headmaster. They considered the matter at a special meeting held on 19 April 1861, following which Temple was sent a formal letter of rebuke.

> The Trustees do not think themselves called upon to offer any opinion on matters of religious controversy connected with the objections made to some parts of that volume, as tending to impair the reverence due to the Holy Scriptures. But they cannot be blind to the fact that such objections are entertained by the highest Ecclesiastical authorities.

The letter asked Temple to furnish the trustees with the substance of statements on the subject he had already made to pupils and others connected with the school. It ended with a stern shot across his bows: 'They [the trustees] are unwilling to remain uninformed of any statements which Dr Temple may have thought fit to make … on a subject which has elicited comment of so grave a character and which might affect the best interests of the School.' Temple defended himself as best he could. He assured the trustees that the boys had been discouraged from reading the book, that no harm had been done to the school, and that, in spite of the national outcry, there had been only three withdrawals. The trustees were mollified – but instructed the headmaster never again to allow his name to be associated with 'speculations of a questionable religious character'.

Temple had survived the first phase of the storm, but he had been bitterly hurt by the attitude of those whom he had supposed to be his friends. Bishop Wilberforce, for instance, who had ordained him and who admitted that Temple's own essay was 'different in tone from those around it and contains nowhere any direct statement of such sophistries or scepticisms as abound throughout the rest', was nevertheless loud in his condemnation of Temple for allowing himself to be associated with such a deplorably unorthodox volume. And even his old friend Tait, by now Bishop of London, urged him to make a public pronouncement of faith in order to allay the fears of Churchmen generally. Temple refused to do any such thing. He felt that he was fighting for religious freedom, and he attempted to justify his stance in a series of letters to Tait. His erstwhile tutor remained unconvinced and accused Temple of a 'somewhat arrogant overestimate' of his own opinion.

Temple of course had his champions. Edward Benson, he who had so admired his ideal of the Christian Church while an assistant master at Rugby, was now Headmaster of Wellington. In a letter to J.B. Lightfoot, the future Bishop of Durham, in March 1861 Benson wrote:

Essays and Reviews is indeed a sad subject. I had a very jolly letter yesterday from Temple about them. He has certainly felt deeply, and we all know how wholly different he is from all but Jowett, from whom he still differs. His manliness and chivalry however ought to prevent, and I am confident will prevent, his renouncing those with whom he has set sail [i.e., his fellow essayists], even if he did not know all about them.

The second and more serious phase of the controversy over *Essays and Reviews* (or rather Temple's connection with it) came eight years later. By now Temple, who had won golden opinions as a Headmaster of Rugby second only to Arnold, was considered by the ecclesiastical powers that be as ripe for promotion. Gladstone had recently succeeded Disraeli as Prime Minister, and when, in July 1869, the deanery of Durham fell vacant, he offered it to Temple. After much soul-searching Temple declined the offer, on the ground that he could do more good at Rugby than at Durham. But his resolve to stay on as headmaster was weakening; so when, two months later, the death of the aged Bishop Phillpotts left the diocese of Exeter vacant and Gladstone offered it to Temple, he this time said yes. His acceptance of the see caused the floodgates to open. Gladstone must have been well aware of the possibility of controversy over the appointment, but could not possibly have foreseen the extent of its virulence. Temple's contribution to *Essays and Reviews* might have been indiscreet, but still, in the Prime Minister's eyes, he possessed many of the qualities thought desirable in a bishop. (He happened also to be a Liberal who backed Gladstone's efforts to disestablish the Church of Ireland.) Gladstone warned Tait, by now Archbishop of Canterbury, that the nomination was not likely to be received 'without some noise'. The noise was deafening. Indeed, it even resulted in an uneasy alliance of High and Low Churchmen determined to oppose the nomination. An attempt was made to block Temple's election by the Greater Chapter of Exeter, but the election went through by thirteen votes to six with four abstentions. At the confirmation of his election in London in December his elder sister had to be summoned to testify that her brother had been born in lawful wedlock (a bastard could not at that time become a bishop). Formal objections to the election were raised, but were overruled by the Vicar-General. At this point Tait, worn out by the controversy, suffered a stroke; and the responsibility for Temple's consecration fell on the Bishop of London, John Jackson. Nine of the seventeen bishops in the province of

Canterbury declined to take part in the ceremony. Luckily, however, only three bishops were required for a valid consecration, and Jackson was able to whip up the necessary quorum. A century and a quarter later the whole affair may seem a storm in an ecclesiastical teacup, but at the time it was a close-run thing.

* * * * *

Shortly before his stroke Tait had attempted to defend the Bishop-elect of Exeter in a letter published by *The Times*. Among the points he made was that the popularity of Rugby as a school indicated the confidence of the public in its headmaster. So how *did* Temple achieve his deservedly high reputation? F.D. How, in his *Six Great Schoolmasters*, sums up the effect of his headship as being mainly in the direction of greater breadth. 'Liberty that never lapsed into licence, independence that never rebelled against discipline, these were the qualities he sought to instil in the boys.' Moreover, 'the tender guidance he personally gave to the religious aspirations of the boys, leading, but never attempting to drive, them towards a higher spiritual level, was a method of which the wisdom was proved by the success.' Finally, says How, 'Temple was one of the first headmasters to apply the common touch and 'to abolish the old idea that "the Doctor" lived, and probably slept, in cassock, gown and bands'.

J.D. Hope Simpson, the Rugby historian, heads his chapter on Temple 'Granite on Fire'. And certainly his rugged, no-nonsense air made an immediate impression. To Henry Scott Holland, 'he always appeared like a great ship, furrowing its way alone through the seas'. In the eyes of F.E. Kitchener he stands out in the list of great headmasters.

> Those who had the joy to work under him may be forgiven if they believe that no other headmaster exercised so close a personal influence over his colleagues, till insensibly the principles that guided him in his work began to guide them and make them act together as one man.

Of course, Temple cannot have been *quite* such a paragon as such testimonials imply. He could at times appear extremely rude, and his brusque accents could frighten as well as inspire. But his vigour, his enthusiasm and his passion for justice all ensured that he was loved as well as respected by boys and masters alike during his time at Rugby.* Perhaps the aptest tribute is one that came from an old school servant:'He was a man as would carry through his business in proper Headmaster's fashion.'

*   *   *   *   *

It might have been supposed that, after such a controversial beginning, Temple's reign at Exeter would have continued in equally lively fashion. Far from it. He had no difficulty in living down the storm aroused by his connection with *Essays and Reviews* and developed into a model diocesan. He did much to promote the cause of Church schools and was also a leading figure in the temperance movement. His addresses to working men on the evils of drink were rivalled in intensity only by his exhortations to the clergy against neglecting their duty. Not the least important thing he did while at Exeter was to marry (at the age of fifty-four): a fruit of that marriage was William Temple, the only son to succeed his father in the fullness of time as Archbishop of Canterbury. Frederick's bride was the aristocratic Beatrice Lascelles (a granddaughter of the second Earl of Harewood), and he used to observe afterwards that every peer now seemed to be a cousin. After 16 years at Exeter he was chosen to succeed John Jackson as Bishop of London. The Prime Minister was again Gladstone, who at first hesitated between

---

* The affection felt by Rugbeians for Temple was reflected in a farewell ode by James Rhoades sung (to music by Sir Hubert Oakeley) at a school concert in 1869 on the eve of his departure. The opening verse read:

> Master, best-beloved and best,
> Ours for ever, as to-night
> Hands at parting may be press'd,
> Tears reluctant dim the sight;
> But, where'er thy name be known,
> Rugby hails thee first her own.

Temple and Lightfoot of Durham. Benson, by now Archbishop of Canterbury, favoured his former Rugby colleague. Lightfoot's growing concern with his own scholarly pursuits, he told Gladstone, lessened his usefulness: Temple, on the other hand, though he would often 'wound and bruise one without knowing it', could be depended on for 'hearty sympathy, outspoken counsel and any amount of time and trouble'. So to Temple went the prize; and he proved as hard-working a diocesan in London as he had been in Devon and (until the formation of the diocese of Truro in 1877) Cornwall. He was then in his late sixties and early seventies, but in spite of his age managed to cope in an average year with 70 confirmations, 500 meetings and 10,000 letters. He may have expected to end his working life as Bishop of London, but, if so, he was to be disappointed. In October 1896 Benson, though eight years Temple's junior, died suddenly in Hawarden Church while on a visit to the Gladstones. The primacy was again vacant; and this time the rival candidates were Temple and the much younger Randall Davidson, Tait's son-in-law, who was by now Bishop of Winchester. A tussle took place between Queen Victoria and the Prime Minister, Lord Salisbury, as to which man to nominate. The Premier pressed the claims of Temple: unquestionably, he assured the Queen, the greatest man on the English bench. 'His great liberality of thought, his energy, his piety, and his great intellect have won for him the confidence of all parties in the Church.' The Queen favoured Davidson, who had become her close confidant during his years as Dean of Windsor; and she was able to point to Temple's age (he was by now seventy-five) as a crucial drawback: her beloved Davidson was 27 years younger. In the end she reluctantly agreed to Temple after Salisbury had persuaded her that it was a question merely of allowing the older man to hold the fort for a few years until the younger was of an age to succeed him.

It can hardly be claimed for Frederick Temple that he was as great an archbishop as he had been a headmaster. He was old, and growing increasingly more doddery. Moreover (as the Queen had pointed out to Salisbury), his eyesight was defective: indeed, he was by now half-blind. He tended more and more to let things be, if he could save himself trouble by such a policy of masterly inactivity. Intractable problems were shelved and letters went unanswered. But he still prided himself on being more than a figurehead. He was much in evidence during the Queen's diamond jubilee celebrations in 1897, and in the same year presided over the fourth Lambeth Conference. His ceremonial swansong came when he crowned King Edward VII in Westminster Abbey on 9 August 1902. But he was by now so blind that he put the crown on back to front, and so frail that after paying homage he was unable to rise and had to be hauled to his feet by the bishops near him. He was game to the last, however, and died, as it were, in harness.

On 4 December 1902 he had first chaired a long meeting of the Ecclesiastical Commissioners and then gone on to the House of Lords to speak in favour of the Government's new Education Bill. In the middle of a sentence, however, he was seized with an attack of giddiness and sank back into his seat. It was the beginning of the end. But even now he was not quite done. His last audible words in the Lords debate had been, 'Let us get to work and see how it acts.' The next day, from his deathbed, he sent a message to the Church to the same effect. He urged that, in carrying out the provisions of the new Education Act, Churchmen should act with the greatest possible consideration towards their Nonconformist brethren. It was only fitting that one of the greatest headmasters of the century should have died with his thoughts still fixed on the education of the young.

E.W. Benson in the garden of the Master's Lodge at Wellington.

5

BLAZING A TRAIL

Edward White Benson: Headmaster of Wellington, 1858–1873

It is a pleasant irony of history that Benson should have owed his appointment to Wellington to the good offices of Frederick Temple, the man whom, though nearly eight years Temple's junior, he was to precede as Archbishop of Canterbury. Had Temple not pressed the claims of his bright young Rugby colleague to the headmastership of the new school founded in memory of the Great Duke, it is probable that Benson would have settled into the uneventful routine of a Cambridge fellowship – and that his subsequent ministry would have taken a very different turn. In fact, the careers of the two headmasters who were to succeed one another in the Primacy of All England followed a similar pattern.

The schools over which they presided to such a remarkable effect were, however, vastly different. Rugby, founded in the reign of the first Elizabeth, had experienced a second spring under Thomas Arnold and celebrated its tercentenary under his able successor-but-two, Temple. Wellington, by contrast, was the brainchild of the Prince Consort: a boarding school which would provide good but cheap education for the sons of army officers. To Benson, torn between the rival claims of schoolboys and scholarship, the offer of the Wellington headship eventually proved irresistible. As he put it to his old schoolfellow, J.B.

Lightfoot, the future Bishop of Durham: 'God has been opening my eyes of late to see that I am not able or worthy to work in his fields of thought, and that my place is among the working classes.'[1] The phrase 'working classes' did not mean quite the same thing to Benson as it did to Temple, who had felt a similar call: the sons of army officers were on a higher social level than the trainee teachers to whom Temple had ministered at Kneller Hall. But Benson was no doubt perfectly sincere in his avowal to Lightfoot, even though he had other reasons to sway him in favour of Wellington.

What had persuaded Temple to propose him for the vacant headmastership? To answer that question it is necessary to go back a few years. The Duke of Wellington had died in 1852; and so great was his fame that a collection was made throughout the country to pay for a suitable national memorial. His son was consulted as to what form this memorial should take – and came up with the not very helpful suggestion that a bronze statue of his father should be set up in every market town in England. This idea was quietly scotched and replaced, at the instigation of the Prince Consort, by a scheme for a new public school which would cater especially for the sons of deceased army officers whose widows had been left badly off. The plan went ahead, and the construction of the new Wellington College began on a wild and heathery site on the outskirts of Windsor Forest in Berkshire. But, as the building proceeded, so did the search for a suitable headmaster.

The initial move was to throw the post open to competition. From among a large number of applicants a short-list was compiled, its members being required to answer a questionnaire on the best method of running a school. None of the candidates provided answers considered satisfactory by the Prince and his colleagues on the embryo school's governing body, so they fell back on personal recommendations; and here Temple proved a key consultant.[2] Even before his appointment to Rugby he had made a name for himself as an educationalist of distinction, and he might therefore be relied upon to come up with a suitable candidate. The name of Benson was suggested to him by James Prince Lee, formerly Headmaster of King Edward's School, Birmingham, and now Bishop of Manchester. Benson had been a pupil of Lee, who recognized his quality and urged his claims on Temple. Benson was now on the classical staff at Rugby under Goulburn. In 1858 Temple succeeded Goulburn and was able to observe his young colleague in action. He realized that Lee's praises were fully justified. On 20 February he sent a message to the Prince Consort:

> He [Benson] seems to me to possess that union of originality and elasticity which is absolutely necessary for working a new scheme. He is intellectually a very superior man; a first-rate scholar, and a very fair mathematician. He is one of the best teachers I have ever met with, and this is a very rare qualification, and peculiarly rare when combined with high attainments such as his.

Admittedly Benson was young, said Temple (he was then twenty-eight); but that was inevitable, as any 'really superior man' tended to stay put and could rarely be winkled out of whatever niche he had established for himself. But in this case youth was a definite advantage. 'The Wellington College will demand a mind singularly free from prejudices which almost invariably seize upon those who have become accustomed to a settled routine.'[3] The Prince sent a copy of Temple's letter to his fellow governors, all of whom agreed to the appointment of Benson. Only the Earl of Derby, as an ex-Prime Minister, felt himself entitled to seek a second opinion. He wrote to his twenty-year-old nephew, an Old Rugbeian who had studied under Benson and who now assured his uncle:

> As a man he was much liked, for he has a very interesting way of talking and teaching, and was ever ready to explain any difficulty... As to a working fellow he was unusually kind, so with an idle one he was more than ordinarily severe. Still as a manager of boys, I think no better man could be found; as a teacher none more talented, or possessed of a more universal knowledge.[4]

In early March Prince Albert, on behalf of the governors, wrote to Benson offering him the headmastership. It was as well that they had delayed no longer, as Benson was already feeling unsettled at Rugby and on 23 February had written to a friend: 'If anything could make me stay here it would be Temple, but I rather believe my days here are coming to a close.'[5] In fact he had accepted a lecturership and tutorship at Cambridge several months previously, but had delayed taking up the posts. He had also considered applying for the vacant headmastership of Marlborough – which, having been founded originally for the sons of the clergy, might have been considered more up his street than a school with an army connection. So, when he received the Prince's offer, he took his time in replying. There were strong arguments against his leaving Rugby. Quite apart from the attraction of continuing to serve under Temple, the move to Wellington would leave him considerably worse off financially.* There were also arguments in favour of Cambridge, where he could have collaborated with Lightfoot on works of New Testament scholarship. He was not really in Lightfoot's class as a scholar, however, and it may well have been the challenge of a pioneering post rather than mere ambition that in the end persuaded him to accept the Prince's offer. As he told Lightfoot when he wrote to him to announce his decision: 'I believe this to be the better solution of the perplexities for myself than either of the others. I do not depart from Rugby, or resign residence at Trinity, without grief, but the latter plan of life grew less hopeful to me when I was with you last.'[7]

To some of Benson's friends, however, his decision seemed hard to understand. His former Rugby colleague, G.G. Bradley, who had just been appointed Headmaster of Marlborough, drew attention to the paradox of their respective choice of schools.

'Strange', I remember saying to him, 'that you, whose interest lies so strongly in Ecclesiastical History, should be called on to preside over a school of soldiers' sons; I, who have so often bored you with the Civil War in England and with Napier's Peninsular War … should be at work at a school founded for the sons of clergy and thronged with boys reared in country parsonages'[8]

---

* His Wellington salary would be a mere £800 a year, as opposed to the £1000 which he received as an assistant master at Rugby. Moreover, as he told a friend, he had refused a house-mastership in order to come to Wellington, which would have raised his income to about £1700 – an excessively handsome salary for those days and one which, as Benson pointed out, showed 'the market value of educational labour'.[6]

But the die was cast – though the school to which Benson went in 1858 was to develop in a very different way from that envisaged by the Prince Consort and his colleagues on the Wellington governing body when they offered him the job.

*   *   *   *   *

According to his son Fred, Benson came of 'an exceedingly long line of ascertained persons, all entirely undistinguished'. His ancestors had settled in the West Riding of Yorkshire during the fourteenth century as leaseholders of Fountains Abbey. According to Fred,

> A few of the women made interesting marriages, but in the direct male line there is no name at all, until my father's, which is even faintly notable. They prospered in a comfortable rural tranquillity, they lived on their freehold farms in small, rather dignified manor houses, they raised and educated large families, they went to York and Ripon for a little gaiety in the winter, and they are only remarkable for having gone on so long and having done so little.[9]

Benson's father, also christened Edward White, forsook farming for trade and migrated from Yorkshire to Birmingham. He had a penchant for chemistry and had discovered new methods of manufacturing both cobalt and white lead. Unfortunately, he had not the same flair for marketing his discoveries as for making them. In 1843 his business failed; he died soon afterwards at the age of forty-two, leaving his widow Harriet to bring up a family of four boys and four girls on the income from a small annuity. Edward White junior, who had been born on 14 July 1829, was the eldest child, and on him fell the burden of helping his mother support his siblings. This need for him to assume a responsibility beyond his years made him into a precocious youth accustomed to getting his own way.

He was by now a pupil at King Edward's School, Birmingham, under its able but idiosyncratic headmaster, Prince Lee. It was Lee who, on his father's death, urged his mother to keep him at the school if she possibly could, and two generous friends of his father's who enabled her to do so. Lee had taught for eight years

91

at Rugby under Arnold and was to have a profound influence on Benson. Indeed, when he was Bishop of Truro, Benson once burst into an impassioned defence of his old headmaster in the face of a disparaging remark made at a dinner party: 'You can hardly expect me to agree to that,' he exclaimed, 'when I owe to him all that I am or ever shall be.' Later that evening he told his son Arthur: 'Lee was the greatest man I have ever come within the influence of – the greatest and the best.'[10]

Lee was not in fact quite the paragon that Benson made him out to be. Star pupils might hero-worship him, but the less bright were made to taste the rough edge of his tongue. In the course of a testimonial to the governors of King Edward's School, Arnold had claimed that Lee's manner with boys was at once firm and courteous: 'They would never, I think, put him in a passion.'[11] If Arnold really thought that, he was mistaken. The less able pupils at King Edward's School undoubtedly put Lee in a passion, and he would attempt to flog them into submission. Admittedly he suffered from attacks of neuralgia and his eyes became inflamed and caused him pain, so his frequent furies could be laid at the door of his physical ailments.* But, on the credit side, he was a brilliant teacher of the classics and an intensely religious man; and it is no wonder that future pillars of the Church like Benson, Lightfoot and Westcott should have risen up and called him blessed. These three formed an inseparable trio with a passionate interest in ecclesiastical affairs. They would carry on long conversations (and, in the holidays, correspond) about such arcane matters as Purgatory, the Council of Trent and the validity of lay baptism; they would recite the Canonical Hours in Benson's father's disused white-lead factory; they even hatched a scheme for a Brotherhood of Holy Living 'to bring the Kingdom of God to the poor, to promote the spiritual unity of the Church and to practise the precepts of the Sermon on the Mount'.[12]

---

* When Lee was appointed Bishop of Manchester in 1847 he was accused by a Birmingham surgeon, Thomas Gutteridge, of corruption and drunkenness during his headmastership. Gutteridge claimed in a pamphlet that Lee would drink two or three bottles of wine at a sitting and then make himself quickly sober by wrapping wet towels round his head. Lee successfully sued Gutteridge for libel. In fact, he took laudanum to relieve his pains and, like many others of his generation, had become a laudanum addict.

From King Edward's School Benson won a sub-sizarship to Trinity College, Cambridge. But he went up to the university in the face of strong opposition from his relatives, who felt that he should at once begin earning his living in order to help his mother meet the cost of educating her other children. Edward was ambitious and turned a deaf ear to such pleas. He knew his academic ability and was determined to make full use of it. After only a year at college, however, he suffered a double blow: the deaths on the same day, from typhus fever, of both his mother and his eldest sister Harriet. By this time the family fortunes were at a low ebb, his mother having lost most of her capital through a rash investment in a company owned by George Hudson, the 'Railway King', which crashed in 1848. The younger Benson children had to be farmed out to various relatives. An uncle, Sir Thomas Baker, a wealthy businessman and a bachelor, offered to adopt his youngest nephew and make him his heir; but Edward Benson, who had by now come of age, refused to give his consent – on the ground that Sir Thomas was a Unitarian. An angry correspondence ensued, Benson standing firm on his principles with a fervour that now seems unbelievably priggish. The peroration of his final epistle reads:

> I shall constantly hereafter as a Priest in the English Church, if God will, several times in every service proclaim 'Glory be to the Father, and to the Son, and to the Holy Ghost': I shall offer humble prayer on my own behalf and on behalf of the Church at large to my Redeemer – with what conscience or with what countenance if ever memory should suggest that in one person's case, and his the dearest that could be, I had robbed those Divine persons of the worship and the praise that should have proceeded from his heart, his mind, his lips, his whole life?... Bigot, thus far, a conscientious Christian must be.[13]

By now Benson was a scholar of Trinity and showing prodigious academic promise. In his own case, too, money was tight; but a 'fairy godmother' appeared on the scene in the shape of Francis Martin, the college bursar, a middle-aged bachelor don who, in the words of Benson's son Fred, 'had a romantic and devoted affection for him'. He furnished new rooms for his protégé, paid all his out-of-pocket expenses, took him on tours and expeditions during the vacations, nursed him when ill, and generally treated him 'with a half lover-like, half paternal adoration'. With his material needs taken care of in this way, Benson could devote himself to his books. He took a brilliant first in the Classical Tripos of 1852 and won the Chancellor's gold medal. His sister prophesied that, if he went on as he had begun, he would soon be Archbishop of Canterbury.[14]

His next scholastic hurdle was the examination for a fellowship at Trinity. He cleared that at the second attempt in 1853 and in the following year was ordained deacon. By this time he was a member of Goulburn's staff at Rugby, having joined it in 1852 soon after taking his degree. He lodged with a widowed cousin, Mrs William Sidgwick, two of whose sons, Henry and Arthur, attended the school as day boys. They had a sister, Mary (Minnie), to whom Benson found himself at once attracted. When she was still only eleven (and he twenty-three) he wrote in his diary: 'As I have always been very fond of her and she of me with the love of a little sister, and as I have heard of her fondness for me commented on by many persons, and having been told that I was the only person at whose departure she ever cried as a child ... it is not strange that I should have thought first of the possibility that some day dear little Minnie might become my wife.'[15] The extraordinary story of Benson's courtship of Minnie has been told by David Williams in *Genesis and Exodus*. Suffice it to say here that they became engaged in 1857 and were married in June 1859, five months after the official opening of Wellington College. To be Benson's wife, in the opinion of Williams, was a 'testing task and workload'. Fred Benson put it more romantically: 'She was the staff on which he leaned and the wings that gave him flight.'[16]

His most important duty at Rugby was to teach the sixth form for an hour every morning. In addition he was responsible for 50 private pupils belonging to the School House. But he refused the offer of a boarding house in spite of its financial benefits – no doubt because he enjoyed lodging with Mrs Sidgwick and being in daily contact with Minnie. She sometimes accompanied him on her pony during his afternoon rides in the countryside. In those days he was a bit of a dandy. For Sunday chapel he would appear in a blue frock-coat, pearl-grey trousers, high collar, expensive silk tie, lilac gloves and silk bachelor's cap and gown. The gown helped to conceal the shortness of his legs, a physical defect on which he felt sensitive.[17] In other respects he was already strikingly handsome. Charles Kingsley, when asked to describe Benson's character, replied: 'Beautiful, like his face.'[18]

*   *   *   *   *

This then was the man who, when not yet thirty, found himself appointed to the headmastership of England's newest public school. In the summer of 1858, before the school opened, he was sent to Germany at the Prince Consort's behest to study the educational methods in vogue there. The Prince hoped he would pick up some useful hints, but Benson was not much impressed by what he saw. He wrote to Lightfoot after his return about the 'vast superiority of English over German classical schools, and (save for a few giants in Germany) scholars also – i.e., our run of scholars vastly superior, in sense, in feeling, and *extent* of reading, to theirs'.[19] No doubt he gave the Prince a tactfully watered-down critique of the schools there. Later that year he arrived by rail to take possession of his kingdom. The porter at the halt nearest to the college undertook to show him the way over the heather. They had not gone far when they met a man with a lantern, a pitchfork and a dog who said: 'If you come a step further I'll set the dog at you and stick the pitchfork into you.' The man turned out to be the night-watchman. On hearing that the intruder was the headmaster, he was suitably grovelling in his apologies.[20]

The school was formally opened on 29 January 1859 in the presence of the Queen and Prince Albert. Nine days earlier the first pupils had arrived: 47 foundationers (as the sons of deceased army officers were called) and 29 non-foundationers. It was a miserable winter's day, sunless and with a steady drizzle. The buildings were not yet fully completed and in proper working order. The boys were given a scratch meal of bread, cheese and beer and dispatched to their dormitories. An odd incident occurred in the small hours of the next day. Benson was awakened about 3 a.m. by the sound of voices and tramping feet. It was a bright, moonlit night; and the

95

boys, not possessed of watches, had mistaken the moonlight for day, had dressed, and had gone downstairs so as not to be late for school. Benson was not amused and sent them smartly back to bed.[21]

In the early days the boys wore an extraordinary uniform invented by the Prince Consort. It consisted of a dark-green coat with brass buttons worn with a shepherd's plaid waistcoat and trousers; the finishing touch was a postman-like cap with a red button on top and a ducal crown in front. Unfortunately, the uniform resembled that worn by the porters on the South-Eastern Railway. The boys disliked it intensely and, after two of their number had been handed used tickets by passengers alighting at the local station, something less obtrusive was substituted.[22] Five months after the school's opening the headmaster was married to Minnie Sidgwick. In those days the number of boys was small enough for her to be on familiar terms with all of them. 'Every evening after the evening service', says Arthur Benson, 'my mother, then a sedate matron of eighteen, used to shake hands with each of them and wish them good night.'[23] She was universally known as Mother Benjy – and was at that time only a year or two older than the senior boys.

*　　*　　*　　*　　*

There is no lack of contemporary assessments of Benson's performance as Headmaster of Wellington. His son Arthur, who wrote the official life of his father, includes a number of these in his chapters on the headmastership. The fullest and most percipient is that by A.W. Verrall, one of Benson's most brilliant pupils at Wellington in the late 1860s and afterwards Senior Tutor of Trinity College, Cambridge. Verrall begins by emphasizing Benson's 'advantages of person and bearing' and goes on to observe:

> He was, first of all and above all, an unsurpassable actor of noble parts; and this he was by virtue of two qualities: first, the extraordinary range of his social and personal interests, and, secondly, his high estimate of spectacular function as an index and monitor of such interests.

(David Williams, in his own study of the Bensons, suggests that this somewhat involved remark could be interpreted as meaning that Benson was a show-off and a climber.) Verrall refers to the number of VIPs with whom the headmaster had to deal in his official capacity.

> The personages with whom he had to act, both then and frequently, made a group in rank and power out of all proportion to the scene and to the natural height of his own office... Yet I never saw ... any personage (with one single exception) over whom, if and so far as it was proper, the Headmaster could not easily take the lead.

The 'single exception' was the Earl of Derby, four times Prime Minister and a leading member of the governing body, 'who certainly could on occasion ... act up to the level of Benson'.

Verrall thought that his 'grandeur in social function' was simply the expression of his vivid interest in persons and their social relations to one another. Although not a particularly acute judge of character, he was amazingly well informed about the doings of his pupils: 'Of the life which many of us lived at Wellington, at least in its external features, he could to the last, I feel sure, have given a much more lifelike account than we could ourselves.' This intimate knowledge, Verrall believed, arose from Benson's 'genuine, unaffected sense of the importance and far-reaching effect which belongs, by the action of society, to the proceedings of every individual, however small'. As for the charge that Benson's 'sense of greatness and dignity in all affairs' implied that he was worldly, Verrall declares:

> The grain of truth in it was just this: he was conscious, as honestly he could not but be, of his power to radiate life and warmth to the furthest circle that he should ever reach, and could not but desire, with the kind of ambition which is inseparable from such an organisation, that this circle might have an indefinite extent.[24]

Perhaps this too is another way of hinting that Benson, for all his high ideals, was indeed a bit of a social climber.

Most assessments of Benson draw attention to his striking appearance. E.C. Wickham, for instance, who succeeded him as headmaster before becoming Dean of Lincoln, emphasizes his 'face of command, with great play of feature, eager but quiet, and giving the sense of a fund both of humour and of determination'.[25] To C.W. Penny, an assistant master who became an intimate friend, Benson had at first seemed absurdly young. 'A second glance showed me that he was older than he looked... With his commanding address, but most suave and affable manner, he soon replaced my first impression of his youthfulness with another feeling of deference and respect towards my future Headmaster.'[26] Elizabeth Wordsworth, daughter of the Bishop of Lincoln and later Principal of Lady Margaret Hall, Oxford, claimed that you could not be with Benson for three minutes without feeling that he was no common man. 'He possessed in an unusual degree that kind of magnetism which makes those who are in company with its owner always conscious of what he is doing, and instinctively disposed to follow his lead.' Elizabeth was particularly struck by Benson's active and eager looks and movements, and by the rapid change of colour in his face which often made him blush with pleasure like a schoolboy. 'He had the hands too of an enthusiast, every finger full of character and vigour. It was a pleasure to see him handle anything'[27] (except, the boys would doubtless have added, a cane).

Another of Benson's striking qualities was stressed by his cousin, Henry Sidgwick, who rose to be Professor of Moral Philosophy at Cambridge. This was his sense of history. But, says Sidgwick, Benson's admiring contemplation of the past was allied to a practical interest in the present.

> I used to say that, in spite of his endless delight in scheming and planning, ... he would have found it difficult to interest himself as he did in the making of Wellington College if it had not been connected with the memory of a great national hero. But here I believe I was wrong: if it had been simply a modern commercial school in a brand-new suburb, his ingenuity would have found some way of sending imaginary roots from it into the past, and surrounding it with historic associations.[28]

Of course, Benson's charisma was not universally effective. Even the admiring Verrall admits that he was not popular with the boys. This would have appeared an understatement to Henry Richards: 'We did not like Benson,' he wrote. 'Nobody did. We thought we hated him, because he had a violent temper; he would turn perfectly white sometimes when flogging a boy; and we thought he toadied to people of title.' But elsewhere Richards tones down his criticism when he remarks: 'The school, taken collectively, disliked, even hated Mr Benson, but, individually, we found much to admire in him and even a small residuum which we could like.'[29]

The future General Sir Ian Hamilton felt much the same. 'Whenever Benson was on view I watched him exactly as a mouse does a cat, and for exactly the same reasons.'[30] To Hamilton, Benson was a 'portentous and terrifying figure', but nevertheless one possessed of a redeeming humanity. 'You never knew where to have him or where he would have you. So we admired his raging fury, whereas the icy smile with which one of his successors caned his rare victims is still, by some of them, unforgiven.' Benson, Hamilton recalls, was 'a masterful Master ... not one of those who creep about dormitories in carpet slippers, or get hold of little boys and in a pi-jaw work upon religious feelings till they confess that Smith Major said d---. Benson would have died sooner than do that.'[31]

Benson's fiery rages were notorious. There was a famous occasion at Rugby when he lost his temper during a Calling Over and proceeded to such extreme measures of punishment that he nearly provoked a riot. It was the same sort of thing at Wellington, at least in his early days. Nor was his irascible temper vented only on the boys. Penny describes an occasion when he found himself on the receiving end of the headmaster's wrath. He had been accused by Benson of having broken a school rule in relation to a boy in his form or dormitory and had rashly replied that, if he had done so, it had been through inadvertence, as he had never heard of the rule in question. Benson's eyes flashed and he at once told Penny to follow him to his study. The sequel can be told in Penny's words:

> For ten minutes he poured out all the vials of his wrath on my devoted head. I was so terrified at his violence that I thought he was going to dismiss me then and there. I felt the injustice of his anger so acutely that I burst into tears and said nothing more in my

defence. This at once mollified him, and before we parted he asked me to forgive him if in his heat he had said more than he ought to have done.[32]

Benson mellowed over the years; and on a later occasion, when Penny had opposed one of his proposals during a masters' meeting, he received a much milder rebuke. Penny comments:

> The contrast between the two occasions – his uncontrollable violence on the first and his much more guarded anger on the second – exhibits the wonderful way in which, as the years advanced, he obtained the complete mastery over what in his youth too often overmastered him... Everyone at Wellington by that time had begun to realize the immense – one might almost say complete – control which Benson had acquired over this tendency to sudden anger.[33]

It was just as well that there were fewer temperamental fireworks to explode when Benson left the narrow world of an English public school for the wider canvas of a bishopric. Nevertheless, although he learned to control his temper, he always found it difficult to brook either contradiction or criticism – which did nothing to ease his relations with his governing body. As David Newsome puts it: 'There was lacking that spirit of mutual trust which should ideally exist between Governors and Headmaster, and this in turn led to misunderstandings and difficulties which might otherwise never have arisen.'[34]

Occasionally Benson could indulge in a moment of self-criticism. 'I wish I were more fit for my work,' he wrote to Minnie in 1861 during a temporary absence.

> It is too great a work for me. I am not as keen and yet not as loving as I ought to be. The burden of all things seems to make me fidgety from head to foot, so that I feel little comfort in leisure. I want a greater soul and a calmer way of looking at things. Where am I to get it?... I don't seem to have the spare minutes to philosophize myself into it.[35]

Benson at intervals gave way to moods of black depression. These were more frequent in his early days at Wellington, when he felt his position as headmaster to be still insecure. Arthur Benson remarks at one point in his biography: 'I believe that he never attended a meeting of the Governors without saying gravely to my mother that this time he expected to receive his dismissal.'[36] Penny recalls an occasion, early in the spring of 1868, when, for the only time in his experience, Benson gave way in his presence to a fit of despondency (it was also the only occasion when Penny saw him in tears):

> One morning he came in to me evidently deeply depressed. I asked what was the matter and if he had bad news. No: but he was feeling utterly baffled. His work here did not prosper. The Governors as a body were hostile and on the lookout for the first sign of failure in his administration. Worse than all, the boys he had to teach were so heavy and unintellectual; he found the Sixth a dead weight which it was impossible to bear up against. And here he burst into tears. 'I cannot think', he said, 'what makes my teaching here so ineffectual. I can only say that it was very different at Rugby.'

Penny did his best to comfort the headmaster with the hope of better things to come. 'It proved to be, as so often happens, that it was the darkest hour that precedes the dawn.'[37]

On one thing all the commentators agree: Benson's indefatigable energy. He was almost always at work by half-past six in the morning and rarely knocked off before midnight. Verrall salutes this prodigious industry: 'There was scarcely an hour of the day or night at which he was not often working hard. He must have known, I think, that in all human probability he would prove to have fore-spent his old age.'[38] This was only too true. Benson was to die well before reaching the psalmist's three score years and ten – unlike his friend Frederick Temple, who was to live into his eighties. Benson himself was well aware that he was overworked. As he told Lightfoot in June 1861: 'I exert myself like Samson at Gaza for the present in the hope of having less to do bye and bye … I spin round like a mop thirsting to get dry'.[39] But his hopes of easing off were doomed to disappointment. In July 1868 he was writing to another friend, Fred Wickenden:

Life is now so full of mere work, with a constant sense of dissatisfaction brooding over the hours, and so little time for enjoyment that the very power of enjoyment goes away fast, and I constantly go off from pleasant things to work which is not pressing, simply because I can't enjoy pleasant things.[40]

Later that year he was again writing to Wickenden: 'You have no idea of what life is becoming to me – a humming-top is the only thing that resembles it, perpetual motion, very dizzy, hollow within, keeping up a continuous angry buzz.'[41]

A graphic description of the gruelling timetable that Benson set himself is given by David Newsome in his history of the school:

His day began at 6 a.m. and he was satisfied with five hours' sleep. He was a voluminous correspondent, keeping copies in his own hand of all his important letters. A secretary was an unheard-of luxury. He taught extensively in school, personally examined each form during each term and personally meted out vigorous punishment on those who failed to impress at this ordeal in his study on Saturday mornings. Hardly ever did he miss a school period, even if this entailed an uncomfortable journey in a cattle-truck in the early hours of the morning. He preached every Sunday in Chapel, and conducted almost every service himself. At the same time he could still find opportunities for hours of labour on the planning of the ornamental detail in the Chapel, and on the preparation of his monumental thesis on Cyprian.[42]

It is hardly surprising that such Herculean labours should sometimes induce fits of black depression – which might have been the more readily dispelled if Benson had realized that the high peaks of his career were still to come.

*   *   *   *   *

In his relations with the boys at Wellington Benson strove for perfection, refusing to see that he was sometimes asking of them more than they could deliver. From his sixth-formers, for instance, he expected an excessively high standard of work. The brighter boys might be stimulated by the pressures into producing

102

the desired result, but those of even average intelligence found it hard to cope with their crushing workload and were often depressed at their failure to live up to their headmaster's ideals. A.W. Verrall, in the course of the reminiscences he compiled for Arthur Benson's biography, regarded this striving for perfection as a major flaw in the Bensonian system. He recalls the occasional visits Benson used to pay to other headmasters – visits from which he would return 'primed with impossible tests, intellectual and moral, over which he believed (here was the point), against likelihood and certainty, that we should radiantly triumph'. The result was only too foreseeable: the Wellingtonians performed no more creditably than the pupils of rival schools. 'Then fell the storm,' says Verrall, 'rousing of course no repentance and not a little resentment.'*[43]

The boys in the Lower and Middle Schools were often in such terror of the headmaster that they failed to do themselves justice. According to Penny, 'his eyes fascinated and paralysed them, and not even his most pleasant smile ever reassured them to do well in the terrible ordeal'.[45] Nearly everyone quailed before him and he would ruthlessly demolish any defence which a boy might try to make. E.K. Purnell recalls only one occasion on which Benson failed to come off victorious. Five boys had been reported to him for using saloon-pistols in a nearby wood. They defended themselves thus: 'You preached such a beautiful sermon last Sunday, in which you told us to put temptation away from us, so we said among ourselves, "We have got all those cartridges; the best thing to do will be to go into Cox Wood and fire them off. Then we shall have no more temptation."' The ingenious defence was accepted.[46]

*   *   *   *   *

---

* After a particularly gruelling set of lessons on Guizot's *History of Civilisation in Europe*, one of the prefects produced a clever parody of Benson's weekly questions which he pinned to the sixth-form noticeboard. It began: '1st Lesson – Saturday. The next two lines and a half in Guizot. A small portion only is set because it is wished that the following illustrative points should be thoroughly got up: 1. The number of words and the number of letters in the passage set. 2. All other forms of meaning which the passage can be made to assume by the permutation of words and letters. 3. The weight and dimensions of the volume... 7. Lives of all the commentators on all the biographies of all the historians of the times referred to.'[44]

When Penny first joined the staff in May 1861 he was met at the station by Benson, who walked up to the school with him. 'I noticed the awe in every Boy's countenance whom we met,' says Penny, 'and with what scrupulous attention each Boy touched his cap in passing us. It was clear to me even by then that Benson was a Master whom the Boys feared, and that wherever he appeared strict discipline was the order of the day.'[47]

Arthur Benson says that, as a schoolmaster, his father was 'one of the sternest and severest disciplinarians that ever ruled a school'[48] – particularly in regard to the infliction of corporal punishment. But there is a paradox here because, according to Arthur, his father was in many respects ultra-sensitive about the infliction of pain and had a deep and instinctive hatred of cruelty. Admittedly, the examples quoted by Arthur all refer to animals – hares, horses, dogs and so on. Nevertheless,

> the problem remains that, though he was himself almost morbid in his detestation of cruelty, he yet had a solid belief in the efficacy of chastisement. I think it did harm to his work, because it made him more formidable than anything else in the eyes of many boys.[49]

Certainly all the Old Wellingtonians whom Arthur met agreed that the headmaster believed in, and used, physical punishment far more than was necessary. As a result, Arthur claims, his father could and largely did rule through fear. 'There is no exaggeration in saying that boys and even masters were greatly afraid of him.' Arthur quotes an old pupil as saying what an awful sight it was to see the headmaster fold his gown round him and cane a liar before the school. 'Awful no doubt it was,' says Arthur, 'But his severity had in it something painful, because it was with him, though he did not fully realise it, so unnecessary: he could have ruled by the tongue, and yet he did believe in and use corporal punishment to a conspicuous degree.'[50]

On one occasion Benson found himself having to defend the use of the cane. This was when Sir Charles Phipps, who had two sons at the school but who also happened to be private secretary to the Prince Consort, expressed disquiet about the possibly excessive use of corporal punishment at Wellington. The key sentences of Benson's reply read:

104

The punishment with the cane as used at Wellington College is most strictly limited and watched. The chief and about the only motive which I have had in employing it is the full persuasion that no other punishment is at once so effective and so really free from cruelty and unkindness. I am confident that the boys in general are with me in this, and for one boy who would choose any other punishment there are 100 who would choose such use as we make of the cane... The cane is quickly over, breeds no spite, spoils no temper. *Every* other punishment I know does all these.[51]

There is a limited amount of support for the claim that the boys upheld the use of the cane. Verrall, for instance (who, being a bright boy, probably experienced it little, if at all), commented: 'As a disciplinarian, and in the infliction of punishment, he [Benson] was thought hard, and perhaps he was. But I do not think his sentences were lastingly resented, which is the true test of justice, at least for boys.'[52] And Ian Hamilton, who received a succession of beatings from Benson for his failure to get up in time for early school, could yet confess (admittedly many years later) to being an admirer of Benson's. 'We all were, I think. He was human. You never knew your luck.'*

It must not be supposed that Benson punished simply for the sake of punishment. In cases of severe delinquency he took endless pains in dealing as mercifully (according to his lights) with the culprit as he could. An instance of this is recorded by an assistant master, Arthur Carr, to illustrate Benson's power to drag out the truth and also his sense of the importance of confession (though a cynic might retort that the process of extraction held echoes of the Inquisition!). A boy of promise had committed a 'grievous sin' (not specified) which he had attempted to conceal under a tissue of falsehood. The misdemeanour had been all but proved, and the only thing remaining was for the boy to confess to it. Carr continues:

---

* In his introduction to J.L. Bevir's book on the early years at Wellington Hamilton gives a graphic description of the effect of Benson's beatings: 'When I went to the bathing lake and stripped, I felt as a peacock must feel when spreading his tail; I became the cynosure and stupor of the crowd. The blues of the previous week had changed to green and yellow, whilst along the ribs, under my arms, where the point of the cane curled, the stripes were dark purple – and yet my dislike to early rising was to remain for many years a constitutional infirmity.'[53]

I was present as the boy's tutor, and I shall never forget the beautiful way in which Benson pleaded with him for more than an hour. At first the hard look and proud lips compressed to conceal the truth seemed to defy confession. But still the pleading went on with the utmost gentleness, till at length the false shame yielded, the hard look vanished, and free confession came with tears. The whole look of the boy altered. It was a great victory and left on my mind a strong impression of spiritual power.[54]

On another occasion a boy had been found guilty of an (again unspecified) 'offence' and his parents had agreed to remove him from the school. The sequel is related by Minnie Benson:

That afternoon my husband and I started for a long walk, as usual, and went to Caesar's Camp, about three miles off, talking of all this... We sat down here as we always did, and in a few minutes he burst into a passion of tears. The whole misery and wretchedness of it overcame him: the bright promise of the poor lad with this blight on it, the love between him and his parents and their broken-hearted but still loving grief, and his own absolute certainty that the boy must go for others' sakes; he lay among the fern, shaken with uncontrollable sobs; I could only sit by him and wait. After a while the storm had expended itself; he was able to walk back quietly with me.[55]

On yet another occasion it was not only the guilty who suffered. Three boys had misbehaved and had attempted to lie their way out of trouble. Two of them were expelled; but the rest of the school were deprived of a half-holiday on the ground that the headmaster had given notice some months previously that, if any member of the school persisted in an untruth, all would suffer. Benson justified his action in the course of a letter to his wife:

Some people would say there was no justice in it, but vicarious suffering not only represents but *is* justice. It is the sinfulness of society which breaks out in the sins of the individuals, and if society punished itself instead of 'making examples' there would soon be no examples to make.

According to Benson, the effect on the school was excellent. 'All say so, even those who were against me.'[56]

Benson loved teaching, especially sixth-formers. Verrall thought that the best part was his talk – 'wonderfully rich, witty and variously adapted to the occasion'. But Verrall suspected even then that Benson was too much of a grammarian and verbalist to be an ideal teacher.[57] Arthur says that his father's mode of instruction was based on the methods of Prince Lee and consisted in a minute analysis of words arrived at by a singular kind of rendering.

> This process certainly excavated and laid bare the shades of meaning in the Latin, but it was cumbrous, because the net result bore no likeness to the progress or literary form of the original. Moreover, it had the additional disadvantage that the rate of advance was very slow, and the boys never got a wide view of a book or an author.[58]

*　　*　　*　　*　　*

Arthur Benson says that his father was 'beloved and admired by his masters for his enthusiasm and generosity, his extreme accessibility, the patience and wisdom of his counsel, and his great personal courtesy'.[59] They were also a bit afraid of him, for, as Penny's experience showed, he had a rough edge to his tongue and could be ferociously angry when crossed. Because of his youth Benson was, at least in his early days at Wellington, much more on a level with his colleagues than most headmasters. 'His attitude towards us', Penny recalls,

> was more that of an elder brother. And, while in the actual government of the school he was from the first as absolute as any Monarch who is the arbiter of his own constitution, yet his everyday intercourse and social relations with us were on an entire equality.[60]

Benson was certainly an absolute monarch; and his dominant personality tended to obscure, and even submerge, the individuality of his subordinates. Arthur compares them to Napoleon's marshals: 'They looked loyally after their own brigades and left the initiative to him.'[61]

Certainly, taken as a whole, the assistant masters at Wellington were not of so high a calibre as those at Rugby under Temple; nor did Wellington send out, as Rugby had done, a stream of headmasters to preside over lesser public schools. Frequent changes in the staff took place, which Benson ascribed to inadequate salaries and slender prospects. But he was no judge of character and made some strange appointments. Moreover, he had a preference for ordained men on his staff. He held that a master who was not in orders would be less effective in carrying out his responsibilities than one who was.[62]

Among his particular phobias was smoking. Here he was far in advance of his times, though he disliked the habit not because he thought that it was bad for the health but because he considered it ungentlemanly and self-indulgent. Members of the staff were forbidden to smoke, which must have been a sore trial for the weaker brethren. Indeed, on one occasion a master, driven to desperation, took refuge behind a hayrick near the college in order to enjoy a surreptitious pipe – only to find a boy there similarly engaged. The result was a non-aggression pact, each party undertaking not to give away the other to the head.[63] Another master dug a pit at the bottom of his garden where he and like-minded colleagues could enjoy their tobacco in peace.[64]

If Benson had a down on smoking, he more than made up for it by his lavish hospitality. When a new master arrived at the school he was always put up at the headmaster's house for a week or two until he had found his feet – and Benson made sure that the rooms into which the newcomer eventually moved were comfortably furnished. He would often entertain his colleagues to dinner at the Lodge. Arthur Benson recalls such banquets with nostalgia. 'The days when there were dinner parties were charged with an almost magical sense of something august in the air. I can recollect my mother coming in to say good-night to us in the night-nursery, a radiant vision in a silk evening dress with a crinoline.' Later, when the party was well under way, young Arthur and his siblings would listen to the sounds of talk below – 'and at last the fairy cascades of music which floated up from the drawing-room – a well-touched piano and Mr Penny, in his flute-like tenor, warbling, "Drink to me only with thine eyes", seemed like a foretaste of the angelic song.'*[65] Nor was Benson's hospitality confined to the masters. He used to bring in a couple of sixth-formers to breakfast every morning. 'They were as much a necessary accompaniment of breakfast as my father himself,' Arthur recalls. A favoured few among the boys were given the run of the house. Among them were Arthur Verrall, who often attended nursery tea, and a Romanian prince who remained a friend of the family for the rest of his life.[67]

*   *   *   *   *

Religion played an important part in the life of Wellington College during Benson's headmastership. From his early boyhood onwards he had been passionately interested in anything to do with the Church and the priesthood – forms of worship and minutiae of ritual as well as deeper matters of faith. When he was only ten years old he had written to an uncle to enquire whether he had a chance of becoming a clergyman when he grew up; and he even made an empty room in his mother's house into an oratory. 'He draped a table for an altar,' his son Fred remembers; 'he got a faldstool to kneel at; he hung the walls with sacred prints; and here, all by himself, every morning and evening he made his devotions.'[68] Later, while still at school, he delved into the study of liturgy and ritual. Canon C.B. Hutchinson recalls:

> With a spirit of devotion and reverence he united a love of order and dignity in Ceremonial; and it was a thoroughly characteristic answer that he gave to a friend who asked him what he would like to be. 'I should like to be a Canon and recite the daily offices in my Cathedral.'[69]

Wellington College chapel might not be a cathedral; but in the ordering of its services Benson could and did behave as autocratically as any dean.

---

* Arthur had a soft spot for Penny, who was his father's closest friend among the staff. He describes him as a 'very tender-hearted, demure man whose large dark side-whiskers tend even now, as I think of him, to divert attention from his delicate and refined features. He was one, I think, who was made by nature to be a sympathetic and dutiful lieutenant.'[66]

109

First, however, the chapel had to be built; and here Benson played a key role. He first persuaded the governors of the need for a chapel and then, in effect, supervised its construction. There were frequent tussles with the governors over the size and shape of the building, and Benson did not always get his way – though he usually found an ally in the Prince Consort. The eventual cost of the chapel was about £9,000, of which the public subscribed £2,500. The architect was Gilbert Scott. In matters of detail, however, Benson reigned supreme, personally compiling a huge volume of cuttings, illustrations, letters and notes devoted to the building of the chapel. As David Newsome sums it up:

> It is a scrapbook recording his happiest moments at Wellington, describing with minute detail the day-to-day progress of the building operations, revealing to the reader to what extent the planning of the interior of the chapel – the windows, the mosaics, the stone carvings and every ornamental detail – was the intensely personal work of one man, drawing from his profound knowledge with a devoted care to the fulfilment of a labour of love... For all its [subsequent] alterations, the chapel remains the most intimate link between the College of today and the person of its first Headmaster.[70]

Benson refused to have a pulpit in the chapel on the ground that it would interfere with the austerity of a narrow building. He would preach instead from a small brass desk set out on the chapel steps. He preached regularly every Sunday morning at the midday communion service, though he seldom put pen to paper before the end of Matins two hours earlier and his final sentences were often written as the chapel bell was ringing. It might be thought that the sermons would have suffered from being written in so short a span of time, but this was apparently not so. As his wife commented: 'It was inconceivable sometimes that what was preached to us at 12 should have been created since 10 – but of course it had been simmering in his mind all the week, and came out with a rush from the pressure of necessity.'[71] Minnie's view is loyally supported by her son Arthur: 'This haste and pressure, not giving him time for revision and compression, is perhaps what makes them such beautiful sermons. I often read them even now' (he was writing in 1923), 'and think them deeply moving and impressive.'[72] The sermons were simple and practical. They often contained explanations and elucidations of points of doctrine, but avoided any catchwords or controversial phrases. There is no record, however, of their having had quite the dynamic effect on the boys that Temple's had at Rugby.

Benson had always been interested in hymnology, so it was not surprising that he should have compiled a special hymn-book for use in the school chapel. It was based on a highly elaborate scheme. The hymns in the book were not numbered, a single hymn (but not more than one) being allotted to each service on weekdays and Sundays alike. The collection abounds in hymns by Tractarian writers such as Keble, Neale and Isaac Williams, and Benson supplied a few of his own composition as well as several translations. In a letter written to a friend many years later he describes his principles of selection, and points out that each hymn had its fixed tune in order to rivet the whole more completely in the memory. 'I have heard the most interesting stories', he says, 'of old Wellingtonians separated by years recognising each other in the Himalayas and on board ship with a "Why, you are an O.W." from hearing the proper hymns for the day or season hummed over.'[73] Not everyone shared the headmaster's enthusiasm for his hymn-book, though J.L. Bevir remarks that no one would ever have thought of criticizing it to his face.

> Englishmen are proverbially long-suffering in the matter of Church Services.... If, as time went on, we became somewhat weary of the sameness and monotony of singing the same hymns over and over again with so little change or variety, we also got used to the strangeness in many of them... Finally, I think, we began to like them, however much we disliked them at first.

Nevertheless, Bevir still considers that the book was a 'real misfortune' for the boys. 'I never heard a voice raised in its favour by a single Assistant Master all the thirty years and more of my life at Wellington.'[74]

From time to time Benson was assailed for his allegedly Tractarian or Latitudinarian views. In fact, his churchmanship was by no means extreme. He was always a convinced and ardent Anglican, believing in the principles of the Reformation and yet holding the Anglican Communion to be by true descent and inheritance a branch of the Catholic Church. At the time of his going to Wellington he could best be described (however much he may have denied it) as a moderate High Churchman – but with no leanings to either Puseyism or theological liberalism. According to his son Arthur he liked the solemnity and dignity of a carefully ordered ritual, felt its artistic charm, but attributed to it no direct spiritual influence. He had, of course, a profound knowledge of ritual, but once confessed to Arthur: 'I'm ashamed to seem to know so much about what is really so unimportant.'[75] The ritual in use in Wellington College chapel was deliberately kept unobtrusive, as was to be expected from a middle-of-the-road Anglican who happened to like a reasonable amount of ceremonial. As David Williams observes, Benson was 'a headmasterly churchman rather than a holy churchman'.[76]

He got into hot water during 1860 for his alleged championship of *Essays and Reviews*, the book which had caused so much trouble for poor Frederick Temple. A long letter appeared in *The Record*, an extreme Protestant journal, complaining that Benson had presented a copy of the book to the boys' library at Wellington. He wrote back at once to say that it was the *masters'* library to which the copy had been presented. This room, he added, was out of bounds to the boys; and, moreover, the nature of the masters' profession made it desirable that they should study works of various tendencies. An editorial footnote attached to Benson's letter commented: 'A Christian Public would certainly not be satisfied with these excuses.' [77]

He had already been assailed from the opposite corner of the ecclesiastical spectrum by a lady who complained to one of the governors that her son, a pupil at the school, had heard a very offensive Tractarian sermon preached in the chapel and that the services as a whole were distressingly High Church in tone. The governor forwarded the letter to Benson, who had no difficulty in clearing himself of the charge. 'It may set Mrs C—'s mind at rest', he wrote, 'to know that the preacher whose views her son … considered to be High Church happened to be *Mr Charles*

112

Kingsley, my neighbour and friend, whose name is well known as a most strenuous opponent of such teaching.' There was nothing High Church about the services in general, he added; they were similar to those found in other major public schools.

> I think nothing of such matters myself, and think it wrong and foolish to offend consciences by trifles. I am myself neither High, nor Low, nor Broad Church, though I hear myself consigned by turns to all – as often to one as to another. But I find too much to do in bringing before boys the weightier matters of honour, truthfulness, industry, obedience, mutual kindness, ever to trouble myself, or them either, with party views, party questions, or party practices.[78]

He defended himself a little later along similar lines when another of the governors received a complaint accusing him of High Church proclivities.

> As to my being High Church it is quite absurd; the plain fact is not so... If the same [Evangelical] party make out that a man is a Puseyite and a Sceptic, he may be considered as pretty well disposed of. The fact is that those who don't like us will attack our mutton or our Chapel or our doctor or anything else that occurs to them.[79]

Admittedly, Benson's churchmanship got distinctly Higher as he grew older; and according to Penny there were signs of this trend even while he was at Wellington. On one occasion, when Benson discovered that Penny had been in holy orders for some years but had apparently never yet had an opportunity of celebrating Holy Communion, he invited him to preside at the next week-day celebration for the college servants, with himself assisting as deacon. At the end of the service he said to Penny in a loud whisper: 'I congratulate you on having celebrated your first Mass.' 'At the time,' Penny comments, 'the word *Mass* jarred upon my ears; but in view of subsequent events I think he used it deliberately as it is used in the First Prayer Book of K. Edward VI.'[80] One may suspect anyway that Benson used it with a twinkle in his eye.

*   *   *   *   *

113

Benson was a fanatically hard worker, but he did at least allow himself *some* time off. Unlike Frederick Temple, who waited until late middle age (long after he had left Rugby) before taking to himself a wife, Benson married his beloved Minnie only a short while after his arrival at Wellington. Their relationship was a complex one, as was that between Benson and his brilliant children, and has been explored in detail by David Williams in *Genesis and Exodus*. As Wiliams observes: 'Minnie was his stay and comfort. He relied on her not so much for advice about what he should do as for confirmation that what he had decided to do was beyond question the right course of action. She supplied this need.'[81]

Soon after her marriage Minnie compiled what her son Fred calls a 'little inner history' of the years of her courtship. From this it becomes apparent that, though she admired and revered her husband and was never in the least afraid of him, she may not have been in love with him. 'She was happiest, she confessed, when she knew he was happy, but not necessarily when she was with him.'[82] Nevertheless, she was always prepared to accompany him on his daily walk, a feature of their early years at Wellington. Every day after lunch they used to ramble over the country for at least two hours. In the summer Benson would take a book with him, and they would halt during the walk for him to read to Minnie. One of his favourite occupations during these daily rambles was to translate hymns, and even compose them, as they went along.[83]

Benson no doubt regarded himself as a model father, but his children had always to dance to his tune. He took a great delight in pasting suitable pictures on the walls of the nursery, an occupation in which they assisted. They would go and talk to him before breakfast while he shaved; and sometimes they would accompany their parents on their afternoon walks – though even here business had to be combined, as it were, with pleasure. Just as their father would occupy his mind by translating hymns, so his offspring were encouraged to compose rhymes on a subject of his suggestion. It seems never to have been a question of walking for walking's sake. Benson's happiest moments, in Arthur's opinion, came in the evening, when the children joined him in the study. He would put away his papers, draw them a picture of a castle or cathedral (often adorned with a little poem) and show them the illustrations in one of his books. He was an accomplished draughtsman, and in the holidays loved to go off sketching. He preferred architectural subjects; he was never at ease with either foliage or foregrounds and used, with artistic licence, to leave out trees. Late in life he took up water-colour painting, but without much success. He always travelled with a pocket-book in which he would jot down inscriptions, odd architectural features and anything else that took his fancy.[84]

In *The Trefoil* Arthur has some frank things to say about his father, from which one may deduce what a burden it must sometimes have been to be one of Edward Benson's children. Arthur allows that he was passionately devoted to them and never punished them, however badly they behaved. The trouble was that he was always too busy properly to immerse himself in their goings-on. He might make token gestures during the evening get-togethers in the study, but always there was a didactic purpose lurking in the background. He used to give them old-fashioned books to read of an improving kind – like *Philosophy in Sport*, 'where the poor boy cannot even throw a stone without having the principles of the parabola explained to him.'* He never attempted to bully or tyrannize his children in any way, yet the thundercloud lay in the background and he was never able really to let himself go in their presence. The diplomatic Arthur was reduced to 'making the sort of remarks to him I thought he would like me to make'. This proved a successful ploy, though what Arthur missed was the enjoyment of easy and confident relations with his father. 'His eager love for us [was] staring me in the face all the time if I could have seen it, or if he could have expressed it. Yet the door remained shut, and not even my mother could open it for him.' Benson senior was so busy that he generally came in late for lunch. 'I am sorry to say', Arthur admits, 'that the later he came in the

---

* Arthur says that he never bothered to read the books 'unless I was to have the honour of a walk with my father, and then I produced some scraps of knowledge for his benefit, and he was so delighted that it only encouraged me to continue'.

better I was pleased, because we chattered freely to my mother, but with him were mostly silent.'[85]

The Bensons had many friends in the neighbourhood, chief among whom were Charles Kingsley and his wife Fanny. Kingsley was Rector of Eversley, a fairly easy walk from Wellington, and Benson saw a great deal of him. The two couples dined together once a month. 'I never knew a couple', Minnie told Arthur, 'who between them made such brilliant conversation.'[86] The children sometimes accompanied their parents on expeditions to Eversley. 'Kingsley wore on weekdays a grey coat and knickerbockers, big boots, a flannel shirt with a black tie,' Arthur recalls. 'He used to come out of his study, crying out a stammering welcome, taking both my mother's hands – he was very fond of her – and led us into the drawing-room, where Mrs Kingsley would be sitting, with her dark complexion, black shining eyes, and a delightful, rather roguish smile.'[87] Kingsley sent both his boys to Wellington and used to preach in the chapel – as on that occasion when Benson was delated to one of the governors for his supposedly Tractarian views. Fanny Kingsley was godmother to Fred, to whom she endeared herself particularly by presenting him with a copy of her husband's *The Water Babies*.

*   *   *   *   *

Almost all Benson's most valuable reforms at Wellington were carried out in the face of strenuous opposition by traditionally minded members of the governing body. Fortunately, he was a sufficiently strong character to persist in his efforts – and he was usually successful in wearing down his opponents. He was lucky, too, in being able to count on the support first of the Prince Consort and then of the Prince of Wales, who succeeded his father as chairman of the governors and who was often able to avert a potential mutiny by remarking crisply: 'I think, gentlemen, that this is eminently a matter which we must leave entirely to the discretion of the headmaster.'[88]

The chief purpose of Benson's reforms was a drastic one: to transform Wellington from an institution catering exclusively for boys with a military background into a public school of a more

116

conventional pattern. He had no wish to see the college stagnate as an academic barracks. Moreover, unless it spread its wings by taking boys from a non-military background who could be charged more than the 'foundationers', it would inevitably be hampered by lack of funds. From the start, therefore, he urged an expansionist policy on the governors. He pointed out the need for an adequate staff. If the school could not afford to pay for more masters out of its original endowment, then additional income must be generated from the non-foundationers. As was pointed out by one of the governors who supported Benson:

> The success of the Institution must depend upon the advantage it holds out as a place of education... The Governors must mainly look to the Non-Foundationers for the future support of the Institution, and they will not obtain a sufficient number of these unless the College takes a high standard as a place of public education.[89]

Benson buttressed his financial arguments with others. He pointed out to the governors that a school of 250 boys (the number originally envisaged) was not large enough to allow of sufficient competition in school work – especially in the senior classes. And, in his opinion, the military element in the school would benefit from contact with the sons of civilians. It was vital to persuade the general public that the teaching at Wellington was as good as that to be found at any other major public school. Benson warned the governors early on in his headmastership: 'Unless the next five years produce some real instances of well-directed talent achieving success, I must believe that the public confidence in the College will wane, that hostile predictions will find more and more acceptance, that our numbers will decline and our finances suffer.'[90] Eventually the number of foundationers, sons of deceased army officers, was whittled down to 81. They were charged very low fees (£10 to £20 per annum, according to their means) and were subsidized out of the Endowment Fund. The non-foundationers were the sons of either living officers or of civilians; the former were charged £70, the latter £100 a year. The principle introduced could be – and was – extended over the years. The number of non-foundationers was increased, as were their fees. But Benson had a long and tough struggle to achieve his goal of transforming Wellington into something approaching a traditional public school. It was not only individual governors who opposed his reforms. He also encountered hostility from army officers who had subscribed to the original appeal in the belief that Wellington would, in addition to low fees, also have a low standard of entrance and an exclusively military intake aiming directly at the military academies of Sandhurst and Woolwich. Under the new dispensation, however, the sons of civilians threatened to swamp the sons of soldiers, who, unless they happened to be orphans, enjoyed the benefit of only slightly privileged terms.

The complaint about higher academic standards was justified. Benson was determined both to raise the standard of entrance for the foundationers (he refused to accept complete dunces, however worthy in other respects), and to improve the general intellectual level of the school by the institution of entrance scholarships and leaving exhibitions to the universities. He complained on one occasion of

> how very difficult I have found it to excite any really liberal interest in literature or the arts in the minds of boys who are aware that in one or two years they will have to pass examinations such as are required for the Army and other services. The subjects which they are to 'take in' engross their whole intellectual interest, and that in the driest possible manner.[91]

The discontent in Army circles about the way in which Wellington was developing rumbled on throughout Benson's headmastership. It came to a head in June 1869, when the Chaplain-General of the Army, the Rev. G.R. Gleig, who was a member of the governing body, emerged as the champion of the military malcontents. He complained to his fellow governors: 'We must all give Dr Benson full credit for having the good of Wellington College at heart, but it seems to me that he loses sight in some measure of the purpose for which that institution was mainly founded.' This, he pointed out, had been to educate a limited number of orphans for almost nothing and living officers'

sons on highly preferential terms. Now, however, a costly building programme had swallowed up most of their funds – 'and the
determination to make Wellington College a rival to Eton and
Harrow seems to me to have completed the process'. The
expenses attending a boy's election to the Foundation meant that
widows living on their pensions could no longer afford to apply,
and even those who did so often found that their sons were not
clever enough to pass the entrance examination. Few regimental
officers could now afford to send their sons to the college, said
Gleig. 'I believe that I see more of the Regimental Officers of the
Army than any of the Governors ... and I can assure you that their
complaints of what they call the misapplication of our funds are
loud and deep.'[92]

The governors on this occasion declined to heed Gleig's plea to
put aside all questions of expansion and concentrate instead on
cutting down the fees of both foundationers and military non-
foundationers in order to enable the college to look 'more what it
ought to be, more what it was meant to be'. But they – and Benson
– had to give way a year later when the commissioners of the
Patriotic Fund argued that some of their nominees (on behalf of
whom they had paid the school £25,000) were being refused
admission if they failed to pass the entrance examination. The
solution adopted was to place a nominee of the commissioners who
failed to pass the exam in a preparatory school for a year, in the
hope that he would then be able to reach the required standard. This
silenced the complaints for the time being, though they were to
resurface under the next headmaster.[93] Benson's constant struggle
with the pro-military element on the governing body was one of
the worst crosses he had to bear during his 15 years as Headmaster
of Wellington.

But it was not the only one. On two notable occasions he found
himself having to justify himself before the governors on moral
issues.

The first occasion was in 1861, when a non-foundationer who
happened to be the son of a major-general was seen to strike
another boy in an allegedly indecent manner. Benson wrote to his
father asking him to remove his son immediately. The father agreed
to the boy's removal, but insisted that Benson should withdraw his

claim that the boy had been guilty of a 'gross indecency to a little boy', so that no slur should be cast upon his character. Benson declined to do so, whereupon the general referred the matter to the Prince Consort and his fellow governors. Benson produced a sheaf of letters in his defence from, among others, Lightfoot, Kingsley and Frederick Temple. The governors sat in judgement on the case. Some of them were less happy than others about endorsing Benson's action,* but in the end, as a body, they agreed to do so. The boy was sent out by his father to India, where eventually he died of drink.[94]

Benson justified his action to the governors by explaining that he had always acted in the belief that there were two moral evils which must, above all others, be guarded against: untruthfulness and indecency.

> To what a height this latter may proceed unless it is thus firmly met in its first indications can be appreciated only by those who are familiar with certain periods in the history of public schools. Wellington is yet free from bad traditions; I believe we have every opportunity of keeping it pure.

Benson was hurt, however, that he did not receive the unqualified support of every governor on what he regarded as a matter of internal discipline – and that they had chosen to sit in judgement on him. He voiced his feelings in an impassioned apologia to Sir Charles Phipps:

> I knew I was in the right, and that I had not chosen the easy course for myself, and I knew also that I had endeavoured to be as kind as I could in the matter of punishment. Still, I felt that this was a crisis for the College, and that on the Governors' decision would turn the good or evil of many generations. Knowing intimately the life of public schools, I could see that we had come to a place where two ways met – the way of public purity or of lax morals... This has been the most anxious seven weeks of my life.[95]

---

* The Duke of Wellington, though not then a governor, disapproved of Benson's action. He told the next headmaster many years later: 'There was a boy ... sent away by Dr Benson "for a grossly indecent offence". He afterwards wanted to enter at Harrow and was refused because the crime argued something sodomitical, whereas it was merely an indecent lark in public. I wanted the father to prosecute, but he had not the pluck. I considered that it was unjust to the boy.'

120

The second occasion on which Benson had to defend his stand on a moral issue was even more serious. He contemplated resigning on the issue, but in the end stayed put. However, his disgust with the governors' attempt to reverse his decision played a part in inducing him to accept the next offer of preferment when it came.

The circumstances were these. Three foundationers living at Surbiton in Surrey were found guilty of a 'grave moral offence' committed during the Christmas holidays of 1871–72. At the house of the mother of one of the three they seduced (or were seduced by) a maidservant, as a result of which the eldest of the three contracted a 'shameful disease'. On discovering the facts at the beginning of term, Benson wrote to the mothers of the three boys requesting their removal from the school – otherwise, he said, they would have to be publicly expelled. The three all agreed to withdraw their sons, but the mother of one of the two younger boys then changed her mind and wrote to the governors asking them to overrule the headmaster's decision. Benson had in fact been perfectly within his rights in requesting the removal of a boy for this type of offence without reference to the governors. Nevertheless, when the mother's appeal was received, he was formally summoned to appear before them to discuss the matter. After kicking his heels in an anteroom for an hour and a half he was eventually admitted to the meeting, but was then chagrined to discover that the governors had already made up their minds without reference to him. Their verdict was that, though the boy who had contracted the disease must go, the two younger boys must be reinstated, on the ground that the offence had been committed during the holidays and that the proposed punishment was unduly harsh. The ever-loyal Penny thought that the governors' deliberate reversal of the headmaster's decision in a matter of school discipline was intended (at least by some of them) to drive him to resignation. Benson certainly contemplated this course during the fortnight in which he was allowed to consider his position, but on reflection decided to fight it out. To gain moral support he wrote to the Headmasters of Eton, Harrow and Winchester, asking what action they would have taken in a similar case. The three heads were unanimous in advising that, for the sake of the school and of the boys themselves, they *must* leave the school. Benson forwarded these high-level opinions to the governors. He told them that, while still believing his course of action to have been right, 'if the Governors … are of the opinion that they [the boys] should be restored, I must, with the greatest and most entire deference to them, request them to replace them in the school by exercise of their own superior authority'. He also suggested that, if the governors thought that the mothers would suffer financial hardship through having to educate their sons elsewhere, they might consider granting them an allowance.

Faced with Benson's refusal to back down but offered a way of saving face, the governors gave way. The boys were *not* readmitted to the school, and instead an allowance was paid to their mothers. But even then the governors acted ungraciously, not bothering to tell Benson personally of their change of heart but sending him notice of it via their secretary. Unfortunately, the whole affair became a matter of gossip in the London clubs. Penny, who was tutor to one of the three boys, observed that the governors had acted 'like a pack of cynical, hoary old sinners who looked upon youthful immorality … as a sort of childish complaint, like measles.'[96] Whether or not one thinks that Benson was being unduly harsh in his punishment of the boys concerned, he was certainly within his rights in proposing to deal with the matter on his own; and his employers' abortive attempt to overrule him may well have been the last straw in persuading him that he must leave Wellington for new pastures.

*   *   *   *   *

For a man of Benson's calibre there would be no difficulty in finding such pastures. The only question was *which*. In April 1870 he had written to a friend who had offered him a living: 'I do not know how long I ought to remain a schoolmaster. I do not think of ending my days in this profession.' Later in the letter, reverting to the hope he had expressed in his youth, he observed:

> I *wish* above all things, if I could choose, to have a Canonry, and if one is offered I should accept it without reference to its value, for I think that at this time the Church of England is in such danger

122

of losing her hold – if it is not lost – on higher education for her clergy ... that we are bound to supplement it, and the Cathedral system offers an ancient, recognised, calm and safe mode of education if only a few more people will give themselves to its development... If a Canonry ever came to me I should give myself entirely to that work.*[97]

The living offered to Benson by his friend was that of Dorking in Surrey. The reason he declined it was partly financial: it was worth only £500 a year, a quarter of his Wellington salary. It might admittedly have been possible to combine it with the cathedral canonry for which he was hankering, but, as one who strongly disapproved of pluralism, Benson would never have considered such a solution. It was a canonry alone that he sought. His friends supported him in his wish to give up schoolmastering for more specifically ecclesiastical work. The previous year, when the headmastership of Rugby had become vacant with Temple's appointment as Bishop of Exeter, he had been tempted to apply – but he had resisted the temptation. At that time he had written to Elizabeth Wordsworth about a recent talk he had had on the subject with his friend Westcott, then a canon of Peterborough. 'Westcott agreed with me, to my great peace, that unless an irresistible call came I should take no school work after Wellington; but that I should, on the first opportunity, give up school work for Cathedral work, and this I shall certainly do.'[98]

Three years later the opportunity came. On 10 December 1872 Benson received from the Bishop of Lincoln, Christopher Wordsworth (Elizabeth's father), the offer of the chancellorship of his cathedral, to which a canonry was attached. He was already an examining chaplain to the Bishop† and he accepted the offer. One of the first to be told was the faithful Penny. He was stunned by the news and wept openly. He then expressed doubts as to the wisdom of Benson's decision.

---

* He was true to his word, and, within a year of his arrival at Lincoln, had helped to set up a theological college near the cathedral.
† Elizabeth noted that, when Benson first appeared in his chaplain's scarf in the school chapel, it was supposed by the junior boys that Mrs Benson had died in the night and that he had promptly adopted this method of going into mourning for her[99]

You are worth a great deal more than this. Ought you to leave Wellington for anything except a Deanery? I should have liked to see you a Bishop, but that I know you want rest sadly, and that you would get as a Dean. It is sure to come if you will only wait.

And then there was the financial side, Penny added. Benson was now receiving £2000 a year as Headmaster of Wellington; 'and you are going to sacrifice one half of that by going to a Canonry at Lincoln just at the time when Martin and Arthur's education will cost you every penny you can spare'. But Benson had counted the cost in every sense, and there were to be no second thoughts. Later that morning, the last day of the term, he told the other masters, who received the news for the most part in stunned silence.[100] The Prince of Wales was informed, and replied on behalf of the governors in suitably grandiloquent and grateful terms.

Benson was installed as Chancellor on Holy Innocents' Day, 28 December, but stayed on at Wellington till the end of the following summer term. He took formal leave of the school on Speech Day, when his health was proposed by the Duke of Wellington in a sadly unimpressive address. 'Our Vice-President', Penny noted, 'was always a halting speaker – but on this occasion he outdid himself in incoherency, hesitation and bathos.' The Duke made amends, however, and, only too conscious of his failure to have done justice to the occasion, took Benson's arm afterwards and, according to Penny (who must surely have been lurking behind a pillar with notebook and pencil to have recorded the Duke's remarks so precisely), addressed him as follows:

Made a hash of it – knew I should. Always do. But I really did try to say something this time. This is what I meant to say. When the money was subscribed for a memorial after my father's death, I and my family hoped that there would be a fine monument set up in his memory in every considerable town in England. And you can fancy what our feelings were when we found that it was all going to be lumped together and a Charity School built with it where scrubby little orphans would be maintained and educated like the Bluecoat School in London… By great good fortune the Governors found you and made you the first Headmaster and *you* have made the

124

College what it is – not a mere Charity School but one of the finest Public Schools in England… There, that's my speech – that's what I meant to have said and so I say it to you. But Lord, when I stood up to speak it all ran out at my heels.[101]

The Duke was not exaggerating. When Benson left Wellington it had indeed established itself firmly in the top rank of England's public schools. And this had come about largely through the efforts of its first Headmaster. As David Newsome justly puts it in his history of the school: 'Never in the course of a lifetime of domination did Benson so dominate a society as he did while he was there. Of all the regimes in Wellington's history, his was by far the most personal.'[102] He had come, as he declared in his farewell sermon, to the newest educational and spiritual work in England, and had been bidden to shape it.

The stages had been gradual: the infusion of the civilian element, the cultivation of a university side and the creation of something of a classical tradition;… the gradual accumulation of a highly distinguished staff; the fostering of a sense of responsibility among the boys themselves; the teaching of sound principles; the stress laid on the importance of spiritual values; the development of a strong corporate sense. Edward White Benson was the force behind all these achievements… Through Benson came reputation and prosperity to Wellington, and through Wellington came high office to Benson… It is to be doubted whether it has since been able to boast of an intimate association with a greater man.[103]

*   *   *   *   *

Benson knew the right people, including both Disraeli and Gladstone – and, of course, the Queen herself through the royal connection with Wellington. So it was not to be supposed that he would be allowed to vegetate in a minor cathedral post for long. Three years after his arrival in Lincoln he was sounded informally as to whether he would accept the bishopric of Calcutta. After agonizing for days he decided against, mainly on the grounds that acceptance would mean leaving behind his six children to be educated in England. However, in December of the same year (1876), the offer of the bishopric of Truro arrived from Disraeli; and though, as Benson complained to Lightfoot, '£3000 a year does not really seem adequate for a person without a private fortune', he was prepared to obey this particular call – especially as it was the desire of the Queen that he should accept it. As David Williams somewhat cynically comments:

> It would not be right to think of Benson as a worldly, ambitious man in any calculating way. It was just, somehow, that he happened to do the right things and say the right things when it was crucially important that the right things should be done and said.[104]

The diocese of Truro consisted of the Cornish section of Frederick Temple's huge diocese of Exeter and, as a new see, was ideal for a vigorous and forceful personality like Benson. Once again, as at Wellington, he did a valuable pioneer job, and six years later he was to reap his reward. With the death of Tait the archbishopric of Canterbury fell vacant, and Benson was one of the two prime contenders.* Gladstone had by now succeeded Disraeli as Prime Minister and was very much pro-Benson. Though 73 himself he felt that the other main contender, Harold Browne of Winchester, was, at 71, too old. Browne had had another champion in the dying Archbishop Tait, who had originally seemed to favour Benson but had then changed his mind. Tait had told his son-in-law, Randall Davidson: 'He [Browne] could do more than any other man to preserve the Church in peace for its real work against sin.'[106] Davidson reported these words to the Queen, who was confirmed in her feelings that Browne would be the right man. If some might consider him too old, she told the Prime Minister, Benson was, in the Queen's view, too young. 'She feels convinced', she wrote to Gladstone, 'that to place a man of only 53, excellent as he is, above all the other Bishops would create a very bad and angry feeling in the Church.'[107] Gladstone per-

---

* Frederick Temple was an outside candidate; but, in a letter to the Queen, the Dean of Windsor, Gerald Wellesley, had dismissed him out of hand. 'There is a want in him, while very liberal, of dignity and refinement.'[105] Two years later Temple was translated to London in spite of his being (presumably) still undignified and unrefined.

sisted, however, in pressing Benson's claims, and in the end persuaded the Queen reluctantly to agree to his appointment.

His reign, like that of most primates, was a mixture of triumphs and shortcomings. He was more liberal than Tait and did much to lower the party temperature of the Church of England. The last dying flickers of the Church Association's efforts to put down Ritualism came in 1888, when Bishop Edward King of Lincoln was accused of conniving in various questionable ceremonial practices during a visit to a church in his diocese. The case was tried by Benson personally, sitting in his own court at Lambeth with five episcopal assessors. His judgment, delivered on 21 November 1890, was basically favourable to the bishop.

As he grew older Benson became more intolerant of opposition and criticism. He even remarked to one of his daughters: 'I came to look upon being angry as the quickest way of getting what I wanted.' He could always be graceful and say the right things on social occasions, but he was never a success in the House of Lords – partly because he was too compressed in his speech-making and never learned the trick of making the same point over and over again. Although he lived only five years longer than Browne, his rival for the primacy, he retained his vigour to the last, thereby justifying Gladstone's choice. And it was while on a visit to the Gladstones at Hawarden that he died on 11 October 1896. He had arrived the previous day after a visit to Ireland and had talked much with his host. On his way to church on the Sunday morning he stopped a lot on the way through shortness of breath. As they knelt to confess their sins a frightened Minnie heard his death-rattle. They clustered round: the saying of the Lord's Prayer began, but, with no time for a parting word, Edward was dead. Gladstone declared: 'It was a soldier's death – a noble end to a noble life.'[108]

William Temple: from a painting by J.W. Nichol.

6

HIS FATHER'S SON

William Temple: Headmaster of Repton, 1910–1914

Like his father before him, William Temple was at first a reluctant aspirant to a headmastership. Frederick Temple, when pressed by Tait on the Rugby School trustees in 1850 as the ideal man to succeed him, had declined the subsequent offer on the ground that he could not so soon abandon the duties which he had recently assumed as Principal of Kneller Hall, the training college for teachers in elementary schools. It was only when the headmastership was offered him a second time eight years later, after the closure of Kneller Hall, that he agreed to accept it. So it was with his younger son William. In 1909 there had been a good chance of his being elected to succeed Albert David as Headmaster of Clifton. Temple, however, by then wedded to his work among undergraduates as an Oxford don, had only agreed to stand if the school's governors 'threw it' at him. In the event the governors had declined to offer him the job on his own terms.[1] A year later, when Lionel Ford resigned to become Headmaster of Harrow, the headmastership of Repton fell vacant. Temple again showed an initial unwillingness to stand, but this time was persuaded to change his mind.

Clifton, as it happened, might well have been better suited to him than Repton. It lay on the doorstep of a large industrial city with its own university, and he would have been left with plenty of scope for out-of-school activities. A previous headmaster, J.M. Wilson, had enjoyed such activities. 'I always felt', he remarked in later life, 'that the school gained and did not lose by my multifarious interests.'[2] But a school just down the road from such interests was very different from one tucked away in a Midlands village not easily accessible to the outside world. And one of the factors which caused Temple to leave Repton after only four years was the large amount of time he was forced to spend in getting to and from the external activities in which he became increasingly involved. It was perhaps a pity that the Clifton governors were not sufficiently convinced of his headmasterly qualities to have offered him the job. He would have been warmly welcomed by the staff, and he had the strong support of a previous Headmaster of Clifton, John Percival (who had been his own headmaster in his early days as a pupil at Rugby), and of Bishop Charles Gore. But it was not to be. Clifton's loss may well have been Temple's loss, whatever gain it may have brought to Repton.

What caused him to overcome his initial disinclination to become a headmaster? There were three factors which each played their part. The first was his belief that he might take the lead in an attempt to reform the public-school system – which, in his view, was helping to perpetuate the country's class divisions. The second was his feeling that he might have a special vocation for the spiritual and educational care of adolescents. The third was the memory of his father's great headmastership and the belief that (as he put it to a Repton master, David Somervell) he was 'glad to have the chance of doing as his father had done'. Whatever his motives, he was sufficiently interested, when Ford announced his resignation in the spring of 1910, at least to consider becoming a candidate for the headmastership of Repton.[3] But it was a reluctant candidature. A day or two before the governors' crucial meeting in June to choose a successor to Ford, he visited the school to take a look round. The next day he wrote to Ford to say that he had decided *not* to stand. He admitted that Repton had charmed him and that, if he *had* felt a vocation to the work of a schoolmaster, he would have opted for Repton before any school other than Rugby. Nevertheless, he said, he felt called to his present work (as a tutor at Queen's College, Oxford) for some time to come.

I believe I am where I ought to be. I can talk to undergraduates so that they will listen: whether or not I could do so to schoolboys no one knows. And there is immense opportunity in the Universities. All but one of those whom I have consulted say that I ought to stay here, and move, if anywhere, to an East End Parish. I think they are right... I should like to come; but I am sure I am meant to go on for a time as at present.[4]

The letter ended by asking Ford not to bring Temple's name before the governors at their meeting the next day. But the governors, who by now had the bit between their teeth, were not so easily deflected. They wanted Temple at all costs. In the light of their strong representations to him to consent to be a candidate, he agreed to stand. He wrote to Ford again on 20 June to announce his change of heart and to point out that he had told the governors that, in the event of his election, he would hope to continue his present work both for the Student Christian Movement and for the Workers' Educational Association so far as his new duties permitted. Moreover, he told Ford, 'I said that the Public Schools seemed to me to reproduce our class-divisions in accentuated form, and that I should hope, after learning the ropes, to find ways of moving towards a system which would tend to diminish them. If they take me, knowing this, I come.'[5]

The governors had noted Temple's frank confession of faith, but still wanted him as headmaster. At this dramatic moment in his career he left England to undertake a six-week tour of the universities of Australia on behalf of the SCM. When his ship docked at Marseilles he heard that the selection committee had recommended him to the governors as the new headmaster. From Port Said he sent a letter on 27 June to his friend Frank Fletcher, then Headmaster of Marlborough, to explain the sequence of events:

My dear Frank, About the time this reaches you, you may have seen the appointment of the new Headmaster of Repton. In case they have taken me, I wish to say that I refused the invitation of the Masters to stand as their candidate, and asked Ford not to bring up my name; others brought it up however and they decided to ask me whether I would accept it if offered. The combination of staff and

Governors was very strong, and after three days deliberation, I wrote and told them my views and hopes concerning English Education; adding that only the hope of support in furthering these would induce me to leave my present work just now; but that if with this letter before them they chose to elect me, I would go. I can't trace the considerations that led to this in a letter; but one was a belief, engendered by you, that the Headmasters' Conference is becoming amenable to reason, which makes me want to be on it! Try not to think me a fool; I was never so sure that I had done right.[6]

Temple shed further light on his motives in accepting the Repton headmastership 20 years after the event, in an address to Oxford undergraduates delivered in St Mary's Church during a mission in 1931, by when he was Archbishop of York. One can confidently follow his biographer, F.A. Iremonger, in attributing this passage in the sermon to the decision he had had to make in June 1910:

I had once to make a choice which I found very difficult. I was much interested in the work I was doing, believing it to be of some value. I was asked to take up another post which certainly was more conspicuous in the eyes of the world. I tried to avoid it. I asked all the friends of whom I could think, and they all said that I had better stay where I was. I had to make a decision in time to write a letter by a certain post, and having weighed up the question as carefully as I could – and we must always do that – and having come to no conclusion at all, I began at eight o'clock in the evening to say my prayers; and for three hours, without a pause, I tried to concentrate all my desires on knowing clearly what was God's Will for me. I do not know how these three hours went; they did not seem very long; but when eleven o'clock struck I knew perfectly well what I had got to do, and that was to accept; and I have never had a shadow of doubt since that it was right.[7]

When the ship taking him to Australia berthed at Aden, Temple found a cablegram awaiting him. It announced his formal election by the governors as Headmaster of Repton. In his absence abroad letters of congratulation were sent to his mother, Archbishop Frederick's widow. They included one from Randall Davidson, Temple's successor as Archbishop of Canterbury, and another from

Michael Sadler, afterwards Master of University College, Oxford, which read in part:

> He is a very great power, with growing force in the national life. Hundreds of thousands of young men will watch his work and be helped by his courage and plainness of mind, and by his moral force... His influence is wonderful, and the most varied characters and the most critical minds respond to it.[8]

$$* \qquad * \qquad * \qquad * \qquad *$$

This was an impressive tribute to a young man of twenty-eight, but then Temple was no ordinary young man. First and foremost, he was his father's son. As Hensley Henson put it, he was 'magnificently endowed by Nature, and all the circumstances of his life favoured him.'[9] He had enjoyed a childhood spent in the privileged security of episcopal palaces, first Exeter and then Fulham. His father was near the top of the ecclesiastical ladder; his mother, the granddaughter through her father of the second Earl of Harewood and through her mother of the sixth Earl of Carlisle, was related to many of the aristocratic families of the land. Young William was to be on terms of intimacy from an early age with the great and the good. His father was sixty at the time of his birth on 15 October 1881, and his mother thirty-six; and he and his brother Freddy (later Colonel Frederick Temple, CIE) were brought up to a large extent by their nanny, Ellen Langdon, the daughter of a Devonian country station-master. But the children remained close to their parents. Every day they attended prayers in the Palace Chapel at Fulham, an experience which left a lasting impression on William. The Bishop would stop to kiss each of his sons as he walked hurriedly into the chapel. Iremonger paints a touching picture of the daily procedure:

> The boys fell in beside their father, who put his arms around them, looking (as was remarked) like a large angel with wings as he entered the chapel. He turned into his stall, and William stepped over his mother's feet to take his place on her left. Going out, the boys chased after their father, who dropped his surplice just outside the door, without looking round, into the hands of the pursuing butler, and again put his arms over the shoulders of his sons.[10]

William stressed the value to him in later life of having heard some verses of the Bible read every day: 'Probably three times out of five we did not directly attend to it, but it was flowing over our growing minds, even when attention wandered, and must have been producing a great effect in making natural and spontan-eous that whole outlook upon life which the Bible expresses.'[11] Bishop Frederick loved to have his sons around him whenever he was at home in the evenings. They would even sit on his knee while he was writing, though on one occasion William disgraced himself by spilling the contents of the inkpot over his father's gaitered legs. Even as a child he had his own robe-case, a diminutive mitre keeping company with a folded surplice.

At the age of nine he began attending a local day school, Colet Court in the Hammersmith Road. Among his schoolfellows was P.T.B. Clayton, the future 'Tubby' Clayton of Toc H fame, and among his masters John Sankey, the future Lord Chancellor, who initiated him into the mysteries of Greek. He early showed signs of academic promise, being head of the school by the age of twelve and winning an impressive array of prizes. On 27 September 1894, shortly before his thirteenth birthday, he entered Rugby, the school over which his father had presided with such distinction a generation ago. At Rugby his brilliant intellectual powers grew and flourished. He managed to complete within half an hour each day preparation work for which two hours were allowed. (He employed his 'spare' hour and a half in reading through the English poets.) He reached the sixth form by the earliest allowable age of fifteen and a half and remained there for the next two and a half years. Like his father, he possessed the gift of a photographic memory which enabled him to recall exactly what he had read weeks, months or even years before. He was not, of course, totally omniscient. He once declared in the course of a lecture: 'My ignorance of all things scientific is so immense as to be distinguished.' And, when a master asked him in discussing one of his essays, 'Are you not a little out of your depth here?' he replied breezily: 'Perhaps, sir, but I can swim!'[12] He wrote a daily letter to his mother, and one to his father every Sunday. Nor were these latter epistles confined to domesticities. He was embarrassed on one occasion when his father, by now Archbishop of

Canterbury, quoted in public a letter from his son in which he had asked: 'Don't you think, Father, that the doctrine of the Communion of Saints is too much neglected by most people?' Frank Fletcher quoted this remark in a letter to William's widow written shortly after his death, adding the telling comment: 'There was nothing priggish, though there naturally seemed to be something precocious, about the question. The interest was genuine and unaffected: the boy was father of the man.'[13] But William must have appeared excessively bookish to his schoolfellows. On Sunday afternoons, when most of them would be out of doors, he would seldom leave his study till the bell rang for chapel; and on summer afternoons, while on holiday in the Lakes at the age of seventeen, he sat in a boat reading Kant's *Critique of Pure Reason* while his brother and his friends were fishing or rowing. During the school holidays he would be perfectly happy to discuss philosophical problems with his father over dinner and after it for an hour at a time.* He was never the complete swot, however, and his hours at his desk were broken by regular bouts of less intellectual activity. Fletcher had pleasant recollections of weekly singles at rackets in which William was always victorious. 'He was more active than his un-athletic figure suggested. He was no cricketer, but he represented School House at football as a useful member of the scrum.'[14] The reference to cricket was correct. Temple once remarked to a group of parents when Headmaster of Repton: 'Personally, I have always looked on cricket as organized loafing.'[15]

From Rugby he won an exhibition to Balliol College, Oxford, to which he went up in 1900. Among his senior contemporaries at college were R.H. Tawney, the Christian Socialist thinker; Raymond Asquith, the future Prime Minister's son; and the future Lord Beveridge. He continued to read classics, and had no difficulty in picking up firsts in both Mods and Greats. He soon became a fluent speaker in Union debates, and in his last year was president of the Union. His tutor at Balliol, A.W. Pickard-

---

* He tended to receive his father's opinions as gospel truths. 'Father will never tell me his views', he wrote to a friend from Balliol, 'because he knows how much I am tempted to accept them without thinking.'

Cambridge, described him as being, while still an undergraduate, 'already the man that he was later ... entirely void of priggishness and pretence'. Other critics were less kind and dismissed him as 'bumptious'.[16]

With his brilliant academic promise confirmed by his first in Greats, he did not remain idle for long after taking his degree. Within 48 hours of the Greats list being published he had received more than two dozen offers of work – including an assistant mastership at Rugby. After weighing up the rival offers he finally settled for a fellowship at another Oxford college, Queen's. His particular niche there was as tutor in philosophy, and his six years as a don often seemed to him in retrospect the happiest in his career. It is hardly surprising that he should later have shown such reluctance to abandon Oxford for a headmastership. His ample leisure left him plenty of time for reading; he also threw himself into many worthwhile outside activities, notably on behalf of the Workers' Educational Association and the Student Christian Movement.

Meanwhile, there was the question of ordination – and this was to raise an unexpected obstacle. It might have been supposed that the son of an Archbishop of Canterbury would have been considered an unimpeachable candidate for holy orders. In Temple's case it was not such plain sailing. In 1906 he had approached the Bishop of Oxford, Francis Paget, with a request to be ordained. But he confessed to Paget that he could accept the doctrine of the Virgin Birth only 'very tentatively'; and, in the light of such an unconfident assertion, Paget declined to ordain him. Luckily, Temple's friends in high places came to the rescue. Randall Davidson, who had succeeded his father as Archbishop of Canterbury, was less rigid than Paget. He regarded Temple's expressed doubts as mere undergraduate arguments. He told Paget that he considered Temple as being

in all essential particulars an orthodox believer both in the Virgin Birth of our Blessed Lord and in His Resurrection. I do not say that he expresses himself respecting either truth with the distinctness (at least as to detail) which has been usual in Orthodox Theology. But I can see no adequate reason why he should not be now ordained.

Davidson later assured Paget that Temple had shown him beyond question that his whole attitude towards the Faith 'has undergone a change or a "deepening", and that *credal* things possess now a reality for him which they did not, to anything like the same degree, possess before'. In the light of these assurances Paget accepted Davidson's offer to conduct the ordination himself. In 1909 Temple was made a deacon and in 1910 (the year of his appointment to Repton) a priest in Canterbury Cathedral.[17] Five years later, during a symphony concert in London, he is said to have experienced absolute certainty about the Virgin Birth.[18]

*   *   *   *   *

Repton School, like Harrow and Rugby, was of sixteenth-century origins. It had been founded in 1557, the last full year of Queen Mary's reign, under the will of Sir John Port, High Sheriff of Derbyshire and a local landowner. He left a bequest for the establishment of a grammar school in the neighbourhood of Repton. His executors accordingly purchased, for £37.10s, the remains of Repton Priory, part of which had been destroyed following the dissolution of the monasteries in 1539. Since England at the time of Sir John's death was Roman Catholic once more, he had stipulated in his will that the headmaster of the new school should say a Mass daily for the repose of the founder's soul: the accession of Elizabeth I, however, soon deprived him of this expected recompense for his generosity.

In the three centuries following Sir John's death the fortunes of the school fluctuated, the number of pupils rising and falling with monotonous regularity. It owed its rebirth, and emergence as a leading public school, to Steuart Adolphus Pears (1815–75), who was appointed headmaster in 1854 and, by the time of his death, had raised the numbers from 50 to 300. (His granddaughter Rosamond was to be the wife of Temple's successor, Geoffrey Fisher.) Pears did for Repton what Arnold had done for Rugby and Thring for Uppingham, and his successors were able to build on the foundations which he had relaid. Such was the inheritance which awaited the youthful Temple.

Because of his Australian tour he was unable to take up residence at Repton until 1 October 1910, a fortnight after the autumn term had begun. The boys were in the middle of breakfast when they heard his car draw up. They at once rose from their tables, hurried outside, and cheered lustily as Temple got out of the car. The head of the Hall (the house over which the headmaster presided) described the scene thus:

> I can see now, vividly, his rotund figure moving round the car to pick up one of his cases, waving to us with his broad grin and a slightly embarrassed air. Some time after, I remember him saying to me, 'I wonder if you all realised what a blue funk I was in?' Within a couple of hours he had met the Staff, and was speaking to the assembled School in Pears Hall. His opening words I have always remembered; 'Here I am, the newest of all newcomers – Pray for me!'[19]

*　　*　　*　　*　　*

'I doubt if headmastering is really my line,' Temple remarked in a letter to his brother shortly after his arrival at Repton. And writing to one of his former colleagues, David Somervell, nine months after his departure, he was frank enough to confess: 'Yes – the Hall has had a fearful crop of failures. I expect Fisher [his successor] will be better than I was in these ways. I have always flattered myself that I was rather good for boys of maturer mind or character … but I was not good with the general ruck.'[20] This was true in a sense, but it was not the whole truth. Most of the boys in fact experienced three separate stages in their relations with the headmaster. When they first arrived at the school they felt vaguely, as Iremonger puts it, that 'in all Olympus none could hold a candle to "The Boss"'. J.D. Harford, who was a small boy in the headmaster's house from 1912 to 1914, vividly conveys the impact left on a juvenile mind by the force of Temple's personality:

> The indelible impression is of vigour, vitality, exuberance, joyousness, friendliness, faith. A unique and unchallengeable gusto. An unchanging constancy of Christian attitude, a superb equipoise of one supremely at home in the spiritual and temporal

138

worlds... The sturdy, erect, quick-moving figure; the imperturbable countenance, rich voice, ready smile, and tremendous, joyful, inimitable laugh; that effortless, unfaltering, oracular delivery from pulpit or platform – all took the young mind by storm and remained in lasting possession... That dazzling embodiment of superhuman excellence was 'Billy' to the youngest boy admitted to his special friendship. That was the essence of the matter.[21]

By the time a boy reached the age of sixteen, however, his relations with the headmaster tended to be less straightforward. At confirmation interviews, for instance, speech would often be replaced by a painful and embarrassed silence. (Temple once confessed to a colleague that he would much prefer to address individual boys, or parents for that matter, as if they were a public meeting.) It was when a boy reached the sixth form that his relationship with the headmaster entered its third and final phase. By then he would be mature enough to exchange ideas with the Head and experience the new world of thought and beauty which Temple was able to open out to him. As one sixth-former enthused in a letter to his mother on Temple's exposition of St John's Gospel: 'Billy has opened up a New Heaven and a New Earth to me.'

Somervell ascribes Temple's success as a schoolmaster to his deep and completely spontaneous love for the boys: 'To him they were not primarily "schoolboys" to be taught and disciplined, but boys. He simply delighted in their boyishness. They knew it, and responded... You may say this was his practical Christianity, but it was something deeper and more primitive; it was the nature of the man.' As for his success with sixth-formers, 'he offered to those who could appreciate it the keys to the splendid storehouse of his intellectual powers – in scholarship, in theology, in literature and art and current affairs ... he did not play down to those he taught; he took them intellectually by the scruff of the neck and drew them up towards him. He was Oxford come to Repton.'[22]

Temple was an exceptionally able teacher who treated his pupils as his intellectual equals and was careful not to parade his own superior learning. He maintained a lightness of touch which came out on such occasions as when he would chant the choruses of the *Agamemnon* to tunes of his own composition. The boys, says

139

Somervell, 'blushed for very shame at witnessing so intemperate a performance'. He enjoyed reading poetry with the boys, especially Browning and Shakespeare's tragedies, when he would take the title role himself.[23] But it was not only the intelligent boys who aroused his interest. He loved the less able as well as the clever ones. As Randall Davidson remarked of him in a different context: 'The worst fault of Willie is that he is so kind-hearted that he can say no to nobody.'[24] And the weakness of his headmastership lay in his unwillingness to administer a firm discipline. He complained in a letter to his brother a year after he had left Repton: 'The better one likes the purely personal relations with the boys, the more one shrinks from the disciplinary.'[25] He hated inflicting pain on a boy, however badly he had misbehaved – which says much for his humanity but little for his common sense.*

In the tricky field of moral (and especially sexual) delinquency, he was an innocent abroad. One of his colleagues maintained that he had never met anyone else who gave the impression of being entirely 'unspotted by the world'. His own innocence and chastity were so exceptional, his biographer remarks, that the sexual malpractices of schoolboys lay outside the general scheme of things which had his immediate and sympathetic interest.

> It can hardly be said that he turned a blind eye to them. Probably the safest conjecture is that he was too far removed from them to be able to see what was required by way of discipline to limit their incidence and the atmosphere that encouraged them, or to understand the treatment which would correct them.[26]

Through his failure to take the necessary tough action Temple left a host of problems to his successor.

In the field of religion, however, he really came into his own. Every morning, at the daily service in chapel, he would give a two-minute commentary on the Bible passage for the day which left a profound impression on his hearers: it would both stimulate their imagination and help the Scriptures come to life. His Sunday

---

* One of his favourite punishments was to make a miscreant work out a series of complicated cross-country railway journeys with the aid of *Bradshaw's* timetable.

sermons were also in a class apart. They were the sermons of a highly intelligent man who respected the intelligence of his congregation. Temple aimed primarily at the older boys; the younger ones, in his opinion, were unlikely to pay much attention or to pick up more than a crumb or two. As one sixth-former explained: 'You had to follow closely until you found yourself led to a point from which some new aspect of the Christian faith stood out clear and strong for all to see and make their own.'[27] J.R. Darling, who went on to become Headmaster of Geelong Grammar School in Australia, recalled, in a letter to Temple's widow, the enjoyment with which the boys had looked forward to the headmaster's sermons. 'These were always printed afterwards, and had a big sale. They were bought, even re-read and sent home. It was, I think, a quite genuine expression of our pride in having as headmaster one whose eminence in the Church and country was already recognized.'[28] In the course of a notice of *Repton School Sermons* in the *Church Times* the reviewer remarked: 'Mr Temple is, we should say, obviously dissatisfied with the religion which is generally taught in public schools, and is determined that things shall be different at Repton.' In the reviewer's opinion the sermons were 'almost exactly what school sermons ought to be'.[29]

Temple's religious influence on the boys was not confined to his daily Bible commentaries and weekly sermons. His sixth-form divinity lessons were also memorable in that he insisted on teaching religion rather than merely teaching about religion. According to Somervell the lessons 'aroused in many boys a degree of enthusiasm that those who entertain conventional ideas about public schools would barely credit.'[30]

Like his father before him at Rugby, William Temple did not marry until after he had left Repton, and his mother kept house for him throughout his headmastership. By all accounts she was a formidable old lady. S.S. Jenkyns, who was Temple's house tutor at the Hall, remembers her as both shrewd and lovable, if also alarming. To have come at an advanced age, the widow of an archbishop and accustomed to the pomp and dignity of a palace, to supervise the running of a headmaster's house containing 80 boys, not to mention a constant stream of guests, was no light undertaking. But she coped magnificently. 'I know', says Jenkyns, 'that she often felt anxious lest he [her son] should allow his gift of speech to run away with him and he should become something of a windbag; her wise criticisms carried great weight with him, and no one could have had a greater love and respect for her advice than he.'[31] She always thought of him as a schoolboy at heart, and he never lost the freshness and exuberance of boyhood. 'I hear William is coming to have supper with you tonight,' she remarked on one occasion to David Somervell. 'Don't give him too much to eat. He always eats such a lot when he goes out to supper.'[32] Her own dinner parties tended to appear both formal and alarming until the headmaster's laugh, following one of the stories from his exhaustive hoard, put the guests at their ease. More domestic, Jenkyns recalls, was the picture of Mrs Temple seated before a table containing the pieces of an enormous jigsaw puzzle. 'William comes in, kisses his mother, rapidly places some quite featureless pieces of sky in their correct positions and retires to grapple with even more puzzling school problems.'[33] Pupils at the Hall saw him at his most relaxed when he rambled through the dormitories at night. He would throw out frank comments on the world at large (such as the need to abolish compulsory Greek at the universities or the iniquity of handing out Oxford DD degrees to all and sundry), punctuated by his rumbustious laugh.[34]

*　*　*　*　*

Those who had hoped that Temple, as a young and progressive headmaster, would revolutionize the public-school system were doomed to disappointment. They had certainly been entitled to such hopes. He had warned the governors that, if appointed, he would try to find ways of easing the social divisions which set public schools in a class apart; but, in the event, the system proved too strong for him. Why did he fail to satisfy the expectations that had been justifiably aroused among advocates of reform? The clue lies in a conversation he once had with his colleague David Somervell:

> I remember Temple telling me, near the end of his last term, that when he wrote the revolutionary letter [to the governors] his ideas of public-school policy were of the vaguest: a mixture of boyhood

recollections and W.E.A. Utopianism. As he said to me on that occasion – 'If there is one thing my time here has taught me, it is that institutions must be run on their own lines or else scrapped. You cannot turn an old institution into a wholly new direction and expect to be able to utilize its running powers as before.'[35]

Somervell must have had this conversation in mind when, nearly 40 years later, he wrote a mature analysis of the dispute between Temple's successor, Geoffrey Fisher, and Victor Gollancz [see the following chapter] in the course of which he compared Gollancz to Temple as another 'elephant' imported into the Reptonian 'birdcage'. Referring to Temple's 'revolutionary' letter to the governors, he continued:

No sooner had he got to Repton than he found that he was a headmaster, responsible for an *institution*. He had his own Geoffrey Fisher inside him, and the revolutionist went down before the G.F.... So in a very short time he found that he had made a mistake in coming to Repton at all. But he loved it, just as Gollancz did; loved the boys and their charming discipleship. He made many of them think about religion and love God as they would never otherwise have done. But there was no revolution.

Later Somervell remarks somewhat cattily:

Both Temple and Gollancz left an awful mess behind them. Put the elephant into the birdcage, and what can you expect? Poor Fisher had to tidy up both the messes and I suppose he did it very well. Repton relapsed into the useful insignificance from which it had momentarily emerged.[36]

Temple had in fact soon admitted defeat. As early as June 1911, when he had been at Repton for less than a year, he had written to his brother: 'Things are going very well here: I have nothing to do except jog the show along.'[37] Those were hardly the words of a reforming zealot. Apart from a few mild innovations in the curriculum, things went on much as before; the duds among the staff remained in office, and it soon became apparent that hopes of a revolution would be stillborn. Temple could have counted on few allies among a largely traditionalist staff who might have supported him in pushing through reforms at Repton itself: Gollancz, who was to prove such a thorn in the flesh of Fisher, had yet to appear on the scene. As for the wider public-school spectrum, any revolutionary moves would have had to be made through the staid medium of the Headmasters' Conference. In spite of his youth, Temple was elected to the HC committee; but he was on it for too short a time to have much say in its policy-making or to make any important contribution to its deliberations.[38]

In his *William Temple* John Kent suggests that, in spite of his frustrated efforts at reform, Temple's experiences at Repton persuaded him that a school could express the spirit of Christ and so the kind of world in which people ought to live. Neither before nor after the First World War did he think of public-school religion as helping to make inequality respectable, any more than he was entirely committed to the common Edwardian vision of the public schools as the source of a stream of gentlemanly Christian bureaucrats and colonial officials deeply opposed to materialism but sound on a Christian empire. In his farewell sermon at Repton he declared that selfishness and even self-centredness unfitted a boy, in proportion to its intensity, for effective membership of his house or school. There were moments in that sermon, says Kent,

> when the preacher's language, if not the preacher himself, was demanding that his hearers anticipate in their own actions a drastic reformation of the economic structure of British society. He talked at times as though the public schools were 'mission schools' dedicated to forming a Christian elite in a foreign land.[39]

As he grew older he became more and more convinced of the divisive effect of public schools on the British educational system. He must sometimes have wished that he had made more of an impact when he had been in a position to do so. In his last major publication, *Christianity and Social Order* (1942), he refers to the 'shocking anomaly' by which the 'so-called Public Schools' were in fact inaccessible to poorer children.

That what is generally thought to be the best form of education should be reserved to those whose parents are able to pay expensive fees, or expensive preparatory-school education with a view to the winning of scholarships, makes a cleavage in the educational and social life of the country as a whole which is destructive of the best fellowship.[40]

Whether or not it was because he considered it hopeless to attempt a reform of the public-school system, Temple soon became immersed in the work of central Church committees. These inevitably encroached on his time, though they also had the effect of keeping his name before the Church authorities. After only two years at Repton he would have accepted the offer of a missionary post in India – as Principal of St John's College, Agra – had it not been for a plea by Archbishop Davidson to turn it down. Davidson considered that Temple's contacts with the Labour Movement and the WEA in Britain were too valuable to be lost by his going abroad. A few months later came an offer which he felt he could hardly refuse: the succession to Hensley Henson as Rector of St Margaret's, Westminster, and Canon of the Abbey. Unfortunately, the authorities had failed to do their homework properly. It turned out that Temple was ineligible for the post through having not been a priest for the qualifying period of six years. The offer was withdrawn; the Archbishop of Canterbury, the Dean of Westminster and the Prime Minister, Asquith, all apologized for their collective if inadvertent gaffe; and Temple turned up at Repton on the first day of the Lent term of 1913 looking (as one wag remarked) 'like a runaway wife who had missed her train'.[41] The authorities finally got it right* in May of the following year, when Temple was offered and accepted the prestigious West End rectory of St James's, Piccadilly.

He excused his departure from Repton after so short a time in a circular letter to the staff. This referred to his growing immersion

* But only just! The living was in the gift of the Bishop of London (two turns) and the Lord Chancellor (one turn). This turn was the Lord Chancellor's. A day or two after he had accepted the offer Temple met Dick Sheppard and told him the news. Sheppard looked at him rather oddly and later explained: 'I was rather startled by your news, because the Bishop of London had just offered the living to *me*!'[42]

145

in general Church politics and to his membership of three key committees. The letter continued:

> My work here has prevented my doing for those Committees the work which was really called for, while the interest of the problems with which they are concerned has drawn my attention somewhat seriously away from the school and its needs. I trust that the school has not yet suffered from this, but it would suffer before long. I have therefore felt bound to accept the offer of a position where I can respond to the claims made upon me without feeling that my primary duty is being neglected.[43]

The die was cast; and William Temple now had his foot on the first rung of the ecclesiastical ladder that was to lead him back, eventually, to Lambeth Palace, the home of his adolescence.

$$* \quad * \quad * \quad * \quad *$$

David Somervell once asked Temple why it was that common-place men often seemed to make better headmasters than stars of the first magnitude. Temple replied ('characteristically'): 'I fancy the answer is that, though the stars can provide the luxuries of education, they are often unfitted to provide its necessities.' He was not a great headmaster, in Somervell's view. 'He was some-thing better, a great man, and it is an uncommon privilege for a school to have, for a few years, a great man in its midst. He gave us, liberally and with enthusiasm, "the luxuries of education".'[44]

Temple certainly put his school on the map. Though headmastering may not have been his real *métier*, his four years at Repton supplied an intellectual stimulus which was of lifelong value to many Reptonians. And for him personally it was, as Geoffrey Fisher said in a broadcast tribute after his death, a 'joyous episode'. His influence on his pupils was often profound and long-lasting. He encouraged the senior boys to take an interest in politics and social conditions, and, through his own numerous contacts, kept them in touch with the world outside. 'In those days it was rather a remarkable thing to do,' J.R. Darling told Temple's widow, but I think that it bore fruit. Many of his best boys were killed in the war;... but, of those who survived, it is noticeable how many took up work of a vocational nature and how many became schoolmasters and are now headmasters in various parts of the world. With all these he managed to keep in touch, first at Oxford on his many visits to address students and later in his various homes and by correspondence, always written in his own hand.[45]

As Iremonger remarks in summing up his headmastership, 'Temple brought with him a distinction in learning, in breadth of interest, in preaching and in teaching which left an indelible mark on Repton, and an intellectual and spiritual vitality of which the infection spread through the whole life of the place.' The school *Terminal Record* for June 1914 declared: 'Both by his great gift for preaching and by his magnetic personal influence he has infused new life into us all.'[46]

*   *   *   *   *

Frederick Temple's contribution to the controversial *Essays and Reviews*, written while he was still at Rugby, caused him immense embarrassment in after years. His son likewise was a contributor during his time at Repton to a book of essays which became the subject of controversy. This was *Foundations*, a symposium edited by a liberal theologian, B.H. Streeter, and published in 1912. Temple's own essay, 'On the Divinity of Christ', was attacked the following year by his friend Ronald Knox in a book entitled *Some Loose Stones*. Knox, then still a High Church Anglican, castigated Temple's essay, and indeed the whole book, as displaying a deplorable liberal tendency. Temple was sufficiently disturbed by Knox's criticisms to send him a letter of many pages replying to them in detail. Fortunately for Temple, *Foundations* caused less of an outcry in the Church at large than had *Essays and Reviews*, and his own contribution was not held against him in the way his father's had been. On a lighter note of criticism Knox also published a long satirical poem, *Absolute and Abitofhell*, in the style of Dryden, in which he took to task the various contributors to *Foundations*. The passage in the poem referring to Temple began:

147

First, from the Public Schools – *Lernaean Bog* –
No paltry Bulwark, stood the Form of OG.
A man so broad, to some he seem'd to be
Not one, but all Mankind in Effigy:
Who, brisk in Term, a Whirlwind in the Long,
Did everything by turns, and nothing wrong.

The poem ended with a satirical dedication to the authors of *Foundations* from

> an humble Friend,
> Praying that Providence this Wind may use
> To Puff your Sales, and to confound your Views.[47]

Temple replied with a postcard to Knox on which he scribbled: 'Ta for Puff: OG.'

*   *   *   *   *

His progress up the ecclesiastical ladder after leaving Repton was smooth and comparatively effortless. From his initial base at St James's, Piccadilly, he embarked on a notable ministry which included much public speaking and journalism. He edited a new Church newspaper, *The Challenge*, which urged social and ecclesiastical reform. He became a secretary of the National Mission for Repentance and Hope. More significantly, in 1917 he resigned St James's and an income of over £2000 a year to become chairman, at £700 a year, of the Life and Liberty Movement, a ginger group formed to press for self-government and the radical renewal of the Church of England. It was a bold move for one who had only recently married (his bride was Frances Anson, the daughter of an old family friend), but Temple's crusading zeal was such that his campaign eventually led to the setting up of the Church Assembly, the forerunner of the General Synod. His role as a reformer, however, led him to hesitate, when offered the succession to Bishop Knox (Ronald's father) at Manchester in 1920, to join the Church establishment as a diocesan bishop. Archbishops Davidson and Lang and Bishop Gore quickly overcame his scruples and persuaded him to accept Lloyd George's offer. When

Lang was translated from York to Canterbury in 1928 Temple was chosen to succeed him. His lively concern with social and international questions made him an admirable partner to the older and more conservative Lang. Nor, in spite of his left-wing views, was there any comparable candidate when the time came in 1942 to choose a successor to Lang at Canterbury. He was head and shoulders above his fellow diocesans – or, in the homely words of Winston Churchill, the Prime Minister, 'the only half-a-crown article in a sixpenny bazaar'. To Bernard Shaw an archbishop of Temple's enlightenment was a 'realized impossibility'.

Temple took office at Lambeth in the middle of the Second World War. He was not fated to survive the war. On 26 October 1944, a bare two and a half years after his enthronement, he died both suddenly and unexpectedly. The nation at large was shattered by the news. 'His death just now', Bishop Haigh of Winchester told his diocese, 'seems like a master-stroke of the Evil One.' Joseph McCulloch, then a radical young priest, said at Temple's funeral service in Canterbury: 'We are burying the hopes of the Church of England.' And R.H. Hodgkin, Provost of Queen's College, Oxford, declared: 'Temple's death seemed to shake the Western world as if one of its pillars had been removed.'[48]

Geoffrey Fisher: Repton School speech-day, 1930.

7

HOLDING THE BALANCE

*Geoffrey Francis Fisher: Headmaster of Repton,
1914–1932*

The choice of Geoffrey Fisher as William Temple's successor at
Repton smacks a little of wire-pulling. In fact, in the circumstances surrounding the appointment, history was repeating
itself. Just as Temple's father, Frederick, had been instrumental in
securing the appointment of Edward Benson as the first
Headmaster of Wellington, so the younger Temple made sure that
his own nominee, Fisher, would succeed him as Headmaster of
Repton. With hindsight the choice may have seemed inspired.
It did not look so at the time to the outside world. Fisher, after all,
was a mere twenty-seven years old, even younger than Temple
had been at the time of *his* appointment; and, although an Oxford
triple first, he had been teaching at Marlborough for only three
years when his name came up before the Repton governors. They
were indeed taking a gamble in appointing another comparative
youngster to the headmastership; but Temple's powers of persuasion were such that it was a gamble that they were quite
prepared to take.

It had all begun when Temple had approached his friend Frank
Fletcher, Fisher's old head at Marlborough but by now Headmaster
of Charterhouse, to ask his advice on the Repton succession. He
set out a long list of the qualifications (especially spiritual gifts)
which he thought the new man ought to possess. It was a

formidable list, and Fletcher replied that he knew only one man capable of measuring up to it – 'but Fisher is too young.'[1] Temple replied at once on an enthusiastic postcard: 'Fisher we must have.' He had been assured that, although only twenty-seven, Fisher already had the mature judgement of a man of forty.

The next stage was to persuade the favoured candidate to apply for the vacant post. He was not lacking in ambition. He had only recently been asked by a boy at Marlborough: 'Sir, will you be a headmaster one day?' On that occasion he replied that he didn't know but that, if ever he did, 'perhaps one day I might become headmaster of Ashby-de-la-Zouch grammar school'.[2] (Ashby was a small town not far from his family home in Leicestershire.) He had set his sights too low. Soon afterwards his headmaster, Wynne Wilson, stopped him in the corridor and told him that he ought to apply for the vacant headmastership of Repton. To Fisher (he claimed many years afterwards) the notion had at first appeared ludicrous. 'I had no idea of doing such a thing, nor had I any kind of idea that I knew how to be a headmaster.' By a happy coincidence, however, he wrote for advice to both Fletcher and Temple, the very two people who were united in supposing him the ideal candidate. They both, naturally (but without revealing their partisanship), told him that he *ought* to apply – which he accordingly did.

He was summoned to attend an interview with the Repton governing body at the Westminster Hotel in London, a building near the Abbey which has since vanished. When he arrived at the hotel he found to his surprise that he was the only candidate to be interviewed. 'That rather alarmed me. I thought I should be one of four or five.' The governors themselves were an elderly lot, quite a number of them 'already on sticks'. The interview appears to have been little more than a formality. Fisher was asked a few questions – did he agree, for instance, that mathematics were the foundation of character? He felt bound to make one confession: that he was not an ultra-pure classicist. Temple at once came to his rescue. ' "Oh, I suppose you mean you don't know when the conditional clause ought to be the subjunctive or the optative?" I said, "Yes." And he said, "Well, I don't know either!" And he laughed, as he *did* laugh, and that got me out of that hole, but at least my conscience was clear. So I was elected.'[3] The date was early in the fateful month of June 1914, at the end of which the Archduke Franz Ferdinand was to be assassinated at Sarajevo.

*   *   *   *   *

Geoffrey Francis Fisher was born on 5 May 1887. He was the youngest of ten children, the two eldest of whom died early. He had three surviving sisters and four brothers.* His father, Henry Fisher, was Rector of Higham-on-the Hill in Leicestershire. That brief sentence, however, tells much less than the whole story. Henry Fisher was in fact Rector of Higham from 1868 to 1910, a period of 42 years. He had succeeded his father, John, who had held the living since 1832, the year of the First Reform Bill. This John had succeeded *his* father, also John, who had been appointed to the benefice in 1772, 60 years earlier. Thus the three successive Fisher incumbents held the rectory for no less than 138 years – a remarkable achievement even by nineteenth-century standards. As the living was in the gift of the family, it was of course a simple matter to keep it in the family. If Geoffrey had been an older rather than a younger son, he might well have succeeded his father as rector in due course – and his subsequent career have turned out very differently. As it was, his brother Legh replaced Henry when the latter retired in 1910.

Geoffrey's childhood was a happy one, spent in the secure environment of a Victorian rectory. His father laboured away devotedly at his parochial duties; his mother appears to have been the pivot of the household, keeping her children under strict control but having a particularly soft spot for her youngest. For a short while he attended the village school, but soon progressed to a local preparatory school, Lindley Lodge, first as a day boy and then as a boarder. He spent six years there, ending up (inevitably) as top of the school in all the main subjects. From Lindley Lodge he won

---

* Two of the brothers, Leonard and Legh, were also ordained, Leonard becoming a bishop in South Africa. Another brother, Harry, was a GP and a sister, Katie, a nurse who served in Palestine with the Church Missionary Society. The eldest surviving daughter, Edith, remained at home to prop up her parents and act as an unpaid parish worker (as happened so often in Victorian households).

153

a scholarship to Marlborough, which he entered in September 1901 and in which his spiritual development really took root. As he wrote later:

> I learned how to tackle everything that came along in what I now recognise was an intelligent Christian way, not consciously borrowing from Christ, not precisely trying to follow his example, but translating into my daily duties and occupations and pleasures and sympathies the spirit which flowed from His revelation of the Kingdom of God.[4]

Academically he turned out a brilliant pupil and multiple prizewinner. In October 1906 he went up as a scholar to Exeter College, Oxford.

At Oxford he proved a good all-rounder. His budding academic promise was crowned with firsts in Classical Mods, Greats and Theology. In athletics a broken collar-bone led him to forsake rugger for the river: he became his college's captain of boats and even rowed in the university trial eights. His social graces led to his election as president of the Junior Common Room. He was exemplary in his attendance at services in the college chapel, and helped with its choir and Sunday school. In his attitude to such indulgences as drinking and smoking he was typically pragmatic. He forswore alcohol to save himself constantly having to decide when and whether he had had enough. Smoking, in the days before it carried a health warning, had no such drawback for him. 'You could smoke as much as you liked and as long as you liked,' he once remarked.[5] So, for the next 40 years, he was an inveterate pipe-smoker.* He spent five years at Oxford, going down in June 1911. But he was never enchanted by the university to the extent that William Temple had been. He summed up his period of residence thus: 'It was a grand time, but it did not make the same impression on me that Oxford had made on so many people. I think the cause lay in the fact that it was only developing, stabilising, enriching the same attitude to life that I had already acquired before leaving Marlborough.'[6]

---

* He abandoned his pipe as suddenly as he had taken it up. One evening, at Lambeth Palace, he felt sick. He was due to go away the next day for a fortnight and left all his smoking materials behind him. He never resumed the habit.

154

In view of his resistance to the charms of the university, it is hardly surprising that he should have chosen the life of a schoolmaster rather than that of a don. He was offered chaplaincies by both Balliol and University College, but turned them both down. Instead he accepted an invitation from his old friend, Frank Fletcher, to return to Marlborough as an assistant master. In later life he defended his decision on the ground that he had not wanted to spend his working life in the field of academic theology.

> I enjoyed it immensely, but I knew quite well that to go on with academic theology would mean to go on asking questions to which there was no answer, and spending most of one's time correcting someone else's answer, and trying to think up some answer of one's own: a very unprofitable and unrewarding thing unless you were just made for that kind of research work.[7]

So 'without hesitation' he accepted Fletcher's offer – even though there were many masters at Marlborough still around who would have taught him as a schoolboy only a few years earlier. It seems strange in retrospect that he apparently never seriously considered the third alternative of the parish priesthood. Coming as he did from such a conspicuously clerical family, it might have been thought an obvious choice. But maybe he would have judged it a waste of his talents to fritter them away on parochial chores. In the fullness of time he was to become a bishop – but his way to the bench was to be via a headmastership rather than the customary rungs of the ecclesiastical ladder.

He returned to Marlborough in the autumn term of 1911. By then, however, Fletcher had left to become Headmaster of Charterhouse, so Fisher served under Wynne Wilson instead. His three years at Marlborough proved a sunny start to what he already looked forward to as a career in schoolmastering. 'I had from the beginning got the hang of the thing. I was absorbed in all my occupations, which exhausted me to the limit of my desires and possibilities.'[8] He loved teaching, he revelled in the community life, and he soon discovered that he would have no difficulties in maintaining discipline. But he was not unmindful of his clerical background and was quite happy to be ordained. He looked on ordination as a perfectly natural culmination to the work of a schoolmaster. His religion had always been matter-of-fact, and he tended to see theological issues in black-and-white terms. 'All my life', he once observed, 'I have been perfectly clear that there was a clear and reasonable doctrine of the Church of England by which all other doctrines must be judged.'[9] His attitude to churchgoing was equally clear-cut.

> The Holy Communion was an essential thing, but never in any kind of isolation from the rest of one's life. As a boy I had grown from going to Communion every three weeks to going every Sunday; and to go to Communion every Sunday remained a constant and constructive feature in my life. I never particularly wanted, except under special circumstances, to go more often than that.[10]

In those far-off days, a two-year spell at a seminary was not considered an essential preliminary to ordination. But Fisher at least paid lip-service to its value by spending the long vacation of 1911 at Wells Theological College in order to pick up a few hints about the technical side of the ministry. He was made deacon in Salisbury Cathedral on 2 June 1912 by Bishop John Wordsworth (the brother of Edward Benson's friend Elizabeth) and was priested in March of the following year by Wordsworth's successor, Frederic Ridgeway, who licensed him to officiate as an assistant chaplain at Marlborough. Fisher felt his ordination as something that would enable him to do more with and for boys, and on a deeper level, then had hitherto been the case. He later confessed to being suspicious of undue emotion in connection with ordination or of any 'waiting for the moment' or 'listening for the call.'[11]

His time as an assistant master at Marlborough was destined to be brief. When he received the news of his election as Headmaster of Repton he went at once to the rooms of a colleague not much older than himself to share the joke. 'We shouted with laughter. It was so utterly absurd. But there it was; and, since by nature I don't like running away from anything if it has to come to me, clearly I had got to go and do it.'[12]

*   *   *   *   *

156

Fisher faced an unforeseen handicap as he prepared to take over as headmaster: the outbreak of the First World War on 4 August 1914. An immediate consequence was the departure of about 60 senior boys to join the army. More serious from the school's point of view was the loss of six masters who had likewise volunteered for war service. The sudden and unexpected depletion of his staff meant that the new head had to spend much of the summer holidays in seeking and hiring new masters (some of whom turned out to be hopeless at maintaining discipline) and in compiling a new timetable to take account of the changes in personnel. When not engaged in these tasks he found himself having to furnish his official residence at Repton. Here he sought the advice of Frank Fletcher's wife. 'She told me what to buy and how to furnish the drawing-room and the dining-room... So I found myself established and the School came back.'[13]

There was a more particular problem with which Fisher had at once to deal: that of re-establishing discipline after the relaxed regime of William Temple. In a taped interview with William Purcell which took place towards the end of his life Fisher minced no words in describing the nature of that part of his inheritance:

> The discipline of the school was very poor... Why was it so bad? For a perfectly simple reason. William Temple, with every other virtue in the world, was not a good disciplinarian, partly because he was too innocent. He had never been inclined to kick over the traces. He was a very disciplined person... In moral matters, he was, by nature, restrained and above reproach. So much so that he really couldn't get down to the level of ordinary school discipline; and this was having some disastrous consequences.[14]

It did not take Fisher long to discover the first disciplinary nettle he had to grasp: that of homosexuality. The Hall, the house for which the headmaster was personally responsible, had gone 'very badly astray.' Charles Smyth describes Fisher's prompt action in this field as 'the cleansing of the Augean Stables'. He certainly didn't shirk his task.

> I was young and enthusiastic, and I was quite clear that I was going to make it evident to everybody that there was no place in the life

157

of The Hall, or the School, for homosexual practices. This wasn't a matter of less or more. In any community it must be none so far as one can secure it.[15]

This of course was over 40 years before the Wolfenden Report and the subsequent more relaxed attitude to homosexuality in the nation at large (though not perhaps in the public schools). In his first term Fisher was ruthless. He expelled two boys near the top end of school – no doubt *pour encourager les autres*. 'I didn't like the look of them. I didn't think we could really carry them and reshape them, and I thought that it was for the general good that they should go.' The boys' parents thought differently. One was an army officer who found it inconceivable that his son should face expulsion. The resultant interviews were painful and embarrassing. However, Fisher remarked, 'I am an obstinate person when I am convinced that I must do something, and obstinate I was.' He describes the result of his tough action as a 'transformation' in the life of the school:

Very soon, so far as one could tell, the thing was gone; and years afterwards, after I had left, a parent who was a boy under me said to someone else, and it reached me, that in his day, while there was dirty talk still, nobody would have dreamt of going any further than that. Well, that is something, and most boys can avoid dirty talk if they want to. At least there is no constant temptation to go too far.[16]

*   *   *   *   *

In his taped recollections of his time at Repton Fisher maintains that his abiding interest was in the boys themselves. 'It was my delight to try and get to know as many boys as I could.' He claims to have known the 90 boys at any one time in his own house very well and to have got to know eventually most of the 400-odd boys in the other boarding houses.

Whenever I passed a boy I would stop and say, 'Who are you?' and ask him a question or two and get something out of him. The chiefest delight I had was trying to win the confidence of the rather

158

slow, shy, slightly eccentric boy who didn't just fit into the ordinary pattern or swim with the ordinary tide, and that was a constant challenge and joy.

Also a joy to Fisher were the clever boys, who were easy to talk to if you were prepared to discuss anything with them without embarrassment.

> That I was always ready to do and it meant argument, endless argument, and all the fun of the chase; and I learnt there always to hold my own, knowing just a bit more, though not necessarily much more, than them about whatever had come up ... and if they got conceited to put them gently in their place.[17]

That was how Fisher himself looked back on his relationship with the boys under his charge – through no doubt partially rose-coloured spectacles. But how did the boys themselves remember Fisher? The evidence is mixed. In a long appreciation published in *Repton 1557–1957*, Charles Smyth, by then an established church historian and a close friend of his old headmaster, recalls his uncanny power of remembering not only faces but also names and even initials.

> His disposition was naturally affectionate, though I can never remember his showing deep emotion, any more than I can remember seeing him lose his temper: he could, however, upon rare occasions, startle us by rising to a pitch of moral indignation which (I fear) appealed to the more ribald instincts of one's unregenerate adolescence, although it was always respected because it was so transparently sincere.

Smyth later remarks that, since it was the traditional temptation of the best schoolmasters and dons to seek to impose their own personalities, prejudices and ideals upon the personalities of their pupils, 'perhaps the greatest tribute that can be paid to Dr Fisher as a headmaster is to say that he never captured our imaginations except at the subconscious level'.[18] Smyth also recalls Fisher's habit of coming round the dormitories before lights-out to see what books the boys were reading. He would perch on the bed, and if he found them deep in Dickens or Conrad or Wells or Masefield, would exclaim: 'Splendid! Hurray! Well done!'[19] Nor did he mind sharing in their recreations. Randall Ellison recalls an occasion during the summer term of 1922 when the headmaster suddenly appeared at the swimming pool, 'stripped off his clothes rather to our amazement and dived in, then splashed about with the rest of us'.[20] But appearances could be deceptive. As Smyth remarks: 'His universal geniality, so genuine and spontaneous, never for one moment compromised his dignity as the Headmaster.'[21]

A churchman even more distinguished than Smyth was also a boy at Repton under Fisher. This was Michael Ramsey, who was to succeed him eventually as Archbishop of Canterbury. Ramsey apparently called his headmaster 'the little snipe'. He regarded him as a distant figure, but as forceful and efficient and later as friendly. He admired Fisher especially as a teacher of Latin and Greek. In the words of Ramsey's biographer, Owen Chadwick: 'Fisher had zest. He rushed them along. He did not delay boringly on points of scholarship. He bubbled along with enthusiasm and humour. He made the dead languages into living literature.'[22] Fisher, for his part, wrote a prescient final report on the young Ramsey: 'A boy with plenty of force of character who, in spite of certain uncouthnesses,* has done good service on his own lines... If he can get over [his uncouth and ungainly appearance] he might do quite well.'[23]

According to Sir Stuart Hampshire, Fisher was very strict, if not abnormally so by the standards of the time. He was also 'very unfeeling and illiberal' and he certainly beat boys excessively – 'by which I don't mean too often, but too hard'.[25] Even Fisher admitted that he could be 'pretty crisp' towards the boys. But Hampton Gervis, who later became a prep-school headmaster, remembered him as 'firm when necessary but never brutal'. Gervis

---

* Arthur Benson, the archbishop's son and biographer (and also, by a coincidence, the writer of the words of the Repton school song), shared Fisher's view of Ramsey's uncouth appearance. By now Master of Magdalene College, Cambridge, and a friend of the Ramsey family, he recorded in his diary: 'Michael, a distressing object, so sharp-faced, dull-eyed, spotted.' But Benson himself had his critics. The undergraduates of Magdalene used to say of him that he spent the morning doing nothing and the afternoon writing about what he had done in the morning.[24]

also found that Fisher could empathize with a boy's feelings. On one occasion he was told to come to the chapel to practise reading the lesson. He arrived early, only to find the headmaster already there. 'You are not late,' Fisher explained. 'I am early because I did not want you to arrive to an empty chapel and become more nervous than you are now by having to wait for me.'[26] Sir Desmond Lee thought Fisher a very good headmaster and an excellent teacher, though 'very conventional and ordinary in his tastes'. Both Gervis and Lee dismissed as a 'travesty of the truth' an incident depicting Fisher as a sadistic brute which appeared in a childhood memoir by the writer Roald Dahl.[27] A contemporary of Dahl's, Denton Welch, in a parallel autobiographical memoir, paints a sympathetic portrait of Fisher on the occasion of his going to take formal leave of him:

> He was soon to be a famous bishop, but I would never have suspected it. In spite of his dog-collar, I never thought of him as clerical.... 'So you're the one who went to visit cathedrals instead of coming back to school!' he began... I blushed. To have my escape explained as an architectural holiday sounded silly. I said nothing, so he went on talking.
> 'My experience is that one must accept one's environment and fit into it as best one can; otherwise life is nothing but beating one's head against a brick wall.'
> I felt his sincerity apart from his ordinary words. Schoolmasters generally never show it. I had never had three words of deeply felt advice before. It had always been argument and parrot-rule. I knew the difference now. I got up, warm inside and admiring.[28]

An anecdote which Fisher himself delighted to tell concerned another boy who had come to take leave of him – a blameless but colourless character who had apparently made no impact or impression on anybody during his time at Repton. Racking his brains for *some* word of encouragement for this dim youth, Fisher was reduced to observing: 'Well, So-and-so, I think you'll be able to stand on your own feet all right'. The sequel can be told in Fisher's own words:

Many years afterwards, when he was a professional man of good standing, I ran into him. He said to me suddenly: 'I don't suppose you remember it, but in fact the thing which you said to me when I was leaving changed the whole course of my life. I was a very diffident boy, very frightened of everything, unsure of myself, and unsure of what life would do with me. I came down to say goodbye to you, and you shook me by the hand and said: "You'll be able to stand on your own feet." That gave me a confidence which changed the course of my whole life.'[29]

In spite of his phenomenal energy Fisher could occasionally relax. It was his custom on Sunday afternoons to endeavour to complete the Torquemada crossword in *The Observer*. But he came to disapprove the policy of the paper's editor, J.L. Garvin, to such an extent that eventually he refused to have the paper in his house. He solved his crossword problem by an arrangement with one of the boys at The Hall, David Paton (the future canon and ecumenist). Paton cut out the crossword from his own copy of *The Observer* each week and passed it over to the headmaster, who paid him a shilling a term in remuneration. Paton commented: 'His combination of extreme competence and lack of self-concern made him extraordinarily easy and attractive.'[30]

Fisher enjoyed teaching, in that he only taught what he enjoyed. He took the Upper Sixth for Latin and Greek because those happened to be his own favourite subjects. He also taught Middle School Divinity;* and on Sunday and Monday mornings he took the whole Sixth for Divinity – 80 or 90 boys in all.

> It was perhaps stupid to take them, but the real thing was that I couldn't divide them. It was my one opportunity of getting some little touch with every boy in the Sixth form… That little touch was a thing I dared not surrender… There were some boys I would have done something with which caught their interest. With the mob, of course, many of them went more or less to sleep; but it did stand, in my mind, for something.[31]

---

* One boy, going home for the holidays, was asked by his father in Ireland whether he had had a good term. His reply was: 'Yes, a lovely term, especially doing Habakkuk with the Boss.' Fisher commented: 'Well, *there* is a testimonial for you!'

It was also the headmaster's job, of course, to have a rough idea of what was being taught throughout the school, and of how it was being taught; and that meant keeping in touch with heads of department and other senior masters, and every so often trying to extract from them how things were going. Like Temple, Fisher was entirely ignorant of science. But he was prepared to recognise that the science laboratories had to be properly equipped, and that a double period, rather than a single period of a mere three-quarters of an hour, was essential for the scientists if they were to make any real progress with their experiments. So he took the bull by the horns and compiled a completely new timetable starting from scratch. The key to the successful running of a school curriculum, in his view, lay in the choice of really good heads of department. He flattered himself that he had been successful in his selection of first-rate men, particularly in the middle period of his headmastership. They helped to ensure a steady flow of university scholarships and a general improvement in the intellectual life of the school. Several members of the Repton staff during Fisher's reign left to become headmasters of other schools.[32]

*   *   *   *   *

Repton during Fisher's headmastership was a 'tough place', in the view of one of those who suffered under the system. Rules and discipline were tight and living conditions 'really spartan'. But, as was the case at most other public schools of the period, much of the discipline was administered not by the masters but by the boys – who, it was calculated, were responsible for 90 per cent of the frequent beatings. The staff, however, were ever-present in the background as a court of last resort.[33]

Fisher reckoned himself a good disciplinarian. 'But I was by no means a ferocious disciplinarian,' he recalled many years after his departure, 'nor did I generally think about it. Before long it had just taken its place as a natural feature of the School, that it was a well-disciplined school.' Fisher considered it his job to see that the rules, so far as there *were* rules, were sensible, and to some extent flexible as well. Two or three years after his arrival he produced a rule-book containing certain directions with which everybody had

163

to be familiar. Rule 1, so typical of his pragmatic approach to life, set the tone for the rest: 'Any breach of common sense is a breach of these rules.' When asked who decided what constitued common sense, he replied that he did – and nobody else. The boys apparently considered this a fair answer. The ghost of the lackadaisical Temple had now been finally laid to rest. Certain matters continued to be referred to the headmaster* and Fisher dealt with them 'not ruthlessly'. Towards the end of this time, he says, such instances grew very rare. 'I should think that the last boy that I caned was perhaps eight years before I finally left Repton.'[34]

In the face of this assertion, what is one to make of the claim made by Roald Dahl, who was a boy at Repton from 1929 to 1935, that Fisher was not only a constant flogger but a brutal one at that? Dahl made his charge in a memoir of his childhood published in 1984, 12 years after Fisher's death. He begins his chapter on 'The Headmaster' by dismissing him as a 'rather shoddy, bandy-legged little fellow with a big bald head and lots of energy but not much charm'. Dahl was ahead of his time in his fervent opposition to corporal punishment. 'All through my school life I was appalled by the fact that masters and senior boys were allowed literally to wound other boys, and sometimes quite severely.' He goes on to describe, in great detail, one of these 'ceremonies' at which Fisher had allegedly administered a severe beating to Dahl's best friend. In between each 'tremendous crack' of the cane, said Dahl, the headmaster would stop to fill his pipe and lecture the kneeling miscreant about sin and wrongdoing. By the end of the account the reader might well have found himself sharing Dahl's indignation at the thought of this clergyman-headmaster preaching about mercy and forgiveness in the school chapel one moment and in the next showing 'neither Forgiveness nor Mercy in flogging some small boy who had broken the rules'.[35] The only flaw in the argument was that Dahl, a best-selling children's author with a

---

* There was a rule against a boy leaving Repton at the end of term on a motor-bike. One boy broke this rule and Fisher sent him a telegram: 'Return at once or not at all.' The boy got the telegram as he arrived home and at once returned. 'It was the only time', Fisher recalled, 'that I had the extraordinary experience of caning a boy in plus-fours.'

marked tendency to fantasize, had picked on the wrong headmaster. His friend certainly received a beating: but it was at the hands not of Fisher but of those of his successor, J.T. Christie, later a canon of Westminster. The beating took place in May 1933, nearly a year after Fisher had left Repton; and the offender was not so much a 'small boy' as an eighteen-year-old prefect who had been caught in bed with a younger boy. The true facts about the beating only came to public light in 1994 with the appearance of a life of Dahl by Jeremy Treglown. The incorrect version of the story had caused a minor sensation on its appearance ten years earlier. Members of the Archbishop's family had been justifiably outraged at this slur on his memory, and they and a number of Old Reptonians complained to Dahl – who was, apparently, unrepentant.[36]

*   *   *   *   *

As a clerical headmaster Fisher found the chapel at Repton 'my special care and my special delight'. In a telling comment he told William Purcell that he could not have done his job at Repton

> unless I had felt not only that I was Headmaster of the School in its general social life and community life but that I was also Headmaster of the religious side of that community life represented inside by the teaching of Divinity, the encouraging of Christian standards and, in the Chapel, the teaching and practice of Christian faith and worship.

He admitted to Purcell, however, that he was speaking only for himself in this respect. Two of his sons, Frank at Wellington and Charles at Scotch College, Adelaide, were both 'first-class Christians and teachers of the Christian faith' but were both lay headmasters. He then adds paradoxically: 'I think it is probably true that they are more effective as laymen than they would have been if they had been ordained.' Members of his own family perhaps constituted the exception that proved the rule. 'I perfectly understand the good Christians who say that they do more good as Headmaster by being laymen than by being clergymen. It may be so. I am not convinced that it is so.'[37]

Fisher endeavoured to keep the chapel services 'alert and alive and fruitful and joyful.'

> Of course boys got bored with parts of them. That didn't worry me. I've never known anything good that I've enjoyed that hasn't had its boring aspects as well... In my day there was still a universal feeling that the Christian faith was something which everybody ought to support, ought to be interested in and ought to absorb something from. And thus there was very little feeling against the chapel services and the like.[38]

Those were indeed the days!

Fisher came to the conclusion, however, that, in the ordinary routine of chapel services, there was 'too much for the ordinary good boy'. Every Sunday there was an 8 o'clock celebration of Holy Communion, followed by an hour's Divinity lesson. Then came Matins at eleven, and in the evening Evensong.

> Well, I knew that most of those boys, if they went to church at all in the holidays, went once on a Sunday and no more; and I realised that, with morning and evening service compulsory, it was really very hard to expect them also to be regular or frequent Communicants at 8 o'clock in the morning.

Fisher's solution was to excuse communicants at eight from having also to attend Matins at eleven. But here, as he admits himself, he was being somewhat devious, and not really expecting that there would be a marked falling-off in attendance at Matins:

> It was a perfectly safe thing to do. He [the early communicant] had got to go to the Divinity hour, and after that it was no hardship really to go for the Matins service, which only took half-an-hour and then left him free; and I reckoned that if he was already meaning business he would get up at 8 o'clock and go to Communion not feeling that he would thereby be getting off something of much moment later on in the day. To make it a little more weighted I put the early service at a quarter to eight just so that it shouldn't be a simple 8 o'clock.[39]

166

The new system, in Fisher's view, worked well. It certainly increased the number of communicants. From time to time there were Saturday-night preparation services which he generally took himself.

> When I tried to make it obvious how serious the Communion Service was, how it was not be taken lightly or wantonly but only with a true Christian purpose. I don't think there was any abuse of this arrangement. I think that the services all through were reasonably enjoyed, that the Communion Service was properly respected, that the boys grew up in a disciplined sense of church membership and church worship, and that preaching by the staff, and I hope by myself, was such as to engage their interest.[40]

Fisher claims not to have enjoyed preaching to the boys. He insisted, however, on never saying anything that he did not personally believe and could explain intelligently. His sermons were appreciated by the *cognoscenti* among the boys, such as Charles Smyth and Michael Ramsey. Smyth claims that Fisher never put a foot wrong in the pulpit ('or anywhere else') but that he had never met any Old Reptonian other than Ramsey who had realised at the time how good Fisher's sermons actually were.[41] (He can hardly, however, have been in the same class as either of the Temples.) Fisher sums up the general effect of his sermons by remarking that, for the most part, people thought that they were 'all right' but were not converted by them. He adds modestly: 'Indeed, I do not think I have ever converted anybody particularly by anything I have happened to say.[42] Some 50 of Fisher's sermons at Repton have survived. Their themes are mainly practical and ethical – for example, the Christian use of money, gambling or Sunday observance.

Smyth subsequently found himself using, as a parish priest, illustrations which Fisher had given when preparing him for confirmation. 'I constantly remember things that he said in casual conversation which cumulatively taught me to understand, as nothing else outside of parochial experience has done, the nature and ethos of the Church of England.[43] Fisher himself had acquired his own basic approach to religion while still a boy at Marlborough, and he retained it for the rest of his life. In his own words:

167

A religion, such as a public school at its best encourages, includes an enormous love for the ordinary services of the Book of Common Prayer, a quite different and far more personal devotion to Christ in the Holy Communion and a very high interest in intelligent discussion of preaching of the Christian faith and a consequent direction of life to good purposes. I am sure that these things stand as the best way of leading people to live according to the kingdom of God.[44]

*   *   *   *   *

Within three years of his arrival at Repton a notable event took place in Fisher's domestic life. He was married to Rosamond Forman, the daughter of a former housemaster at Repton who had died prematurely in 1905 and the granddaughter of the school's 'second founder', Steuart Pears. Like her husband, she came of a large family. He had been the youngest of ten children; she was the ninth of fourteen, all of whom had been born at Repton (her own six sons were to share a like distinction).

Their courtship had some hurdles to surmount. In 1916 Rosamond, who was then 26, was paying a final visit to old friends at Repton before going off to train as a missionary. During the visit she met her future husband for the first time, in the art school. Something clicked immediately for both of them. He apparently declared: 'Repton belongs to you more than to me, really, and I know all about your father and grandfather.' A few days later he remarked to his sister Katie, herself an ex-missionary, who was then keeping house for him: 'If I marry at all, I shall marry Miss Forman.' In October he proposed to her; but she was at first doubtful whether she ought to put the prospect of personal happiness before her missionary vocation. She wrote for advice to her college principal.

I told her that I had met a man, that I had fallen in love with him, that I thought he had fallen in love with me, and that, if I saw him again, I should almost certainly not become a missionary. What ought I to do? Should I go and see him again?

168

The principal sensibly wired back, 'Go.' Fisher subsequently declared that he had sent back to the mission field a wonderful missionary in his sister and saved the mission field from a very bad missionary in his wife.[45]

The boys at Repton were intrigued by the progress of the headmaster's courtship. During the winter of 1917 the river Trent was frozen over for some days. Charles Smyth recalls:

> One afternoon in the middle prep. we looked out of the window and observed the Boss, in a black trilby and black overcoat, walking gingerly, with the aid of a stick, into the centre of the ice, followed, to our enchanted gaze, by his fiancée on skates. He stood there, a stocky little figure, occasionally rotating on his axis while she skated round him, gracefully cutting circles in the ice.[46]

They were married on 12 April 1917, three weeks before Geoffrey Fisher's thirtieth birthday. Looking back many years later, he declared: 'My wife, Rosamond, entered into the life of the School in all its aspects as to the manner born! She identified herself with the interests of the masters' wives – and did much for the village community.'[47]

*   *   *   *   *

The early years of Fisher's headmastership were overshadowed by the First World War. Many of the young subalterns who were slaughtered in such numbers in France and Belgium came from the public schools; Repton supplied its full quota, and the mounting casualty lists brought home to the school the effects of the war as nothing else could. The records show that 1912 Old Reptonians fought in the war, of whom no fewer than 355 were killed or died on active service. The many decorations they won included one VC (Jackie Smyth, the future MP) and 73 DSOs.[48] Long casualty lists appeared in successive issues of *The Reptonian*. Vacant places appeared in chapel as boys were called up. Letters from ORs on active service were received by their old schoolfellows. There were longer and more strenuous OTC parades – the older boys were required to do up to ten hours' military training a week during term.

169

These were the outward signs of the impact of the war on the school. How did the staff and boys themselves react to the pace of events? According to Victor Gollancz, the radical young master who was at the centre of a controversial episode soon to be described, many of the staff were reactionary in their views. As he recalled many years later in his autobiographical *More for Timothy*: 'They specialized in hatred of "the enemy": they were out of sympathy with the working class: their minds were closed: they felt by rote: and they had lost the early freshness and enthusiasm, the joy in living and sense of adventure, that we ought ever to keep undimmed.'[49] A particular bugbear of Gollancz's was Guy Snape* (thinly disguised in his book as 'Pruke'), whom he once overheard say to a colleague: 'It's our solemn duty, mah dear chap, to instil into the boys such a hatred of the Hun that for the rest of their lives they'll never speak to one again.'[50] But it was not only the masters who, in Gollancz's view, were at fault. Many of the boys were tarred, to a greater or lesser extent, with the same ultra-patriotic brush.

Nor was the headmaster entirely immune from it. In the very first sermon he preached in the school chapel after taking office he declared, in a passage which today seems both naive and simplistic but would then have been lapped up unthinkingly by most people:

The cause of this War is arrogance and, alas, we see the fruit that grows from it. The facts compel us to condemn our enemies of an arrogance that is unchristian and too often inhuman. They arrogate to themselves a superiority of intellectual power which justifies force as the handmaid to increase its dominion…. We fight because we are fighting God's cause against the Devil's.[52]

The sermon, delivered when the war was a mere seven weeks old, was printed 'by request of the Prefects' and went on sale in the

---

* Their ideological differences did not prevent Gollancz and Snape from being on friendly personal terms. Snape had a son, Paul, to whom he was devoted but who had contracted polio and, as a result, was behind in his work and needed extra tuition in Latin. This Gollancz willingly agreed to give. 'Our sessions, which never failed to give me pleasure, were uninterrupted, if I remember rightly, by the development of the row between father and coach. We both regarded them, I think, as above the battle.'[51]

school bookshop. Such a black-and-white analysis of the causes of the war had obviously been meat and drink to the youthful congregation.

*   *   *   *   *

It was the war which indirectly brought in its wake a problem of 'immense difficulty and immense importance' for Fisher to resolve. It became known as the 'Somervell–Gollancz row' and its reverberations spread far beyond the confines of Repton. The controversy is discussed briefly and objectively by Fisher's two biographers, and even more briefly and diplomatically in the history of the school published in 1957. Four years earlier Victor Gollancz, by then a highly successful publisher, had issued his own version of the dispute. It occupies the central section of his autobiographical volume, *More for Timothy*, and runs to fifty thousands words or so. As is to be expected, it is a highly subjective account. It contrives, however, to be mainly fair and even generous to Fisher, who began by supporting the Gollancz–Somervell experiments but found himself in the end having to suppress them in an atmosphere charged with bitterness and acrimony. A more objective version of the dispute appears in Ruth Dudley Edwards's biography of Gollancz, published in 1987. Fisher gave his own side of the affair in his taped interview with William Purcell, on which both Purcell himself and Edward Carpenter draw heavily in their lives of the Archbishop.

The affair began in February 1916, when Fisher, in desperate need of a good classical master, applied to an agency and was told about Gollancz. He was then a young man of twenty-four who had won a brilliant first in Mods at Oxford but, because of the war, had left to join the army without taking his degree. As he was confined to home service, not being considered fit enough to go abroad, the War Office raised no objection to releasing him for work as a teacher. He had a preliminary interview with Fisher, who offered him the charge of the Classical Sixth, together with a commission in the school's OTC. At this stage Gollancz was referring to Fisher in letters as a 'charming man'. It was only later, as the situation soured, that the charmer was transposed into 'the little man' or 'the

171

old man' (Fisher would then have been thirty). For his part Fisher in later years praised Gollancz as

> a brilliant man ... full of vitality, full of energy, very very sensitive, as though he lacked one skin, with all the best kind of idealism moving him in every single thing that he thought of; but at that stage not yet at all aware as to how to be a respectable idealist in such a community as a school.[53]

From the start Gollancz won the hearts of many of his pupils, especially those with liberal leanings. In later life some of them recalled the qualities in him that had specially attracted them. James Harford, for instance, describes his impact on the Classical Sixth as 'cataclysmic, messianic. He seemed to be the incarnation of all the godlike elements in the spirit of man... Notions of discipline and status were completely foreign to Victor's nature. To us he was an undergraduate among undergraduates – a fourth-year man among "freshers"'.[54] James Darling thought that the 'tremendous range of his intellect may have been his greatest quality, but it was the enthusiasm which carried all before it, and enthusiasm is the one indispensable quality in a good teacher'.[55]

Gollancz's relations with his fellow masters were less happy. He found it difficult at times to co-exist with the 'morass of High Toryism' he found in the staff-room, personified by the Hun-hating Snape. But there were a few kindred spirits, chief among whom was David Somervell, the senior history master. History to Somervell was not a bundle of dry bones but a living entity, and he had the rare gift of being able to inspire his pupils with his own enthusiasm.* In Gollancz's view Somervell was a historian second and a schoolmaster first – 'a man dedicated utterly, but without bother or selfconsciousness, to the vocation of schoolmastering'.[57] Somervell was nine years older than Gollancz and had his feet planted rather more firmly on the ground.

---

* In an article, 'Repton Remembered', published in the *Church Times* of 26 July 1957, an Old Reptonian, Christopher Palmer, recalled that Somervell had inspired him with a love of history which he had never lost. 'Though I have never seen him since I left over forty years ago, my memory of him and his kindness and inspiration to me I shall never forget.'[56]

It was not to be supposed that Gollancz's easy relations with his pupils had escaped the notice of his headmaster. Their first major brush occurred in the summer holidays of 1916, when Fisher wrote him a line 'to pull you up in the path you are pursuing before it is too late'. Friendliness between masters and boys was all to the good, the letter went on, but there was a certain line that should not be passed, and a certain dignity and reserve that every master should maintain. Gollancz summarizes the rest of the letter thus: 'I had to realise that there were two distinct classes in a Public School – the teachers and the taught; classes having constant relations with one another, no doubt, but distinct and separate nonetheless. The "popular" master was suspect, and rightly so, by his colleagues and the more thoughtful among the boys.'[58] Gollancz was perturbed by Fisher's letter and wrote to ask where exactly he had gone wrong. A fortnight later the reply arrived:

> I refuse to write long letters from the tops of Welsh mountains. I will give you two instances of what I mean. You had some boys up to dinner last term, and borrowed the prefects'-room gramophone to amuse them with. You also went with a lot of boys to Derby on the last morning, and gave them a feed there. This sort of thing will never do.

> Yours sincerely,
> G.F. Fisher[59]

Gollancz later attempted to justify, in a personal interview with Fisher, his allegedly over-friendly relations with boys at Repton, but without any success. He complained in a letter to a friend: 'I found his mind tiny and cold, and his views on education deplorable... But the boys are a joy – and I'm not going to allow any miserable little pedantic parson of a schoolmaster to make me alter my attitude towards them.'[60] In spite of his misgivings, however, the 'little pedantic parson' had no doubts about Gollancz's teaching abilities and promoted him to the Upper Sixth.

The scene was now set for the first act of a drama that was to end with the enforced departure of Gollancz from the Repton stage. For some time he had been disturbed by the reactionary nature (as it seemed to him) of the political views of his pupils – even of those of his most devoted disciples. He reports one remark which had particularly appalled him: 'I say, isn't all that *radical*, what you're saying? The radicals are *bloody* people. They ruin the country and teach the working classes to put on airs.' Such a comment Gollancz must have thought more worthy of Snape than of one of his own favourite pupils. He reacted accordingly.

> I was flabbergasted. Here was a set of boys, nearly all of whom I knew to be decent and generous, even perhaps great-hearted; and yet not one of them, to judge from their talk, had the smallest degree of sympathy with people less well-off than themselves, or any stomach for an argument that ran counter to their prejudices.[61]

The obvious answer was to increase the boys' political awareness; and so, in due course, the Civics Class was born. It was the joint brainchild of Somervell and Gollancz. It was not confined to the study of civic institutions, but tackled the war and other great issues of the day such as imperialism; militarism and the League of Nations; and capitalism *v* socialism. Enrolment in the class was to be voluntary, with an undertaking to attend weekly for at least a term. When all had been arranged, says Gollancz, 'we went down to see Fisher. David was bland. I was eloquent. Quite a series of interviews followed. In the end, just as Christmas was looming, Fisher laughingly agreed.'[62] In fact, he was being both bold and liberal-minded in giving the go-ahead to the experiment. Such a project a generation later would be commonplace. At the time that it was launched, in January 1917, it was considered a radical innovation – and was regarded with the deepest suspicion by the more conservative members of the staff. However, 32 boys enrolled for the inaugural sessions; they were treated to a series of lectures on such issues as parliamentary reform, the position of women and the future of the Empire. The experiment was off to an unflamboyant start and soon became highly popular.

The next significant development arose directly out of the Civics Class. It was the launch of a political journal, *A Public School Looks at the World* – or, as it soon became known, *The Pubber*. This was intended to supplement the official school magazine, *The*

174

Reptonian, which confined itself to reporting facts and was basically non-controversial. *The Pubber*, by contrast, never shrank from controversy – though it looked on itself as a serious and high-minded journal which had been founded, in the words of its opening editorial, 'in the belief that the study of politics is the most absorbing study in the world.' Once again the headmaster's consent had been sought in advance by Somervell and Gollancz, and once again he had 'laughingly agreed' – convinced, no doubt, by Somervell's assurance that those behind the magazine had no desire to revolutionize society. Certainly no exception could have been taken to the first issue, which appeared in June 1917 and which included an article by the previous headmaster, William Temple, calling for widespread educational reform. The second issue likewise appeared blameless: it reproduced a Speech Day sermon by Fisher urging self-sacrifice in war and peace in order to bring about a better world governed by Christian principles and brotherhood.

Soon, however, the storm clouds were gathering. First, a letter appearing in the normally staid columns of *The Reptonian* attacked Somervell and Gollancz by implication for 'turning Repton into a collection of little prigs'. This was followed by a schoolboy essay on patriotism in the issue of *The Pubber* for November 1917 which declared it to be worthless if inspired by narrow self-interest but noble if it was based on a genuine love of humanity. The piece was denounced for vitiating the school's healthy patriotism. The upshot was that subsequent issues of *The Pubber* printed an assurance that 'nothing that appears in this paper is to be taken as expressing the opinion of the school as a whole'. Every word in *The Pubber* was read by Fisher as censor prior to publication; and the issue of December 1917, which had been intended to include letters for and against the article on patriotism, carried instead a letter from the headmaster himself (in addition to an irenic editorial which had won his approval):

Sir, it is perhaps desirable that I should state in your columns that I have censored three letters sent to you by correspondents, of which two severely criticised, the third warmly commended, this paper. I censored the three impartially because I thought that the

175

chief cause of adverse criticism and the necessity of commendation to balance it were removed by your editorial, and that anything likely to perpetuate an undesirable controversy should not appear in your columns simultaneously with that which is designed, and, in my opinion, well designed, to remove all cause for it.[63]

The controversy was now rapidly approaching its climax. On 19 February 1918 an impassioned discussion took place in the school debating society on the motion that, 'In the opinion of this house, it is disgraceful that Conscientious Objectors, whether genuine or not, should be disfranchised.' The audience was five times the normal size, scores of younger boys having been dragooned by reactionary prefects into attending in the hope that they would then vote as 'patriots' against the motion. The hope was only partially realized. The motion was won in the Upper House by twelve votes. In the Lower House it was lost – but by only twenty votes, which showed that many juniors had defied orders and voted according to their liberal consciences. The atmosphere of the debate had not been helped by a statement issued beforehand by one of the masters, a priest named Alfred Agard-Butler. He had declared, 'on behalf of himself and all other Reptonians', that it was a disgrace to Repton that the motion had been permitted at all; that, in the days when he had been at Repton, the proposers would have been ducked in the horsepond; and that it would be a 'crying scandal' if the motion were passed in either house.[64] Unfortunately, his suggestion of a ducking was heeded. A senior boy who had spoken in favour of the motion was thrown into the Steinyard, a local stream, to the open delight of Snape and like-minded militants. Other boys were mercilessly bullied. A deputation from the opposing camp (including Somervell but not Gollancz, who was considered too fiery) waited on the headmaster to protest against such acts of hooliganism, Fisher, conscious that the situation was getting out of hand, endeavoured to tread a middle way. He addressed first the masters and then the boys on the unfortunate nature of their divisions. According to Gollancz's account,

he lectured us all pretty severely: allotted blame – a fifth to David and me, the rest to Pruke [i.e., Snape] and his confrères: and

176

announced penalties – in inverse proportion. I was to be forbidden, for a period unnamed, to address the Civics Class: and a conservative boy was to be associated with Amyas [Ross, the current editor] in the editorship of *The Pubber*. A peroration, relieved by touches of humour, exonerated David and me from the charge, now insistent, of pacifism.[65]

By this time the fifth (and final) issue of *The Pubber* was about to go to press. It included a leader denouncing the Versailles declaration, which put an end to any hope of peace by agreement, as a blunder. A second leader, arguing the declaration's merits, was hastily cobbled together by Fisher and Somervell and inserted as a counterweight to the first.

If that particular issue of the journal had appeared in Repton alone, all might yet have been well and the two radical ringleaders, Somervell and Gollancz, have retained their positions on the staff. Unfortunately they were misguided enough to allow it to be put on sale in addition at a radical bookseller's in London's Charing Cross Road known as the 'Bomb Shop'. This at once brought it to the attention of the War Office and sealed its promoters' fate. For, once the affair had passed outside the narrow confines of Repton, it ceased to be a merely domestic matter and became one of which the military authorities felt that they must take cognisance.

How much pressure they actually put on Fisher is difficult to determine. They had certainly for some time had their eye on Gollancz, who was supposed to be justifying his release from normal military duties by helping with the Repton OTC but who was now suspected of pacifist leanings. According to Gollancz they had concluded 'not only that Repton was a hotbed of pacifism but that the entire neighbourhood from Derby to Burton-on-Trent and between the other two points of the compass was aware of it'.[66] The incident of *The Pubber* and the Bomb Shop seemed to them the final straw. According to some accounts they threatened to disqualify the Repton OTC and refuse a commission to any member of it unless Fisher got rid of Gollancz. Whether the threat was quite as drastic as this or whether some other form of military pressure was applied, Fisher (who may also have been motivated by the dissension among the staff) decided to act. Three days before the beginning of the summer term Gollancz, who was taking part in an OTC course at Chelsea Barracks, received a letter from the headmaster informing him that his services at Repton would no longer be required. The news could hardly have come as a surprise to him, though even then he refused to submit without a struggle. He sent a telegram to Fisher requesting an immediate interview in London. Fisher agreed, and the interview took place in Gollancz's lodgings. 'I remember feeling that I rather liked him. I remember two, but only two, of his sentences: "I have supported you consistently for a year and a half" and "David Somervell is the most obstinate man I've ever had to deal with".'[67] Following his dismissal Gollancz forsook teaching for publishing, and enjoyed immense success in his new career. For him dismissal may, in the long run, have been no bad thing. And, from his publishing pinnacle, he was able to look back in 1953 and be surprisingly generous to his erstwhile opponent: 'He gave us our chance, and few others would have done so. My major emotion, accordingly, is one of gratitude.'[68]

Meanwhile, back at Repton, Fisher had to pick up the pieces. The Civics Class was suspended for the duration of the war and *The Pubber* suppressed. The news of Gollancz's dismissal came as a tremendous shock to the boys. Fisher announced it formally to the school on the first day of term. 'The Boss's speech,' a boy wrote to Gollancz afterwards, 'went down awfully badly. It sounded as if he didn't believe what he said about you, but hadn't the guts to face criticism in county circles.'[69] Gollancz himself received many letters of condolence from both boys and masters – including even one from his old opponent, Snape.

Fisher found Somervell a less straightforward nut to crack – it would have been awkward to have sacked a senior master of established position outright. He dealt with him as fairly as he could. He began by asking him to refrain from any political discussion, whether in school or out of it. Somervell refused to give such an undertaking, and Fisher accepted his refusal. Somervell was even allowed to start up a small and unofficial kind of civics class. But then, on the rumour of fresh demands from the War Office, things took an uglier turn. Fisher felt compelled to order that all political activites in the school should cease immediately.

178

His demand was met with protests. 'These boys are impossible,' he complained to Somervell. 'They will take nothing on authority.' Somervell was again asked for a pledge of silence on all political matters. He refused to give such a pledge, and eventually agreed to leave the school voluntarily 'for the duration'. He took a temporary job with the Ministry of Munitions and then a mastership at Tonbridge School. He never returned to Repton. Snape told the Army Class (according to Gollancz): 'We've got rid of the last of the traitors.'[70] Somervell blossomed out into a historian of distinction. He wrote lives of Gladstone and Disraeli, an account of George V's reign and a one-volume abridgement of Toynbee's ten-volume *Study of History*. He had earlier collaborated with Gollancz in two accounts of their Repton experiment, *Political Education at a Public School* and *The School and the World*, published in 1918 and 1919 respectively – though, in deference to Fisher's wishes, the name of the school was omitted.

Although the row with Gollancz and Somervell occupied only a small proportion of Fisher's headmastership, it has seemed right to chronicle it in considerable detail. It throws much light on his powers of judgement and on his ability to deal with a complex situation made much more complex because of its arising in the middle of a world war. It must be remembered that Fisher was three years younger than Somervell and only six years older than Gollancz, though infinitely more mature in judgement – had not Temple, back in 1914, credited him with the maturity of a man of forty? Looking back on the affair in old age, he described it to William Purcell as an 'invaluable experience'. He had, he emphasized, consulted none of his colleagues on the staff throughout the controversy because of their own acute divisions.

There was no single master that I felt I could pick out to give me advice which I could accept... I had to face it entirely on my own, weighing it this way and that way; and I think I can say that, when the moment came I *could* act, I seized it with both hands and was perfectly clear what the action should be. Now that was a lesson which has lasted me for the rest of my life.

The nub of the problem, as Fisher saw it, was to balance the liberal and conservative elements in the controversy: he felt that he must neither quench the 'smoking flax' of the progressive nor refuse to allow reactionary forces their say. The lesson he had learned then was 'not to make up my mind too quickly, not to apply any fixed principle or any fixed rule or any fixed attitude, but to weigh and consider the liberal and the conservative: the two great forces, if I might almost say, of the Gospel as against the Church'.[71] It was a lesson that Fisher was to apply in future years as he grappled with the massive ecclesiastical controversies that were to overshadow his reign as Archbishop of Canterbury.

It is tempting to think that both Somervell and Gollancz might have fared better under Fisher's predecessor, William Temple, with his more progressive ideas. This may well not have been the case. Temple became a governor of the school after ceasing to be its headmaster; and throughout the controversy Fisher received the loyal backing of the governors. Indeed, Somervell, who had been a close friend of Temple at one time, admitted to the Archbishop's widow after his death that they had drifted apart after 1917, 'partly because we got rather annoyed with each other over the "Repton row"... I think my feeling was that he was so anxious to be loyal and correct in his relations with his successor that he was rather less than fair to me.'[72] And, in any event, the 'institution' would probably have proved in the end too much for Temple, whatever his personal feelings might have been. As indeed it had proved for Fisher. He had, as Gollancz admitted, allowed him an inordinate amount of rope – but in the end was content to let him hang himself. It was chiefly the war, and all the impassioned feelings that the war engendered, that brought the Somervell–Gollancz experiments to a premature end. To a more enlightened generation it may seem incredible that such a sensible and unsensational programme of political education should have been deemed unpatriotic and its advocates traitors. But, in the climate of 1914–18, such must almost inevitably have been the case; and it is doubtful whether any other public-school headmaster of the period would have behaved any differently from Fisher. Charles Smyth, a boy at Repton at the time, must have recognized this. He doubtless spoke for many of his more thoughtful contemporaries when he later

180

observed: 'It was only during the Somervell–Gollancz crisis that we suddenly woke up to the moral strength and power of his [Fisher's] personality, and regarded him with an entirely new respect, enhanced by the awareness that he was handling a momentarily unruly team of older men.'[73]

*　　*　　*　　*　　*

After all the excitements of the wartime years Fisher was able to settle back in 1919 into the comparatively uneventful routine of a public school at peace with itself in a world at peace. The 1920s proved a prosperous period in the history of Repton. Numbers rose steadily in the post-war boom that affected most public schools. Repton shone both academically and athletically. There was an increasing flow of scholarship-winners to the universities following significant changes to the curriculum in 1921 which made possible a longer period of specialized scholarship work for those capable of benefiting from it. Fisher remained in the background, the efficient administrator waving his organizational wand to ensure the smooth functioning of the school. As one Church dignitary is alleged to have remarked: 'When Geoffrey was Headmaster of Repton everybody said, "What a good school Repton is", but nobody ever said, "What a great headmaster Fisher is!"' By the early 1930s, however, he was beginning to feel the strain of his task.

In the summer of 1932 Temple, by now Archbishop of York, came to Repton for a meeting of the school governors; when it was over, Fisher accompanied him on a walk through the grounds in the course of which he unburdened himself to the older man. He told Temple that he had been at Repton for 18 years, which he thought was long enough. He had no desire to leave, but felt that he ought not to go on. When Temple asked if there was a particular reason, Fisher replied: 'When a boy gets seriously ill, as occasionally happens, I cannot stand the strain. Once upon a time I could.' He had in fact only recently gone through a period of acute anxiety. The school had been hit by an epidemic of measles and mastoids. Three boys had died and two others had only just survived. Fisher was still feeling the strain.

181

Temple asked him what he wanted to do instead and Fisher, no doubt looking back nostalgically on his childhood, replied: 'I would like to be a country parson.' Temple advised him to apply for a rural living to any bishops he happened to know, and went on without a pause: 'The man I want to succeed you is John Christie.' Fisher's immediate reaction was (as he recalled it to William Purcell): 'Upon my word, not only does he think I have been here long enough, but he has already chosen my successor! Certainly it is time I got out!' He said that he had never felt more deflated than at that moment. He did not know, nor could Temple tell him, that at that moment his name was before the Prime Minister for a senior appointment in the Church. 'Well, the deflation lasted for I suppose a fortnight or so, and then one morning, before going into first lesson, I opened a letter from the Prime Minister offering me the bishopric of Chester.'[74] Fisher's nomination had in fact come about largely through the efforts of Temple. He had pressed his claims on the Archbishop of Canterbury, Cosmo Lang, who, in a letter to the Premier, Ramsay MacDonald, had bracketed Fisher equal first with the Bishop of Gibraltar, Nugent Hicks, in his list of possible successors to H.L. Paget as Bishop of Chester. Lang dutifully sang Fisher's praises to MacDonald – 'a man of very distinguished academic career at Oxford, with very broad sympathies ... would probably make an excellent bishop' – though he would really have preferred Hicks.*[75]

Fisher himself had no hesitation in accepting the Prime Minister's offer. He went through the motions of consulting Temple, but apparently wrote off to MacDonald before receiving Temple's reply. The reply, when it came, was suitably flattering. Temple wrote that he very much wanted to see Fisher in charge of a diocese. Of all the sees in the province over which he presided, he said, Chester would probably suit Fisher best in its combination of town and country and in its varying brands of churchmanship.

---

* He wrote to MacDonald's secretary after hearing that Chester would go to Fisher: 'I am rather sorry for the Bishop of Gibraltar's sake that he has been passed over as he finds the continuance of his present ceaseless travelling [the diocese covered all southern Europe] very bad for his health.' MacDonald made amends later in the year by appointing Hicks Bishop of Lincoln.

The school was genuinely sorry to see him go. In his Speech Day address in June Temple declared: 'His skill and efficiency was subordinated to clear educational principles and high idealism.'[76]

$$* \qquad * \qquad * \qquad * \qquad *$$

Just how good a headmaster was he? Victor Gollancz reports his Repton landlady as dubbing him 'not a bad man, though he *has* raised himself from nothing'. Gollancz himself pays tribute more than once in his book to Fisher's administrative ability: 'first and foremost a brilliant executive (a far better one, for what that is worth, than the saintly Temple), he was doing a businessman's job and doing it with remarkable efficiency.'[77] Later, in a long descriptive passage, Gollancz paints a graphic picture of a masters' meeting at which Fisher had displayed 'the clear-headedness, the grasp of detail, and the ability to mug up a boring subject that would have made [him] so admirable a civil servant or business executive.'[78] Efficiency was the quality in Fisher's make-up that struck almost all observers. In a tribute to his old headmaster Charles Smyth remarked:

How he got through all the work he did with only a part-time secretary remains a mystery and a legend in the history of Repton. Looking back, it is obvious that he was gifted with a phenomenally quick and active brain, and with that faculty of recognising at once the real issue, and sifting non-essentials from essentials, which is supposed to be the intellectual precipitate of Oxford Greats.[79]

One of the most penetrating analyses of Fisher's character comes not from an admiring disciple but towards the end of Victor Gollancz's account of the row in which they were the two main protagonists. Fisher, in his opinion, was

passionless, at any rate in the realm of ideas… He believes, but with a belief itself devoid of excess, in [the golden mean]. He distrusts sentiment, which he confuses, or is apt to confuse, with sentimentality… His kindliness, which no one could question, stops just short, just a little, of warmth. Order, efficiency, discipline … are the values that tend to frighten the more glowing ones away from his spiritual landscape. Ranks, classes and hierarchies, within reasonable limits, seem inherent, in his vision of reality, in the nature of things.

Gollancz is prepared to concede that Fisher was a moderate liberal.

To call him intransigent, narrow-minded, would be unfair: he sees the other man's point of view. His preference, too, is against oppression, cruelty, injustice, racial discrimination, all the rest of it, but he would never really *battle* against them – battle with his whole being as Shaftesbury battled, as Wilberforce battled. He resembles, perhaps, the average foreigner's idea of the typical Englishman.[80]

Gollancz recalls a remark that Fisher once made to him at a moment of crisis: 'If it's a choice between all this turmoil and what you call deadness, I prefer deadness.' Political education, therefore, says Gollancz, could have made little appeal to such a personality as this. 'It meant noise, enthusiasm, difficulties, controversy; and these were repugnant to him.' And yet he had given the would-be reformers their chance. 'Why? Because he is fair and, up to a point, open-minded, and *wanted* to give us our chance. He suspected, I think, that our experiment would succeed in a humdrum sort of way; and both the success and the humdrumness would have pleased him.' The nub of Gollancz's critique comes in the following passage.

Schoolmastering, with its struggles and strivings, was by no means his vocation, any more than priesthood is. He was called to something quite different; to the work, first and foremost, of preserving institutions, and then, should he be able, of enhancing their prosperity... With a different background he could have become, quite as easily, a top civil servant or a distinguished proconsul: but always a cautious and 'safe' (albeit impeccably honourable) one, and always devoted above everything ... to the stability and prosperity of the institution he served.[81]

Let the last word remain with Charles Smyth:

184

When all is said, it is chiefly the impression of complete integrity and of ordinary human friendliness that abides: and perhaps no one who has never as a boy felt the Boss put his arm around his shoulders and heard him chuckle, 'Khh! Ha-ha! Well done!', can fully relish the late Canon Leonard Prestige's characterisation of the present Primate of All England [this was written in 1957] as 'the greatest schoolmaster – and the greatest schoolboy – who has ever sat upon the Chair of St Augustine.'[82]

*   *   *   *   *

Early on in his episcopate Fisher was shown a copy of a parish magazine in which the vicar had remarked that he could not quite understand *why* the new bishop had been appointed. He had had no parochial experience, nor did he apparently possess any particular abilities to qualify him for the job. However, the vicar concluded, as they had been praying about the matter, and as this was apparently the answer to their prayers, he supposed that they must make the best of it. Fisher quoted these observations in his inaugural address to his diocesan conference – and was off to a flying start.[83] Indeed, so successful was he in his seven-year reign as Bishop of Chester that it was soon to be a case of 'Friend, go up higher.'

The new diocese was London, and for some time it was a question of whether Fisher or Bishop Cyril Garbett of Winchester, who was twelve years older, would be chosen. The scales were evenly balanced at Downing Street between these two front-runners, but eventually Archbishop Lang came down definitely in favour of Fisher. He recommended him to the Prime Minister, by now Neville Chamberlain, who hesitated, however, before taking the plunge. His doubts centred on the spiritual, as opposed to the intellectual, side of Fisher's character. Lang was soon able to reassure the Premier on this point. The Bishop of Chester, he had discovered, was undoubtedly a man of genuine deep personal religion. 'His piety is that of the best type of English Layman... His religious life is not easily seen for two reasons: (*a*) he is very shy and humble about it (very English), and (*b*) because his other gifts of intellect and administration are vastly more obvious to the world.'[84] Fisher was duly nominated. His new diocese, after nearly 40 years of the popular but lax rule of A.F. Winnington-Ingram, who had held it since 1901, was in a state of ecclesiastical chaos. The task of coping with the administrative backlog was likened to the cleansing of an Augean stable. It was, of course, tailor-made for an organizational wizard like Fisher, though he could hardly have foreseen, when he accepted the post, that almost the whole of his London episcopate would be spent under the shadow of the Second World War. So well did he perform there that he was even considered in 1942, when Lang resigned, as a possibility for Canterbury – an influential section of the Conservative Party pressing his name on Winston Churchill as a preferable alternative to William Temple, whose left-wing ideology they disliked. Temple, however, was so much the stronger candidate that he was Churchill's obvious choice and Fisher had to wait.

But not for long. Temple's premature death in October 1944 again left Canterbury vacant, and Fisher's chance had come. His chief rival for the primacy was the Bishop of Chichester, George Bell. But Bell was now a marked man as far as Churchill was concerned – marked with the Prime Minister's disapproval for his wartime speeches in the House of Lords denouncing as immoral the RAF's 'obliteration bombing' offensive. So, in spite of his great reputation abroad as well as at home, he paid the price of his outspokenness and stayed put at Chichester – and the ex-headmaster rather than the prophet was chosen for Canterbury. In the oft-quoted words of Donald MacKinnon, 'The historian of the Church of England may yet recognise that the worst misfortune to befall its leadership at the end of the war was less the premature death of William Temple than his succession by Fisher of London and not by Bell of Chichester.'[85] That must remain a matter of opinion. The burden of being an archbishop could well have lessened Bell's effectiveness on the ecumenical stage, for which his lighter work in Sussex gave him the necessary freedom. Moreover, as Fisher's *Church Times* obituary put it, 'The hand of providence can be seen in giving the Church an administrator when the work of the prophet [i.e., Temple] was done.'[86]

In many ways he was indeed the man for the hour. He tackled the multifarious post-war problems which beset the Church of

England with his customary energy and efficiency. If, in retrospect, the Church during his primacy gives the impression of a Church obsessed with its own domestic problems, at the time those problems seemed urgent of solution. Fisher's friendliness, good humour and lack of pomposity always went down well at the humbler level, though the headmaster remained very much in the background – and sometimes pounced on malefactors with the equivalent of a summons to the study. On the wider Anglican stage he presided with distinction over two Lambeth Conferences. On the ecumenical front he set in motion the long (and eventually abortive) series of efforts to achieve organizational union with one or more of the Free Churches. And, at the very end of his primacy, he paid his historic visit to Pope John XXIII at the Vatican.

He resigned at the end of May 1961; and a mild element of controversy entered the behind-the-scenes negotiations concerning his successor. The most obvious candidate was the Archbishop of York, Michael Ramsey, Fisher's old pupil from Repton days, of whom he had prophesied in that final school report that he 'might do quite well'.*

The Prime Minister, Harold Macmillan, backed Ramsey, an Anglo-Catholic. Fisher would much have preferred the Evangelical Bishop of Bradford, Donald Coggan. He had been perfectly happy to see Ramsey succeed Garbett at York, but since then had come to feel that he was suspicious of reunion schemes and would not therefore play a leading part in the Ecumenical Movement. Moreover, Fisher doubted Ramsey's ability to cope with the Lambeth workload – he was more interested in 'theologizing' than in administration. Macmillan, on the other hand, felt more of a rapport with Ramsey than with any other of the potential candidates. He admired his capacious intellect and deep spirituality. In the end, after all the due processes of consultation had been studiously observed, he stuck to his guns

---

* The combination of an Old Reptonian Archbishop of York and an Archbishop of Canterbury who had been his headmaster at Repton must have been unique. Even more remarkable was the occasion when *three* future Archbishops of Canterbury, none of them yet consecrated, attended a service in Repton School Chapel in June 1919 at which Temple preached. Yet another coincidence took place in York Minster ten years later, when Temple was enthroned as Archbishop by the man he had succeeded as Headmaster of Repton, Lionel Ford, by then Dean of York.

and chose Ramsey. In his own words, 'I thought that we had had enough of Martha [i.e., Fisher] and that it was time for some Mary.'[87]

Fisher bore the setback philosophically enough, but Ramsey had a memorable conversation with the Prime Minister a few days after his appointment had been announced. 'Fisher seems to disapprove of you,' Macmillan began. 'Yes,' said Ramsey, 'he was my headmaster and headmasters often know the worst.' To which Macmillan retorted: 'He may have been *your* headmaster, but he is not going to be mine!'[88]

Just as Fisher had been born in a country rectory, so he was destined to spend his last years in one. It was in fact a redundant rectory, that of Trent, near Sherborne, Dorset; and, in return for being allowed to occupy it, Fisher gave what pastoral help he could to the rector, a housemaster at Sherborne School. His retirement was far from idle, and he could often be seen, an elderly man in a cloth cap, on his way to the village to post the many letters he wrote every day. 'My correspondence is voluminous,' he would explain with a chuckle, 'and some of the people who get it don't like it!'[89] He delighted during those twilight years to wade into ecclesiastical controversies, and caused his successor no small embarrassment in the matter of the Anglican–Methodist reunion scheme by advocating a course diametrically opposed to that being urged from Lambeth. Indeed, towards the end of his life, it was said that, for the sake of the peace of the Church, his wife Rosamond was quietly suppressing most of the letters he put in his out-tray each day. It was the headmaster at work still, wanting to have his finger in every pie.

On 14 September 1972, being then 85, he suffered a mild stroke; and it was characteristic of his practical mind that, when Rosamond rushed to assist him as he lay prostrate, he exclaimed to her: 'Don't bother me, dear, I'm busy dying.'[90] He died in hospital the next day and was buried in a vault beneath the churchyard at Trent. It had been a busy, fulfilled life – and in death, as in the moment of birth, he was to lie beneath the shadows of a country church.

EPILOGUE: STEPPING-STONES TO LAMBETH

How do our six candidates rank in the league table of public-school headmasters? Perhaps only one of the six, Frederick Temple, would quality for the epithet 'great': he was undoubtedly a greater headmaster than he was an archbishop. But two others, Benson and Fisher, came very near to greatness. Benson just failed because, although he put Wellington firmly on the public-school map, he ruled to a large extent through fear rather than love. Fisher just failed because, although he maintained Repton as a great public school, he lacked the spark to set it on fire. Of the remaining three archbishops-in-waiting, William Temple was a great man but emphatically *not* a great headmaster, while Longley and Tait were middle-of-the-road heads who kept their respective shows on the road without breaking any box-office records.

All six, however, were exceptionally *able* men. Intellectually they were all in the top class, acquiring their firsts in Classics at Oxford or Cambridge with nonchalant ease. They all enjoyed good health – and sufficient stamina to maintain a schedule of work which would have left most men gasping for breath. Tait was always at his desk by 7 a.m. and seldom in bed before midnight; Frederick Temple would correct exam papers in an uninterrupted stint lasting 17 or 18 hours; Benson's Herculean labours reduced him, he told a friend, to a humming top in perpetual motion. But all six were men of ambition who were motivated by an urge to succeed in the top scholastic job to which they had been promoted.

How professional were they by modern standards? In one sense they were highly *un*professional, in that not one of them had undergone any specific training in the art of teaching. But in their day, of course, a good university degree was considered more than adequate, and a double first in Classics an automatic passport to the highest educational appointment. Academics would glide from school to university and then, after perhaps a few years as a don, straight back to school again with no questions asked about their ability to *teach*. Benson and Fisher were the most professional of the six in the sense that they had experience of other schools, so the governors of Wellington and Repton were at least appointing teachers to the top job. But Longley was a simple parish priest at the time of his appointment to Harrow, and appears to have been chosen as one totally unconnected with the warring factions among the staff. Tait and William Temple were Oxford dons who went straight to the headmaster's study at Rugby and Repton without any intervening period in which to learn the scholastic ropes. Frederick Temple was also an ex-don, but more recently had been a college principal; he at least was already a big name in educational circles at the time of his appointment to Rugby.

Why did our six characters choose to go into teaching in the first place? It had been with reluctance in the case of both Tait and William Temple: Tait because he had doubts about his capacity to measure up to the job, Temple because he was so wedded to the life of an Oxford don as to be loath to exchange it for that of a schoolmaster. Tait was eventually talked into it by his friends, and Temple by the combined importuning of the Repton staff and governors. But both Tait and Temple also looked for divine guidance in the matter. Tait told the Almighty that his decision to apply for the Rugby headship was a step which might lead to 'much good or much evil' and that the responsibility of the job seemed 'every day more aweful'. Once he had secured it, however, he looked forward to dedicating 'my whole life to the grand work of Christian education'. William Temple prayed for three hours and then 'I knew perfectly well what I had got to do, and that was to accept.' Frederick Temple had few qualms; he told Tait that the Rugby headship was the post on earth which he would most like to fill. But, as Principal of Kneller Hall at the time of Tait's resignation, he was too conscientious, and too dedicated to his vocation of training working-class teachers, to wish to forsake it for the fleshpots of Rugby. So it was not until the headship had been offered him a second time round that he found himself able to accept it.

Benson was another who found it difficult to make up his mind. For long he dithered between the headmastership of Wellington and a don's life at Cambridge. In the end it was the challenge of a pioneering job in shaping a new school to his own image, rather than mere ambition, which persuaded him to accept Wellington. The simplest reaction to the offer of a public-school headship came from Fisher. He rushed into a colleague's room and collapsed in laughter – at the absurdity of a 27-year-old being appointed to a post of such fearful responsibility. He was the youngest of the six at the time of his appointment, though William Temple had been only a year older, Benson 29 and Tait 30. Longley and Frederick Temple, the oldest of the six, were still only in their mid-thirties when they went to Harrow and Rugby.

Having advanced to the top of the educational tree at such an early age, all six men were still young enough to rise a lot higher when they laid down their headmasterships. Longley, Frederick Temple and Fisher stepped straight from the head's study to the bishops' bench; Tait arrived there after a few years as Dean of Carlisle. Only Benson and William Temple suffered demotion in the short term. Benson, indeed, accepted a substantial cut in salary to take up a cathedral canonry: he seems to have been genuinely inspired to devote his energies to the higher education of the clergy, though it was not long before the prospect of another pioneering job persuaded him to exchange Lincoln for Truro. In the case of William Temple, his growing reputation as an anti-establishment gadfly caused him to think long and hard before accepting Lloyd George's offer of a mitre.

There can be no doubt that all six of these headmasters were aware of the spiritual opportunities awaiting them at their schools. Thomas Arnold once informed the Rugby trustees that he must ever feel himself, as headmaster, the 'real and proper religious instructor of the boys'; and his successor, Tait, told his future wife that there was no situation of so directly pastoral a nature as his – 'how very few clergy have parishioners who are so willing to be led as my boys!' Although Longley at Harrow was handicapped by the absence of a chapel and had to rely more on his personal contacts with the boys, Tait was able to exercise a great deal of religious influence on the school through his sermons. He may not have been in the same preaching league as the two Temples, but, on set-piece occasions such as the death of a boy or master, he would give rein to his feelings and exercise a profound effect on his congregation.

Frederick and William Temple were in a class very much of their own as pulpit orators. According to one colleague the former held the whole school in his hand with his religious fervour and preaching power. He would give reign to his feelings with the tears streaming down his face in a manner that went straight to the hearts of the boys as he strove to instil in them a 'quiet sense of duty'. It was in his chapel services that he really let himself go, though his classroom lessons in divinity were, in their way, equally memorable. His formidable powers as a preacher were inherited by his son William, who, like his father, really came into his own in the field of religion. His sermons too were in a class apart. If Benson's sermons were not quite so powerful, at least he took immense trouble in their preparation and they impressed observers as deeply moving. As for Fisher, he says that, as a clerical headmaster, he found the chapel at Repton his special care and delight. Of course, one may argue that he could have found it an equal delight and preached just as effectively as a layman; but Fisher felt that for him personally the fact of being ordained added immensely to his power to influence the religious life of the school. Certainly all the six headmasters discussed in this book exercised such an influence in their different ways, whether or not such influence derived from their possession of holy orders.

How then did they rank overall as headmasters? Of course, they were all men of their time who in many ways reflected the close-knit, élitist world of the public schools over which they presided. One cannot pretend that, with the exception of the younger Temple, any of them was reformist at heart. Benson set out to shape a school which, in its conception, was to be different from the others; but, in the event, he turned it into one very like its fellows. William Temple began at Repton full of reforming zeal, but found the system too much for him and achieved little or nothing in transforming the public-school pattern he inherited; Fisher regarded it as his duty to preserve that pattern inviolate.

*   *   *   *   *

Longley may be dismissed as a well-bred gentleman whose inability to maintain discipline led to unlimited 'skylarking', and Tait damned by faint praise or stigmatized as 'hardly a success'; but Frederick Temple was indisputably a great head. Stern but just, he was a hero to the boys and revered by the masters as their 'glorious chieftain'. He believed in liberty without licence and, in his dealings with the school, delighted to apply the common touch.

Benson is perhaps the most complex character of the six. He may not have been as great a headmaster as Temple, but he was certainly a great actor – and an undeniable social climber. He suffered both from fiery rages and from fits of depression (though, by the time he arrived at Lambeth, he had learned to keep both weaknesses under control). He had undoubted charisma, but it was ineffective in securing him popularity among the boys. He was an immensely dominant personality. He dominated his wife and family, and he dominated Wellington throughout his long association with the school. In this he contrasts sharply with Fisher at Repton, who resisted the temptation to implant his own personality on his pupils. As a headmaster he never captured their imagination except at the subconscious level – but this was considered by at least one pupil as a good thing. Fisher would have been classed by David Somervell as one of those 'commonplace' characters who often seemed to make better headmasters than 'star' performers. The latter, as William Temple put it, could provide the luxuries of education but lacked the power to provide its necessities. Temple himself was less successful as a headmaster, though greater as a man.

So we have our six headmasters: men of immense ability and of talent who, in the fullness of time, were each promoted to sit on St Augustine's throne at Canterbury. They formed an educational apostolic succession of their own: six archbishops out of eight almost in a row, Davidson and Lang being the odd men out.

It is a rare coincidence, unlikely to be repeated, that six headmasters should have been elevated successively to the supreme position of power within the Church of England. It cannot be denied, however, that all six shone out among the episcopal ruck and were of obviously primatial mettle. Their promotion at particular moments in the Church's history may have depended on who happened to be Prime Minister at the time, but none of them was noticeably inferior to his potential rivals. A headmaster, then as now, exercised immense power and influence in his own narrow world. It would be a natural transition from one such sphere of influence to another: from Harrow, Rugby, Wellington and Repton to Canterbury and Lambeth. Their fellow diocesans may at times have seemed like the staff and their clergy like the boys, but at least the motivation was the same: to bring them all that much nearer to the Kingdom of Heaven.

REFERENCES

CHAPTER 1: PASTORS AND MASTERS

1. P.G. Wodehouse, *Meet Mr Mulliner* (1956 edn), p.68.
2. David Newsome, *Godliness and Good Learning*, p.2.
3. *ibid.*, p.2.
4. J.R. de S. Honey, *Tom Brown's Universe*, p.311.
5. *ibid.*, p.308
6. *ibid.*, p.313.
7. H. Hensley Henson, *Retrospect of an Unimportant Life*, Vol. 1, p.20.
8. T. Balston, *Dr Balston at Eton*, pp.51–2.
9. Honey, pp.310, 312.
10. *ibid.*, p.312n.
11. Grahame Greene (ed.) *The Old School* (1984 edn), pp.117–18.
12. Honey, p.318.
13. *ibid.*, pp.319–20
14. F.A. Iremonger, *William Temple*, pp.14–15.
15. Honey, p.320.
16. *ibid.*, pp.240–1.
17. Newsome, p.x.

CHAPTER 2: TEACHER OF TROLLOPES

1. Anthony Trollope, *An Autobiography* (1946 edn), p.33.
2. *ibid.*, pp.23–4.
3. *ibid.*, p.24.
4. *ibid.*, pp.29–30.
5. A.M.G. Stephenson, *The Victorian Archbishops of Canterbury*, p.19.

6.   Percy M. Thornton, *Harrow School and its surroundings*, p.274.
7.   Stephenson, pp.19–20.
8.   E.W. Howson and G.T. Warner (eds), *Harrow School*, p.81.
9.   Thornton, pp.264–5.
10. John Rodgers, *The Old Public Schools of England*, p.75.
11. Trollope, p.33.
12. *ibid.*, p.30.
13. Rodgers, p.76.
14. Charles Mallet, 'Old Harrow Days', in *The Nineteenth Century and After*, January–June 1931, p.90.
15. J. Fischer Williams, *Harrow*, pp.74–5.
16. *ibid.*, p.78.
17. Mallet, p.91.
18. P.H.M. Bryant, *Harrow*, pp.60–4.
19. Howson and Warner, p.81.
20. *Church Times*, 23 September 1898.
21. Trollope, p.33.
22. *Letters of Queen Victoria*, 2nd Series, Vol. 1, p.545.
23. Thornton, p.267.
24. J.G. Cotton Minchin, *Old Harrow Days*, p.94.
25. Howson and Warner, p.82.
26. Minchin, p.94.
27. Williams, p.86.
28. Thornton, p.267.
29. *ibid.*, p.275.
30. Minchin, p.95.
31. Bryant, p.59.
32. Thornton, p.276.
33. *ibid.*, pp.276–7.
34. Howson and Warner, p.86.
35. *ibid.*, p.84
36. Trollope, pp.34–5
37. Anthony Trollope, 'Public Schools', in *The Fortnightly Review*, Vol. 2, August–November 1865, pp.482–3.
38. N. John Hall, *Trollope: A Biography*, p.387.
39. Trollope, 'Public Schools', p.483.
40. *ibid.*
41. *ibid.*
42. Richard P. Stebbins, 'Trollope at Harrow School', in *The Trollopian,* No. 1, Summer 1945, pp.42–3.

43. Bryant, p.59.
44. Minchin, p.92.
45. Howson and Warner, p.84.
46. *ibid.*
47. *ibid.*
48. *ibid.*
49. Hall, p.17.
50. Thornton, p.268.
51. Peter Hinchliff, *John William Colenso*, pp.29–30.
52. *ibid.*
53. Bernard Palmer, *Gadfly for God*, pp.32–3.
54. A.M.G. Stephenson, *Anglicanism and the Lambeth Conferences*, pp.38–41.
55. J.R. de S. Honey, *Tom Brown's Universe*, pp.297–8.
56. Williams, p.82.
57. *ibid.*, p. 86
58. *ibid.*
59. R.T. Davidson and W. Benham, *Archibald Campbell Tait*, Vol. 1, p.206.
60. Philip Guedalla (ed.), *Gladstone and Palmerston*, p.232.

CHAPTER 3: IN THE SHADOW OF ARNOLD

1. A.C. Bickley, *Archibald Campbell Tait*, p.13.
2. David L. Edwards, *Leaders of the Church of England: 1828–1944*, p.104.
3. J.B. Hope Simpson, *Rugby Since Arnold*, p.12.
4. *ibid.*, p.11.
5. Katharine Lake (ed.), *Memorials of William Charles Lake*, pp.34–5.
6. W.C. Lake, 'Rugby and Oxford: 1830–1850', in *Good Words*, October 1895, p.666.
7. Rowland E. Prothero, *The Life and Correspondence of Arthur Penrhyn Stanley*, pp.315–6.
8. R.T. Davidson and W. Benham, *Life of Archibald Campbell Tait*, Vol. 1, p.110.
9. *ibid.*, p.111.
10. *ibid.*, p.112.
11. *ibid.*, pp.111–12.
12. *ibid.*, p.113

13. *ibid.*, pp.113–14
14. *ibid.*, p.114.
15. John Rodgers, *Old Public Schools of England*, pp.77–8.
16. Lytton Strachey, *Eminent Victorians* (1948 edn), p.194.
17. Rodgers, p.79.
18. Davidson and Benham, p.110.
19. Isabel Quigly, *The Heirs of Tom Brown*, pp.36–7.
20. John Chandos, *Boys Together*, p.251.
21. *ibid.*
22. *ibid.*, p.252.
23. *ibid.*, p.265.
24. Quigly, p.27.
25. W.C. Lake, p.667.
26. Chandos, p.255.
27. Edwards, p.18.
28. Chandos, p.255.
29. *ibid.,* pp.254–5.
30. Quigly, p.31.
31. Prothero, p.317.
32. *ibid.*, p.318.
33. Davidson and Benham, pp.114–15.
34. Bickley, p.14.
35. William Benham (ed.), *Catharine and Craufurd Tait*, p.14.
36. *ibid.*, p.6.
37. *ibid.*, p.14.
38. *ibid.*, pp.229–30n.
39. *ibid.*, pp.228–9.
40. *ibid.*, p.18.
41. A.P. Stanley, *Letters and Verses*, (ed. R.E. Prothero), p.78.
42. Benham, pp.233–4.
43. *ibid.*, p.16.
44. Strachey, pp.192–3.
45. W.H.D. Rouse, *A History of Rugby School*, p.276.
46. Hope Simpson, p.13.
47. Rouse, p.277.
48. Davidson and Benham, p.118.
49. *ibid.*, p.117.
50. *ibid.*, p.143.
51. Hope Simpson, p.13.
52. Davidson and Benham, p.117.
53. *ibid.*, p.144.

54. *ibid.*, p.121.
55. Hope Simpson, pp.15–16.
56. Davidson and Benham, p.140.
57. J.P.L., 'Recollections of Rugby under Tait', in *Leisure Hour*, 20 March 1875, p.183.
58. Davidson and Benham, pp.141–2.
59. *ibid.*, pp.133–4.
60. *ibid.*, p.134.
61. *ibid.*, p.135.
62. Benham, pp.28–9.
63. Davidson and Benham, p.144.
64. Hope Simpson, p.17.
65. Davidson and Benham, p.146.
66. *ibid.*, p.148.
67. Stanley, p.142.
68. Davidson and Benham, pp.137–8.
69. Hope Simpson, p.21.
70. Davidson and Benham, pp.147–8.
71. *ibid.*, pp.126–30.
72. *ibid.,* pp.131–3.
73. *ibid.* pp.152–3
74. Edwards, p.107.
75. Davidson and Benham, p.192.
76. *ibid.*, pp.271–2.
77. *Letters of Queen Victoria*, 2nd Series, Vol. 1, pp.545, 549.

CHAPTER 4: BENEVOLENT AUTOCRAT

1. J.B. Hope Simpson, *Rugby since Arnold*, p.41.
2. E.G. Sandford (ed.) *Memoirs of Archbishop Temple by Seven Friends* (F.E. Kitchener, 'Rugby Memoir'), Vol. 1, p.152.
3. *ibid.*, p.152.
4. *ibid.*, p.158.
5. *ibid.*, p.153.
6. F.D. How, *Six Great Schoolmasters*, p.185.
7. *ibid.*, p.183.
8. David L. Edwards, *Leaders of the Church of England: 1828–1944,* p.290.
9. Hope Simpson, p.41.

10. *ibid.*, p.42.
11. Sandford, p.159.
12. A.C. Benson, *The Life of Edward White Benson*, Vol. 1, p.185.
13. Edwards, p.289.
14. Hope Simpson, p.41.
15. How, pp.183–4.
16. Edwards, p.290.
17. How, p.184.
18. Katharine Lake (ed.), *Memorials of William Charles Lake*, p.176.
19. *ibid.*, p.175.
20. Hope Simpson, pp.24–5.
21. Sandford, p.158.
22. How, p.187.
23. Sandford, p.175.
24. How, pp.188–9.
25. Sandford, pp.158–9.
26. How, p.190.
27. *ibid.*, p.195.
28. Sandford, p.173.
29. Henry Scott Holland, *The Commonwealth*, February 1903, p.34.
30. How, p.191.
31. *ibid.*, pp.192–3.
32. *ibid.*, p.205.
33. Sandford, p.179.
34. How, p.191.
35. *ibid.*, p.219.
36. Hope Simpson, p.62.
37. *ibid.*, p.44.
38. How, p.196.
39. Sandford, pp.163–4.
40. *ibid.*, pp.160–1.
41. *ibid.*, pp.165–6.
42. *ibid.*, p.167.
43. *ibid.*, p.167.
44. *ibid.*, pp.167–8.
45. How, p.199.
46. *ibid.*, p.202.
47. Sandford, p.212.

48. How, p.204.
49. Sandford, pp.174–5.
50. *ibid.*, pp.174n–175n.
51. How, p.194.
52. Sandford, p.173.
53. *ibid.*, p.227.
54. *Public Schools Commission Report*, 1864, Vol. 2; Answers, p.311.
55. How, p.194.
56. Sandford, p.181.
57. *ibid.*, p.182.
58. How, p.200.
59. Sandford, p.163.
60. *PSC Report*, ii, p.311.
61. *ibid.*, Answer 197
62. Hope Simpson, p.50.
63. Sandford, p.175.
64. A.P. Stanley, *The Life and Correspondence of Thomas Arnold* (7th edn), p.126.
65. Sandford, p.164.
66. *ibid.*, p.217.
67. *ibid.*, pp.216–7.
68. *ibid.*, p.216.
69. How, pp.206–7.
70. Sandford, p.217.
71. How, p.208.
72. *ibid.*, p.209
73. Sandford, p.219.
74. *ibid.*, p.164.
75. *ibid.*, p.212.
76. How, p.205.
77. Sandford, p.208.
78. *ibid.*, pp.209–10.
79. How, pp.202–3.
80. Sandford, pp.211–12.
81. *PSC Report:* Evidence, Rugby, Answer 392.
82. Sandford, p.186.
83. *PSC Report:* Rugby, p.249.
84. Sandford, p.187.
85. *PSC Report*: Minutes, p.251.
86. Hope Simpson, p.49.

87. How, p.213.
88. W.H.D. Rouse, *A History of Rugby School*, p.301.
89. Sandford, pp.192–3.
90. Hope Simpson, p.97.
91. *ibid.*, p.90.
92. *ibid.*, pp.56–7.
93. Sandford, p.228.
94. *ibid.*, p.232.
95. Hope Simpson, pp.57–8.
96. Sandford, p.220n.
97. *ibid.*, p.176.
98. *ibid.*, p.220
99. *ibid.*, p.224.
100. Hope Simpson, p.55.
101. *ibid.*, p.56.
102. How, pp.220–1.
103. Benson, p.196.
104. This summarization of the Exeter Bishopric controversy is based on Bernard Palmer, *High and Mitred*, pp.92–5.
105. How, pp.215–16.
106. Henry Scott Holland, *A Bundle of Memories*, p.166.
107. Sandford, p.183.
108. How, p.216.
109. *ibid.*, p.210.
110. Edwards, p.288.
111. G.K.A. Bell, *Randall Davidson*, Vol. 1, pp.169–70.
112. Edwards, p.295.
113. *Letters of Queen Victoria*, Third Series, Vol. 3, pp.94–5.
114. How, p.224.

CHAPTER 5: BLAZING A TRAIL

1. A.C. Benson, *The Life of Edward White Benson*, Vol. 1, p.136.
2. J.L. Bevir, *The Making of Wellington College*, p.3.
3. David Newsome, *A History of Wellington College, 1859–1959*, pp.52–3.
4. *ibid.*, p.54.
5. *ibid.*, p.56.
6. *ibid.*, p.88n.

7   A.C. Benson, *Life*, p.136.
8.   Newsome, p.88.
9.   E.F. Benson, *As We Were*, p.40.
10. A.C. Benson, *Life*, pp.39–40.
11. David Williams, *Genesis and Exodus*, p.3.
12. E.F. Benson, p.53.
13. *ibid.*, p.58.
14. *ibid.*, pp.56–9.
15. Williams, p.11.
16. E.F. Benson, p.66.
17. Williams, pp. 12–13.
18. A.C. Benson, *Life*, p.188.
19. Williams, p.17.
20. Bevir, p.5.
21. A.C. Benson, *Life*, p.98.
22. *ibid.*, p.162.
23. *ibid.*, p.164.
24. *ibid.*, pp.215–20.
25. *ibid.*, p.247.
26. *ibid.*, pp.192–3.
27. *ibid.*, pp.275–7.
28. *ibid.*, pp.253–4.
29. Newsome, p.158 and n.
30. Ian Hamilton, *When I Was a Boy*, p.154.
31. Bevir, pp.vi, viii.
32. *ibid.*, pp.30–1.
33. *ibid.*, pp.31–2.
34. Newsome, p.90.
35. Williams, p.34.
36. A.C. Benson, *Life*, p.206.
37. Bevir, pp.83–4.
38. A.C. Benson, *Life*, p.226.
39. *ibid.*, pp.196–7.
40. *ibid.*, pp.257–8.
41. *ibid.*, p.260.
42. Newsome, p.151.
43. A.C. Benson, *Life*, pp.221–2.
44. *ibid.*, pp.214–15.
45. Bevir, pp.27–8.
46. *ibid.*, pp.117–18.
47. *ibid.*, p.27.

48. A.C. Benson, *Life*, p.202.
49. A.C. Benson, *The Trefoil*, p.53.
50. A.C. Benson, *Life,* pp.202–3.
51. Newsome, p.115.
52. A.C. Benson, *Life*, p.223.
53. Bevir, p.vii.
54. A.C. Benson, *Life*, pp.245–6.
55. *ibid.*, p.244.
56. Newsome, p.159.
57. A.C. Benson, *Life*, p.225.
58. A.C. Benson, *Trefoil*, pp.48–9.
59. A.C. Benson, *Life*, p.209.
60. Bevir, p.28.
61. A.C. Benson, *Trefoil*, p.39.
62. Newsome, p.153.
63. A.C. Benson, *Life*, p.205.
64. Newsome, p.153.
65. A.C. Benson, *Trefoil*, pp.40–1.
66. *ibid.*, p.39.
67. *ibid.*, p.41.
68. E.F. Benson, pp.52–3.
69. A.C. Benson, *Life*, p.32.
70. Newsome, p.111.
71. A.C. Benson, *Life*, p.177.
72. A.C. Benson, *Trefoil*, p.46.
73. A.C. Benson, *Life*, pp.175–6.
74. Bevir, p.54.
75. A.C. Benson, *Trefoil*, pp.54–5.
76. Williams, p.43.
77. Newsome, p.126.
78. A.C. Benson, *Life*, pp.178–9.
79. Bevir, p.11.
80. A.C. Benson, *Life*, p.174.
81. Williams, p.31.
82. E.F. Benson, p.65.
83. A.C. Benson, *Life*, p.241.
84. *ibid.*, pp.241–4.
85. A.C. Benson, *Trefoil*, pp.43–6.
86. A.C. Benson, *Life*, p.188.
87. A.C. Benson, *Trefoil*, pp.36–7.
88. A.C. Benson, *Life*, p.353.

89. Newsome, p.96.
90. Bevir, p.12.
91. Newsome, p.104.
92. *ibid.*, pp.143–4.
93. *ibid.*, pp.144–5.
94. *ibid.*, pp.108–10.
95. *ibid.*, pp.109–10.
96. *ibid.*, pp.166–9.
97. A.C. Benson, *Life*, pp.316–17.
98. *ibid.*, pp.310–11.
99. Williams, pp.44–5.
100. A.C. Benson, *Life*, pp.354–5.
101. *ibid.*, p.357.
102. Newsome, p.90.
103. *ibid.*, pp.174–6.
104. Williams, p.47.
105. *Letters of Queen Victoria*, 2nd Series, Vol. 3, p.331.
106. G.K.A. Bell, *Randall Davidson* (3rd edn), Vol. 1, p. 53.
107. *ibid.*, p.57.
108. Williams, p.107.

CHAPTER 6: HIS FATHER'S SON

1. F.A. Iremonger, *William Temple*, pp.131–2.
2. *ibid.*, p.149.
3. i*bid.*, p.132.
4. *ibid.*, p.133.
5. *ibid.*, p.147.
6. *ibid.*, p.134.
7. *ibid.*, pp.134–5.
8. *ibid.*, p.135,
9. David L. Edwards, *Leaders of the Church of England, 1828–1944*, p.286.
10. Iremonger, p.5.
11. *ibid.*, p.5.
12. *Bloomsbury Dictionary of Quotations*, p.343.
13. *William Temple Papers*, Vol. 48, p.153.
14. *ibid.*, p.152.
15. Bloomsbury, p.343.
16. Iremonger, pp.57–8.

17. *ibid.*, pp.108–27.
18. *ibid.*, p.488.
19. Bernard Thomas (ed.), *Repton 1557 to 1957*, p.100.
20. Iremonger, p.128.
21. *ibid.*, p.142.
22. Thomas, p.103.
23. Iremonger, pp.143–4.
24. Edwards, p.300.
25. Iremonger, p.146.
26. *ibid.*, p.147.
27. Thomas, p.101.
28. *William Temple Papers*, Vol. 48, p.139.
29. *Church Times*, 18 April 1913.
30. Iremonger, p.143.
31. Thomas, pp.101–2.
32. *ibid.*, p.104.
33. *ibid.*, p.102.
34. 'Repton Remembered': article by C.H. Palmer in *Church Times*, 26 July 1957.
35. Iremonger, p.148.
36. Ruth Dudley Edwards, *Victor Gollancz*, p.124.
37. Iremonger, p.148.
38. *ibid.*, p.149.
39. John Kent, *William Temple*, p.19.
40. *ibid.*, p.18.
41. Iremonger, p.150.
42. *ibid.*, pp.150–1.
43. *ibid.*, p.151.
44. Thomas, pp.102-3.
45. *William Temple Papers*, Vol 48, p.140.
46. Iremonger, p.152.
47. Ronald Knox, 'Absolute and Abitofhell': reprinted in *Essays in Satire*, pp.57, 61.
48. Bernard Palmer, *High and Mitred*, pp.221, 224.

CHAPTER 7: HOLDING THE BALANCE

1. Bernard Thomas (ed.), *Repton 1557 to 1957*, p.104.
2. William Purcell, *Fisher of Lambeth*, p.50.
3. Lambeth Palace Library MS 3467, ff.34–6.

4. Purcell, p.44.
5. Edward Carpenter, *Archbishop Fisher*, p.11.
6. *ibid.*, p.14.
7. Lambeth MS 3467, f.29.
8. Carpenter, p.16.
9. Purcell, p.46.
10. *ibid.*, p.48.
11. *ibid.*, p.49.
12. Lambeth MS 3467, f.35.
13. *ibid.*, f.36.
14. *ibid.*, f.36.
15. *ibid.*, f.37.
16. *ibid.*, f.37.
17. *ibid.*, f.55.
18. Thomas, pp.112–14.
19. Carpenter, p.25.
20. *ibid.*, p.25.
21. Thomas, p.112.
22. Owen Chadwick, *Michael Ramsey*, p.11.
23. *ibid.*, p.15; Michael De-la-Noy, *Michael Ramsey*, p.56.
24. Chadwick, pp.15–16.
25. Jeremy Treglown, *Roald Dahl*, p.22.
26. De-la-Noy, p.51.
27. *ibid.*, pp.49, 51.
28. Denton Welch, *Maiden Voyage*, pp.77–8.
29. Purcell, p.60.
30. Carpenter, p.28.
31. Lambeth MS 3467, f.51.
32. *ibid.*, ff.51–2.
33. Treglown, p.19.
34. Lambeth MS 3467, ff.37–8.
35. Roald Dahl, *Boy*, pp.130–2.
36. Treglown, pp.21–2.
37. Lambeth MS 3467, f.57.
38. Purcell, p.62.
39. Lambeth MS 3467, f.58.
40. *ibid.*, f.59.
41. Thomas, p.114.
42. Lambeth MS 3467, f.60.
43. Thomas, p.114.
44. Purcell, p.48.

45. *ibid.*, pp.57–8.
46. Carpenter, p.27.
47. *ibid.*, pp.27–8.
48. Thomas, p.106.
49. Victor Gollancz, *More for Timothy*, p.172.
50. *ibid.*, p.170.
51. Gollancz, p.194.
52. Carpenter, p.18.
53. Lambeth MS 3467, f.40.
54. Ruth Dudley Edwards, *Victor Gollancz*, pp.104–5.
55. *ibid.*, p.106.
56. *Church Times*, 26 July 1957.
57. Gollancz, p.238.
58. *ibid.*, p.184.
59. *ibid.*, p.187.
60. Edwards, p.107.
61. *ibid.*, p.101.
62. Gollancz, p.240.
63. *ibid.*, pp.288–9.
64. Edwards, p.119.
65. Gollancz, p.292.
66. *ibid.*, p.298.
67. *ibid.*, p.295.
68. *ibid.,* p.309.
69. *ibid.*, p.309.
70. *ibid.*, pp.299–300.
71. Lambeth MS 3467, f.40.
72. *William Temple Papers*, Vol. 48, f.167.
73. Thomas, p.113.
74. Lambeth, MS 3467, f.61.
75. *Lang Papers*, Vol. 110, ff.255, 261, 263.
76. Thomas, p.112.
77. Gollancz, p.156.
78. *ibid.*, p.190.
79. Thomas, p.113.
80. Gollancz, p.306.
81. *ibid.*, pp.306–7.
82. Thomas, p.114.
83. Purcell, p.65.
84. *Lang Papers*, Vol. 169, ff.241–2.
85. *Theology*, March 1963, p.102.

86. *Church Times*, 22 September 1972. The anonymous obitu-
    arist was Bishop J.W.C. Wand.
87. Chadwick, p.107.
88. *ibid.*, p.107; Carpenter, p.750.
89. Carpenter, p.752.
90. *ibid.*, p.762.

BIBLIOGRAPHY

1 *Unpublished Sources in Lambeth Palace Library*

Fisher Papers
Lang Papers
William Temple Papers

2 *Published Sources*

Balston, T., *Dr Balston at Eton*, London 1952.
Bell, G.K.A., *Randall Davidson, Archbishop of Canterbury*, Geoffrey Cumberlege, Oxford University Press, 3rd edn, 1952.
Benham, William (ed.), *Catharine and Craufurd Tait – A Memoir*, Macmillan 1879.
Benson, A.C., *The Life of Edward White Benson, sometime Archbishop of Canterbury*, Macmillan, 2 vols, 1899.
——*The Trefoil*, John Murray, 1923.
Benson, E.F., *As We Were: A Victorian Peep-Show*, Longmans, Green, 1930.
Bevir, J.L., *The Making of Wellington College*, Edward Arnold, 1920.
Bickley, A.C., *Archibald Campbell Tait*, James Nisbet, 1882.
Bloomsbury Dictionary of Quotations, Bloomsbury, 1987.
Bryant, P.H.M., *Harrow*, Blackie, 1936.
Carpenter, Edward, *Archbishop Fisher – His Life and Times*, Canterbury Press, 1991.
Chadwick, Owen, *Michael Ramsey: A Life*, Oxford University Press, 1990
Chandos, John, *Boys Together: English Public Schools, 1800–1864*, Oxford University Press, 1984.

Dahl, Roald, *Boy: Tales of Childhood*, Jonathan Cape, 1984.

Davidson, R.T., and Benham, William, *Life of Archibald Campbell Tait, Archbishop of Canterbury*, Macmillan, 2 vols, 1891.

De-la-Noy, Michael, *Michael Ramsey: A Portrait*, Collins, 1990.

Edwards, David L., *Leaders of the Church of England, 1828–1944*, Oxford University Press, 1971.

Edwards, Ruth Dudley, *Victor Gollancz: A Biography*, Gollancz, 1987.

Fraser, George Macdonald (ed.), *The World of the Public School*, Weidenfeld and Nicolson, 1977.

Gollancz, Victor, *More for Timothy: the second instalment of an autobiographical letter to his grandson,* Gollancz, 1953.

Greene, Graham (ed.), *The Old School: essays by divers hands*, Oxford University Press, 1934.

Hall, N. John, *Trollope: A Biography*, Clarendon Press, 1991.

Henson, Herbert Hensley, *Retrospect of an Unimportant Life*, Oxford University Press, 3 vols, 1942–6.

Hinchliff, Peter, *John William Colenso, Bishop of Natal*, Nelson, 1964.

Honey, J.R. de S., *Tom Brown's Universe: The Development of the Victorian Public School*, Millington Books, 1977.

How, F.D., *Six Great Schoolmasters* (Hawtrey, Moberly, Kennedy, Vaughan, Temple, Bradley), Methuen, 1904.

Howson, Edmund, W., and Warner, George Townsend (eds). *Harrow School*, Edward Arnold, 1898.

Iremonger, F.A., *William Temple, Archbishop of Canterbury: His Life and Letters*, Geoffrey Cumberlege, Oxford University Press, 1948.

Kent, John, *William Temple: Church, State and Society in Britain, 1880–1950*, Cambridge University Press, 1992.

Knox, Ronald, *Essays in Satire*, Sheed & Ward, 1928.

Lake, Katharine (ed.), *Memorials of William Charles Lake, Dean of Durham 1869–1894*, Edward Arnold, 1901.

Minchin, J.G. Cotton, *Old Harrow Days*, Methuen, 1898.

Newsome, David, *Godliness and Good Learning: Four Studies on a Victorian Ideal*, John Murray, 1961.

——*A History of Wellington College 1859–1959*, John Murray, 1959.

Palmer, Bernard, *High and Mitred: Prime Ministers as Bishop-Makers*, SPCK, 1992.

Prothero, Rowland E., *The Life and Correspondence of Arthur Penrhyn Stanley, D.D., late Dean of Westminster*, John Murray, 2 vols, 1893.

Purcell, William, *Fisher of Lambeth: A Portrait from Life*, Hodder & Stoughton, 1969.

Quigly, Isabel, *The Heirs of Tom Brown: The English School Story*, Oxford University Press, 1984.

Rodgers, John, *The Old Public Schools of England*, Batsford, 1938.

Rouse, W.H.D., *A History of Rugby School*, Duckworth, 1898.

Sandford, E.G. (ed.), *Memoirs of Archbishop [Frederick] Temple by Seven Friends*, Macmillan, 2 vols, 1906.

Simpson, J.B. Hope, *Rugby since Arnold: A History of Rugby School from 1842*, Macmillan, 1967.

Stanley, A.P., *Letters and Verses Between the Years 1829 and 1881* (ed. Rowland E. Prothero), John Murray, 1895.

Stephenson, A.M.G., *Anglicanism and the Lambeth Conferences*, SPCK, 1978.

——*The Victorian Archbishops of Canterbury*, Rocket Press, 1991.

Strachey, Lytton, *Eminent Victorians*, Chatto & Windus, 1948 edn.

Thomas, Bernard (ed.), *Repton 1557–1957*, Batsford, 1957.

Thornton, Percy M., *Harrow School and its Surroundings*, W.H. Allen, 1885.

Treglown, Jeremy, *Roald Dahl: A Biography*, Faber & Faber, 1994.

Trollope, Anthony, *An Autobiography*, Williams & Norgate, 1946 edn.

Welch, Denton, *Maiden Voyage*, Routledge, 1943.

Williams, David, *Genesis and Exodus: A Portrait of the Benson Family*, Hamish Hamilton, 1979.

Williams, J. Fischer, *Harrow*, George Bell, 1901.

Wodehouse, P.G., *Meet Mr Mulliner*, Herbert Jenkins, 1961 edn.

INDEX

Aberdeen, George Hamilton Gordon,
  4th Earl of, 13n
'Absolute and Abitofhell', (R.A.
  Knox), 147
Agard-Butler, Alfred, 176
Albert, Prince Consort, 87–91, 95, 96,
  104, 110, 116, 120
Arithmetic for Schools (J.W. Colenso),
  22
Arnold, Matthew, 27, 52
Arnold, Thomas, Headmaster of
  Rugby, 2, 5, 7, 20, 25, 27, 28, 29,
  30, 31–4, 38, 39, 41, 45, 48, 49, 52,
  54, 56, 57, 60, 63, 68, 72, 73, 81,
  87, 92, 137, 191
Ashby-de-la-Zouch Grammar School, 152
Asquith, Herbert Henry, 1st Earl of
  Oxford and Asquith, 145
Asquith, Raymond, 135

Baker, Sir Thomas, 93
Balliol College, Oxford, 26, 27, 54–5,
  135, 155
Balston, Thomas, Headmaster of Eton, 3
Barchester Towers (A. Trollope), 24n
Batten, Samuel, 12
Bell, George Kennedy Allen, Bishop of
  Chichester, 186
Benham, William, 37
Benson, Arthur Christopher (son of
  E.W.B.), 92, 96, 101, 103, 104, 107,
  108, 109, 110–1, 112, 114–6, 124,
  160n

Benson, Edward Frederick ('Fred'; son
  of E.W.B.), 91, 93, 94, 109, 114, 116
Benson, Edward White, Headmaster of
  Wellington and later Archbishop of
  Canterbury; appointment to
  Wellington, 87–91; family
  background and early career, 91–5;
  takes up office, 95–6; qualities and
  characteristics as headmaster,
  96–102; relations with boys, 98–9,
  102–3; as disciplinarian, 104–7;
  relations with masters, 107–9;
  religious teaching and preaching,
  109–111; religious partisanship
  alleged, 111–13; marriage and
  family life, 114–6; pushes through
  reforms, 116–9; clashes with
  governors on moral issues, 119–22;
  appointment to Lincoln canonry,
  122–4; assessment of headship,
  124–5; later career, 125–7;
  mentioned, xi, 5, 7, 54, 63, 68,
  80–1, 84, 151, 156, 189–94
Benson, Edward White (father of
  E.W.B.), 91, 92
Benson, Harriet (mother of E.W.B.),
  91, 93
Benson, Harriet (sister of E.W.B.), 93
Benson, Martin (son of E.W.B.), 124
Benson, Mary ('Minnie', née
  Sidgwick; wife of E.W.B.), 94, 96,
  100, 106, 110, 114, 116, 123n, 127,
  193

215

216

220

Stanley, Edward, Bishop of Norwich, 44
Stephen, James Fitzjames, 33
Strachey, Lytton, 31, 32, 38n
Streeter, B.H., 147
Student Christian Movement, 131, 136
Study of History, A. (A. Toynbee, abr.
  D.C. Somervell), 179
Sumner, John Bird, Archbishop of
  Canterbury, 24

Tait, Agnes (daughter of A.C.T.), 49n
Tait, Archibald Campbell, Headmaster
  of Rugby and later Archbishop of
  Canterbury: appointed to Rugby, 25,
  27–30; family background and early
  career, 26–7; takes up office, 34–5;
  marriage, 35–8; building on
  Arnold's foundations, 38; not a born
  schoolmaster, 39; religious teaching
  and preaching, 39–40; relations with
  boys, 40–4; sudden illness, 41–3;
  appointed Dean of Carlisle, 43–4;
  assessment of headship, 44–5; in
  dispute with W.G. Ward, 45–6; and
  Hampden controversy, 47;
  champions Highton book, 47–8;
  Carlisle tragedy, 48–9; later career,
  49–50; mentioned, xi, 2, 3, 5, 7, 24,
  51, 55, 56, 57, 72, 80, 81, 94, 126,
  127, 129, 189–94
Tait, Catharine (née Spooner; wife of
  A.C.T.), 35–8, 40, 42, 48, 49n, 50
Tait, Catharine ('Catty'; daughter of
  A.C.T.), 37, 48
Tait, Charlotte ('Chatty'; daughter of
  A.C.T.), 48
Tait, Craufurd (father of A.C.T.), 26
Tait, Craufurd (son of A.C.T.), 37, 49n,
  50
Tait, Edith (daughter of A.C.T.), 49n
Tait, Frances (daughter of A.C.T.), 48
Tait, James (brother of A.C.T.), 47
Tait, Lucy (daughter of A.C.T.), 48
Tait, Mary, ('May'; daughter of
  A.C.T.), 37, 48

Tait, Susan (dauther of A.C.T.), 48
Tawney, R.H., 135
Teaching methods: Harrow under
  Longley, 17–21; Rugby under Tait,
  38–40; under F. Temple, 61–3,
  67–8, 73; Wellington under Benson,
  107; Repton under W. Temple,
  139–40; under Fisher, 162–3
Temple, Beatrice (née Lascelles; wife
  of F.T., mother of W.T.), 83, 132,
  133, 141–2
Temple, Dorcas (mother of F.T.), 53, 77
Temple, Frances (née Anson; wife of
  W.T.), 135, 141, 148, 180
Temple, Frederick, Headmaster of
  Rugby and later Archbishop of
  Canterbury: appointment to Rugby,
  51–2; family background and early
  career, 52–6; takes up office, 57–8;
  qualities and characteristics as
  headmaster, 58–61; as teacher,
  61–3; as disciplinarian, 63–5;
  relations with staff, 65–7, 73–4;
  attitude to school curriculum, 67–8;
  religious teaching and preaching,
  68–71; encourages games, 71–2;
  introduces reforms, 72–4; and Royal
  Commission on Public Schools,
  74–6; private life, 76–7; *Essays and
  Reviews* controversy, 77–82;
  assessment of headship, 82–3; later
  career, 83–5; mentioned, xi, 1 , 3, 5,
  7, 27, 87–90, 101, 108, 111, 112,
  114, 120, 123, 126 & n, 129, 132,
  133–5, 147, 151, 189–94
Temple, Frederick (brother of W.T.),
  133, 138, 143
Temple, Jennetta ('Netta'; sister of
  F.T.), 77
Temple, Octavius (father of F.T.), 53
Temple, William, Headmaster of
  Repton and later Archbishop of
  Canterbury: appointment to Repton,
  129–33; family background and
  early career, 133–7; takes up office,

ABOUT THE AUTHOR

Scottish-born painter and esotericist Benjamin Creme has for over 30 years been preparing the world for the most extraordinary event in human history – the return of our spiritual mentors to the everyday world.

Benjamin Creme has appeared on television, radio and in documentary films worldwide and lectures throughout Western and Eastern Europe, the USA, Japan, Australia, New Zealand, Canada and Mexico.

Trained and supervised over many years by his own Master, he began his public work in 1974. In 1982 he announced that the Lord Maitreya, the long-awaited World Teacher, was living in London, ready to present Himself openly when invited by the media to do so. This event is now imminent.

Benjamin Creme continues to carry out his task as messenger of this inspiring news. His books, 14 at present, have been translated into many languages. He is also the editor of *Share International* magazine, which circulates in over 70 countries. He accepts no money for any of this work.

Benjamin Creme lives in London, is married, and has three children.